Inner Music

Santa Cecilia
Sigfrido Martín Begué

Inner Music

*Hobbes, Hooke and North
on Internal Character*

JAMIE C. KASSLER

**ATHLONE
LONDON**

First published 1995 by
THE ATHLONE PRESS LTD
1 Park Drive, London NW11 7SG

© Jamie C. Kassler 1995

British Library Cataloguing in Publication Data
*A catalogue record for this book is available
from the British Library*

ISBN 0 485 11407 0

All rights reserved. No part of this publication may be reproduced, stored in a retrieval system, or transmitted in any form or by any means, electronic, mechanical, photocopying or otherwise, without prior permission in writing from the publisher.

Typeset by
Bibloset

Printed and bound in Great Britain by the
University Press, Cambridge

The author and publishers gratefully acknowledge a grant from the Australian Academy of the Humanities towards the publication of this book.

Contents

List of Illustrations	ix
Acknowledgements	xiii

Chapter 1: Conceiving the Inconceivable	1
I Musical Models	1
Introduction	1
1 Acoustical resonance	5
1.1 Oscillations, energy, sympathy	5
1.2 Musical vibrators and resonators	11
2 Human resonance	16
2.1 Physiological resonance	16
2.2 Ethical resonance	20
2.3 Philosophical resonance	25
II Musical Ethos	28
Introduction	28
3 Ancient harmony theories	30
3.1 The cosmos as a harmony	30
3.2 Health as a harmony	33
4 Toward new harmony theories	36
4.1 The self as musical activity	36
4.2 The body as an instrument	43
Chapter 2: The Paradoxes of Power	49
Introduction	49
I Nature's Fiat	61
Introduction	61
1 Not in our power	62
1.1 Nature's government: motion inward	62
1.2 The natural life: Hobbes and Harvey	66
2 In our power	69
2.1 Self-government: motion outward	69
2.2 The happy life: Hobbes and Cowley	73

II Nature's Law	76
Introduction	76
3 Body as a deformable system	79
3.1 Matter as endeavour to cohere	79
3.2 Motion as virtual power and actual work	82
3.3 Matter as a point, motion as a way	85
4 Body as a habit	88
4.1 Nature's habit: what is given at birth	88
4.2 Our habit: things to be done and known	91
III Nature's Guide	93
Introduction	93
5 Philosophy as method	95
5.1 Teaching by example	95
5.2 Finding the image	99
5.3 Learning by making	103
Conclusion: The virtuous life	105
Chapter 3: Calling to Mind	108
I Memory as a Place	108
Introduction	108
1 Discordant theories	113
1.1 Localisers vs. non-localisers	113
1.2 The soul as a recollection	115
2 Localising memory	117
2.1 As traces	117
2.2 As liquid or as species	121
II Memory as a Time	124
Introduction	124
3 Processing frequencies	129
3.1 The work of the periphery	129
3.2 The work of the interior	133
3.3 The work of the point	137
4 Understanding vibratory patterns	139
4.1 In musical strings	139
4.2 In bells	143
III Forging the Memory	147
Introduction	147
5 Ringing the bell	151
5.1 The mechanics	151
5.2 The pneumatics	157

Chapter 4: The *Daimon* Within	160
I The Musical Man	160
Introduction	160
1 Organised body	168
1.1 As the consort	168
1.2 As the conductor	174
2 Animating principle	181
2.1 As the composer	181
2.2 As the musical score	184
II The Unmusical Man	185
Introduction	185
3 Disorganised Body	188
3.1 As flatus	188
3.2 As ructus	192
4 Elastic Limit	196
4.1 The scale	196
4.2 In expansions	201
4.3 In contractions	205
Chapter 5: Sounding the Depths	208
I Body Music	208
Introduction	208
1 Playing and listening	212
1.1 Techniques	212
1.2 Instruments	216
2 Creating theories	219
2.1 Naming	219
2.2 Classifying	226
2.3 Explaining	229
Conclusion	231
Notes	233
References: 1 Works of Roger North	271
2 Other Works	272
Index	288

List of Illustrations

Frontispiece: Sigfrido Martín Begué, *Santa Cecilia*, oil on linen, 195 x 165 cm, 1988 (privately owned)

Chapter 1
1.1 Simple bullet pendulum
1.2 Motion of the bullet pendulum
1.3 Simple harmonic motion
1.4 Simple harmonic motion
    (a) as positions of a boat moving through the waves
    (b) as positions of a point on a vibrating string
1.5 Waveforms
    (a) of a sine wave
    (b) of several sine waves superposed
1.6 Standing waves of a rope
    (a) vibrating as a whole
    (b) vibrating in seconds
    (c) vibrating in thirds
1.7 The human ear
1.8 The *clavecin*, from M. Mersenne, *Harmonie universelle* (Paris, 1636–37)
1.9 Pythagorean harmony of numbers
1.10 The monochord and its geometrical representation, from M. Mersenne, *Harmonie universelle* (Paris, 1636–37)
1.11 The sentient as a monochord, from R. Fludd, *Utrius cosmi...historia*, II (Oppenheim, 1619)
1.12 The cosmic monochord, from R. Fludd, *Utrius cosmi...historia*, I (Oppenheim, 1617)
1.13 The damned tortured on musical instruments, detail from H. Bosch, *Garden of Earthly Delights* (Prado, Madrid)
1.14 Mental representation as line lengths, from R. Descartes, *De homine figuris* (Leyden, 1662)
1.15 Neuro-muscular function, after R. Descartes, *Discours de la méthode* (Leyden, 1636), from M. Mersenne, *Harmonie universelle* (Paris, 1636–37)

Chapter 2
2.1 King over all the children of pride, from T. Hobbes, *Leviathan* (London, 1651)
2.2 The hoop or rigid pendulum
2.3 The compound pendulum
2.4 Seventeenth-century lute, from M. Mersenne, *Harmonie universelle* (Paris, 1636–37)

Chapter 3
3.1 Descartes' theory of brain function, after K. Digby, *Two Treatises* (London, 1645)
3.2 Pythagoras as symbol of Vulcan, from M. Agricola, *Musica instrumentalis Deudsch* (Wittenberg, 1528)
3.3 Pythagoras, from F. Gafori, *Theoria musice* (Milan, 1492)
   (a) with the canon as a set of bells
   (b) with the canon as a monochord
3.4 Hooke's theory of brain function
3.5 Vibrating segments of square plates
3.6 Vibrating segments of a bell
3.7 The bell (*la cloche*), from M. Mersenne, *Harmonie universelle* (Paris, 1636–37)
3.8 Seventeenth-century English striking clock
3.9 Internal regulator, from R. Hooke, *Lampas* (London, 1677)
3.10 Hooke's Law demonstrated, from R. Hooke, *Lectures de potentia restitutiva* (London, 1678)
3.11 Vibrating segments of circular membranes

Chapter 4
4.1 Microscopic particles of elastic bodies, from R. Hooke, *Lectures de potentia restitutiva* (London, 1678)
4.2 Tube trumpet, showing longitudinal vibrations, from R. North, *Theory of Sounds...1728* (BL Add MS 32535: f.138)
4.3 [facing pages] Method of representing musical pitches as a temporal flow of coincident pulses, from F. North, *A Philosophical Essay of Musick* (London, 1677)
4.4 Mental representation as rules of vibration, illustrated by a 'punctation' of the full accord, from R. North, *Theory of Sounds...1728* (BL Add MS 32535: f.113)
4.5 Key to Figure 4.4

4.6 Chord inversion
4.7 True and false strings, from M. Mersenne, *Harmonie universelle* (Paris, 1636-37)
4.8 Scale of degrees of tension, detail from W. Hogarth, *Credulity, Superstition and Fanaticism* (London, 1762)

Chapter 5
5.1 Firm stethoscopes (wood, ivory, metal), from S.S. Alison, *The Physical Examination of the Chest* (London, 1861)
5.2 Flexible monaural and binaural stethoscopes, from S.S. Alison, *The Physical Examination of the Chest* (London, 1861)
5.3 Percussion hammers
(a) from H.I. Bowditch, *The Young Stethoscopist* (New York and Boston, 1846)
(b) from S.S. Alison, *The Physical Examination of the Chest* (London, 1861)
5.4 Hydrophone, from S.S. Alison, *The Physical Examination of the Chest* (London, 1861)
5.5 Graphic representation of humming murmur, from R. Laennec, *A Treatise on Mediate Auscultation* (London, 1846)
5.6 Graphic representation of the pulse, from F.N. Marquet, *Nouvelle méthode facile et curieuse, pour connoitre le pouls*, 2d edn. (Amsterdam and Paris, 1749)
(a) the norm
(b) deviations from the norm
5.7 Other methods of representing body sounds
(a) Heart motions, from H.I. Bowditch, *The Young Stethoscopist* (New York and Boston, 1846)
(b) 'Wavy respiration', from S.S. Alison, *The Physical Examination of the Chest* (London, 1861)
(c) 'Oscillating respiration' in pulmonary consumption, from S.S. Alison, *The Physical Examination of the Chest* (London, 1861)
5.8 Representation of heart sounds, from C.J.B. Williams, *The Pathology and Diagnosis of Diseases of the Chest*, 4th edn. (London, 1840)
(a) Laennec's rhythm
(b) Williams' rhythm

Acknowledgements

The frontispiece that graces this book is reproduced from the marvellous painting, *Santa Cecilia*, by Sigfrido Martín Begué and is used by his permission. The detail from Hieronymus Bosch's painting, *Garden of Earthly Delights* in Figure 1.13, and the illustrations from Roger North's manuscripts in Figures 4.2 and 4.4 are reproduced by permission, respectively, of Museo del Prado, Madrid, and the British Library, London. The reproduction from Thomas Hobbes's *Leviathan* at Figure 2.1 is from the copy in the Rare Books and Special Collections, University of Sydney Library.

Some parts of this book have appeared in different forms and as preliminary studies in *New Perspectives on the History of Medicine* ed. H. Attwood, R. Gillespie and M. Lewis (Parkville, Vic.: University of Melbourne and Australian Society of the History of Medicine, 1990); *Metaphor – A Musical Dimension* ed. J.C. Kassler (Sydney: Currency Press, 1991); *The Uses of Antiquity: The Scientific Revolution and the Classical Tradition* ed. S. Gaukroger (Dordrecht: Kluwer Academic Publishers, 1991); and *Musical Humanism and Its Legacy: Essays in Honor of Claude V. Palisca* ed. N.K. Baker and B.R. Hanning (Stuyvestant, New York: Pendragon Press, 1992).

Special acknowledgments are due to the Australian Academy of the Humanities, for subsidy toward publication; to the Australian Research Committee, for enabling the research to be undertaken; to members of the School of Science and Technology Studies, University of New South Wales, for encouragement along the way; to Warren D. Anderson, James Franklin, Stephen Gaukroger, Pierre Laszlo, William Sacksteder, Alan E. Shapiro and John Sutton for congenial discussions and constructive criticisms on related topics; and to Michael Kassler, for his joyful outlook that kept me buoyant during a period when my goal seemed particularly elusive.

McMahons Point, N.S.W.

Chapter 1
Conceiving the Inconceivable

I. MUSICAL MODELS

> ...gut intuitions and aesthetic reactions
> call the tune in science
> until someone figures out
> a conversation-stopping proof....
> Daniel C. Dennett, *Liber* (1989, No. 2: 89)

Introduction
Since the time of the ancient Greeks, technology of various sorts has supplied models for studying animal behaviour and, particularly, behaviour that cannot be observed directly.[1] In humans, for example, there is no way of studying mental functioning – an internal event – except by inferring it from overt responses such as speech and gesture. Since the 1950s the most popular model of mental functioning has been the electronic computer, which includes a controlling mechanism called a 'central processing unit'. This unit, which operates on data obtained from the computer's memory, is connected by way of an intermediate interface to a number of input or output devices, for example, a card reader, a card punch, a printer, a magnetic tape unit, a magnetic disc and a keyboard terminal. All data are represented – that is to say, encoded – within the computer in binary form as sequences of 0s and 1s, corresponding to the on or off states of constituent circuits. The action of a computer is then fully specified by a program and data, the former of which presents the specific sequence of basic operations that a computer carries out on given data.

The computer model of human mentation is a symbol of the belief that many higher processes are computational and presuppose an internal medium of mental representation or 'language of thought'.[2] Before the advent of the computer, there were other models that symbolised similar as well as different beliefs not only about mental functioning but also about other internal events. For example, there was the ancient gustatory model of ingestion/sensation, digestion/thinking, cold storage/memory; the light model of sun/soul, radiations/spirits, reflection/brain; various versions of the political economy model – e.g., city centre/heart, sentinels/senses, council/brain, record/memory; and, from the mid-nineteenth century, the telegraph and, later, the telephone-exchange models.[3]

Many of these models have been the subject of comment by historians of science, literature and other specialities; but one model, despite its prevalence, has not been fully analysed. This model is the musical instrument, the sounds of which are generated by the actions of a performer playing upon it.[4] Traditionally, musical instruments were grouped into one of three classes: strings, percussion and wind. Modern organologists (those who specialise in the classification of musical instruments) sometimes refer to these three kinds, respectively, as chordophones, idiophones and aerophones. Instruments within all three classes also have been modified in such a way that organologists group them under mechanical, or electro-acoustic, musical instruments.[5] The piano, for example, is a chordophone; but the automatic player piano is a mechanical musical instrument which includes a 'transmitter' on which messages are 'written'; that is, the instrument itself contains a device on which music has been encoded into symbols. Like any technology, therefore, musical instruments have changed over time. Nevertheless, instruments within each of the three major classes – strings, percussion and wind – may be characterised as resonating systems.

This book tells how, during the seventeenth and early part of the eighteenth centuries, three English writers – Thomas Hobbes, Robert Hooke and Roger North – used resonating systems as controlling metaphors for the development of internal character, thereby conceiving self-knowledge and self-restraint as musical activities – the inner music of my title. This is my main plot. From time to time, however, I contrast the theories of these men with those of the so-called 'mechanical philosophers', who also utilised controlling metaphors from the technology and semantic field of music. From a modern perspective, therefore, we might describe all such theories as mechanistic.[6] But this description would obscure fundamental differences between the mechanical philosophers and Hobbes, Hooke and North. A brief summary of their respective concepts of force and definitions of mechanics will bring out more clearly one of the subsidiary plots which emerged during writing and which, sometimes, threatened to take over my main plot.

In conceiving how mechanical action might be transmitted from one point to another, the mechanical philosophers chose an explanation of action by impact and pressure, in which impenetrability was taken to be an ultimate property of real, but insensibly small, indivisible bodies. On this approach, motion proceeds by jerks from point to point in a line or trajectory; force manifests itself as a series of impacts; and mechanics is defined as a theory of percussion. In short, the mechanical philosophers relied on a simple and commonsensical concept − discreteness, so as to describe the world in terms of recognisable individual elements, like the numbers 1, 2, 3..., or like the letters of the alphabet a, b, c..., or like a row of billiard balls x_1, x_2, x_3....

Individualised elements are not the appropriate image for Hobbes's mechanics, which relies on the concept, continuity − that is to say, infinite divisibility or no-nextness. Against the mechanical philosophers, Hobbes argued that action takes place in a strictly continuous medium, in which the propagation of action takes time, and its velocity depends on the mechanical properties of the medium. Since he conceived bodies as highly deformable and mutually penetrable (i.e., superposed), elasticity and compressibility are properties of every portion of the medium, however small, so that even if the medium is divided indefinitely, it still will be strictly continuous. On this approach, force is all-pervading but continuously differentiated, like bundles of elastic strings stretched under different tensions, and mechanics is defined as a theory of vibration.

It is well known that the reception of Hobbes's work was extremely hostile, though the reasons for this have yet to be fully investigated.[7] From the point of view taken in this book, however, two reasons may be adduced that commentators have ignored. First, Hobbes's mechanics was indebted to two sciences that were new to the seventeenth century and that Hobbes introduced to

English readers. These sciences were elasticity ('strength of materials') and acoustics ('music'), which today are important studies within engineering and physics. Initially, however, acceptance of these sciences came slowly, for they competed with the old mechanics of Aristotle, still taught in the universities, as well as with the new theory of percussion of the mechanical philosophers.

Second, since Hobbes conceived the internal structure of bodies as elastic substances that vibrate, a central feature of his mechanics was a theory of restitution: organic as well as inorganic bodies have a power to restore themselves. Hobbes's most severe critics, the mechanical philosophers, had restricted the kinds of explanatory analogy admitted into physics.[8] On the one hand, only those actions which produce, or tend to produce, locomotion were to be accepted as fundamental. On the other hand, change of motion in bodies was to be explained only by communication from outside and not by any innate power or striving within the bodies themselves. Hence, the mechanical philosophers singled out for attack Hobbes's theory of restitution, because they understood it as a re-instatement of innate powers. Nevertheless, Hooke and North both developed Hobbes's notion that there are continuous forces of tension in body, because their musical researches convinced them that bodies are more or less elastic and consist of parts in continual vibration.

In telling my story, I offer a re-interpretation of the ontology of Hobbes, who traditionally has been treated as a mechanical philosopher.[9] I also offer a modification of, and refinement on, currently accepted notions about the mechanisation of the world picture, according to which there was only one seventeenth-century mechanical philosophy before Isaac Newton.[10] But these are merely by-products of my method, which presents an analysis of changes in a single metaphor. This method, I believe, can claim certain advantages over other methods of historical research. First, an analysis of a single metaphor allows a multi-disciplinary treatment that reflects more adequately the state of old, as well as emerging disciplines during the period in question. Second, since the changing metaphor contains both constant and variable elements, an analysis of the variables can be precise and can make clear both similarities and differences between theories that extend the metaphor. Third, a metaphor not only tells a story but also constrains the story to be told within certain well-defined limits.

My first task, however, is to 'attune' the reader to aspects of the metaphor, which is drawn from the technology and semantic field of music. In this chapter, therefore, I begin with resonance, a conception that had its origin in musical acoustics. After outlining the general principles of resonance and of musical instruments as resonating systems, I provide two examples of the application of musical instruments as models in physiology and ethics. These examples in turn lay the groundwork for understanding musical ethos, which is the focus of the second part of the chapter and which forms an introduction proper to the re-interpretation of internal character that took place from the seventeenth century.

1. Acoustical resonance

> ...all things are subject to the laws of nature,
> by which they are ordered in the best possible way.
> Cicero, *Nature of the Gods* (2.80-82)

1.1. Oscillations, energy, sympathy

By resonance is understood the phenomenon that structures capable of oscillation will oscillate in sympathy with relatively feeble external forces which act periodically and whose oscillation period coincides with that of the resonating structure. While it is resonating, the structure stores up energy. From this description, there are three aspects of a resonating system that require further comment: oscillation, energy storage and sympathy. The first two aspects, oscillation and energy, may be illustrated by the example of a simple pendulum: a bullet tied to the end of a string (Figure 1.1). To displace the pendulum from its equilibrium position, you give the bullet an initial pull or push. If you continue to push it in the swinging direction each time it reaches its maximum deflection, the amplitude, or extension in space, of the oscillations increases progressively. It is this energy build-up that scientists call 'resonance'. Without a periodic push, the to and fro oscillations do not increase indefinitely, because the pendulum is damped, that is, limited by energy losses that eventually return the bullet to a position of rest or equilibrium.

The bullet/pendulum goes back and forth on the arc of a circle, not a straight line; and its to and fro motion takes time (Figure

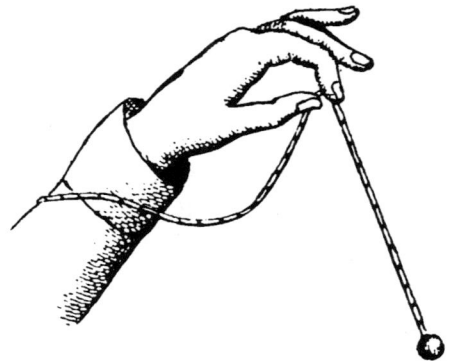

Figure 1.1   Simple bullet pendulum

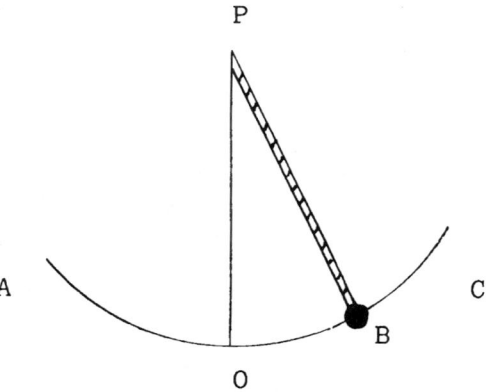

Figure 1.2   Motion of the bullet pendulum

1.2). Consequently, it is an example, though not an exact one, of simple harmonic motion. This type of motion may be represented by projecting on to the diameter of a circle the uniform motion of a point round its circumference (Figure 1.3), where the position of equilibrium is at O and the end points of the to and fro motion of the swinging bullet, at A and B. We could say that the bullet

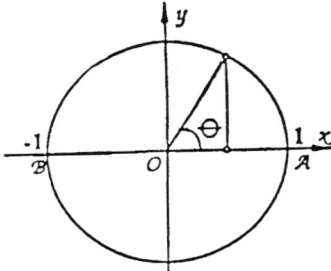

Figure 1.3 Simple harmonic motion

'stops' instantaneously at A and B and is fastest passing through O. But the word 'stop' is misleading, since pendular motion is continuous motion. Hence, it is more precise to describe what happens instantaneously at A and B as an acceleration, or change of speed, which is greatest at A and B and least at O. Suppose, for example, that the bullet takes one second to go from point A to point B and back again to point A. This second of time is called 'the period' of simple harmonic motion. You can change the period of simple harmonic motion by changing the length of the pendulum. In the case of the bullet/pendulum, for example, you can shorten or lengthen the string.

Another way of representing simple harmonic motion is by a sine curve, where the displacement varies with time. Waves shaped like sine curves — sinusoidal waves — are an example of harmonic motion; and the motion is simple harmonic if there is only one sine curve involved. The up and down motion of a boat on the sea is close to simple harmonic. Although there is no circle, the wave surface is modelled well by a sine curve moving horizontally. Suppose, for example, that the sine wave moves forward one period every second. Then the boat moves from the top of one crest to the top of the next one via the trough in between in 1 second. It is the same as a point on a vibrating string, providing the string is producing shapes like sine curves as it vibrates (Figure 1.4a, b). But waves may be made up of several sine curves of different periods or amplitudes superposed on one another (Figure 1.5a, b).

(a)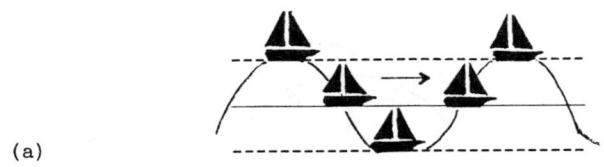

(b)

Figure 1.4 Simple harmonic motion
 (a) as positions of a boat moving through the waves
 (b) as positions of a point on a vibrating string

Since the world we live in is immersed in a huge elastic ocean of air, the agitation of the air produces waves, when, for example, you clap your hands and a volume of air is rapidly compressed. Because of its elasticity, the air expands again at once to compress an adjacent volume of air. This air also tends to expand again, and so an invisible wave moves on and on. Upon reaching your ear, it strikes the eardrum or tympanitic membrane and causes it to vibrate. Its tremors are then transmitted through the drum membrane to the auditory nerve, and along the auditory nerve to the brain. There you feel what is called a sound (your clap), but sound is only a name for the elastic wave that has travelled through air to your brain.

In antiquity, Zeno, the first head of the Stoic school of philosophy, suggested an analogy between the propagation of water waves and the transmission of sound waves through the air: 'We hear when the air between the sonant body and the organ of hearing suffers a concussion, a vibration, which spreads spherically and then forms waves and strikes upon the ears, just as water in a reservoir forms circles when a stone is thrown into it'.[11]

Conceiving the Inconceivable 9

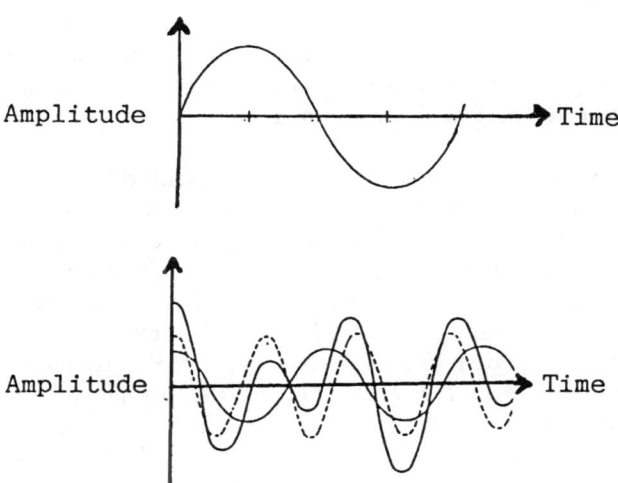

Figure 1.5   Waveforms
  (a) of a sine wave
  (b) of several sine waves superposed

This comparison was repeated in 1633 thus:

> As when a stone, troubling the quiet waters,
> Points in the angry stream, a wrinkle round
> Which soon another and another scatter
> Till all the lake with circles now is crown'd;
> All so the aire struck with some violence nigh,
> Begets a world of circles in the skie;
> All which infected move with sounding qualitie.
> These at Auditus' palace soon arriving,
> Enter the gate and strike the warning drum;
> To which three instruments fit motion giving,
> Which every voice discern; then that third room
> Sharpens each sound and quick conveys it thence;
> Till by the flying poast 'tis hurried hence,
> And in an instant brought into the judging sense.[12]

Here you find undulatory motions described after the manner of throwing a stone into calm water. Round the spot struck there forms a little ring of wave, which, advancing equally in all directions, expands to a constantly increasing circle. Corresponding to this ring of wave, sound also proceeds in the air from the excited point and advances in all directions as far as the limits of the mass of air extend.

The process in the air is almost identical with that on the surface of the water. The crests of the waves of water correspond in the waves of sound to spherical shells where the air is condensed and the troughs to shells of rarefaction. Accordingly, a sonorous wave consists of two parts, in one of which the air is condensed and in the other, rarefied. The motion of the sonorous wave must not be confounded with the motion of the particles which at any moment form the wave. During the passage of the wave, every particle concerned in its transmission makes only a small excursion to and fro, the length of which is called 'the amplitude of vibration'. Consequently, scientists make a distinction between phase and amplitude. Phase refers to a particular stage or point of advancement in a cycle – the fractional part of the period through which the time has advanced, measured from some arbitrary origin; amplitude designates the distance or range from one extremity of an oscillation to the middle point or neutral value. Any finite and continuous periodic motion may be represented by a series of simple harmonic motions of suitable phases and amplitudes.[13]

From the foregoing account, it is obvious that the propagation of sound is solely the business of mechanics and that sound itself has no real existence but is simply a sensation in the brain. Nearly all sounds in nature are noises, the sensation of which is produced by elastic waves travelling in a random manner. For the sensation of musical sound, the elastic waves of air must travel in a definite order. When this happens and a steady train of waves following each other at regular intervals passes through the air, you hear a continuous sound of a definite pitch. As the waves grow more frequent, they become shorter in length, and the sound rises in pitch. The lowest musical sound humans can hear has a frequency of 16 vibrations per second, whereas frequencies above 20,000 become ultrasound, which consists of sound waves too frequent to be heard by humans.

Until a means was found for creating vacuums, the existence of the invisible air and sound waves was demonstrated by the third aspect of a resonating system – the phenomenon of sympathetic resonance. Although this phenomenon was well known to the ancient Greeks, its scientific principles were not understood until the early part of the seventeenth century. According to these principles, sympathetic resonance refers to the transmission of vibrations from a vibrating body to another non-vibrating body, a phenomenon that cannot take place unless the two bodies are capable of vibrating at the same frequency (or a harmonic of that frequency). For example, when the strings of two violins are tuned in exact unison and the string of one violin is bowed, the string on the second violin will begin to vibrate.

The vacuum experiments, which began in the early 1640s, were supposed to demonstrate that sound was interdicted when the surrounding air is withdrawn from a vibrating body. One of the fiercest critics of these experiments, Thomas Hobbes, seems to have been the first to appreciate that the experiments demonstrated no such thing.[14] Indeed, as Frederick Vinton Hunt points out, although an erroneous interpretation of the experiments has adhered 'with stubborn tenacity' from the time of their first performance in the seventeenth century down to their present and continued use in elementary physics classes, 'these experiments do not prove the inability of a rarefied medium to *transmit* acoustic energy, but only the extreme difficulty of *imparting* any appreciable amount of vibratory energy to such a medium'.[15]

1.2. Musical vibrators and resonators

Musical performers, using highly skilled actions, make the air vibrate, quickly or slowly, violently or only slightly, because the musical instruments on which they play are physico-acoustical contrivances that impart various combinations of oscillatory motion to the surrounding air. In all musical instruments, two things are necessary for the production of strongly audible sounds: first, an exciting cause or vibrator and, second, a resonator. If you are to understand how people have been conceived as musical instruments, you will have to learn what these two things are. Let us begin with vibrators.

Science gives the name 'vibrator' to anything that can be set vibrating by an impact, a blow or friction. For example, pendula and springs are vibrators. But musical-instrument vibrators must be acoustic vibrators, that is, they must be capable of sending out sound waves through the air with a frequency rate of tens, hundreds or thousands per second. To do this, an acoustic vibrator must be elastic or, to use a seventeenth-century term, 'springy'. Metal or cane tongues, stretched films, gut or wire strings make excellent acoustic vibrators. Let us use the musical string as our exemplar, since this is one of the most common acoustic vibrators. But let us represent the string as a long, heavy rope stretched between two posts, since the action of the rope is slower than that of the string and, hence, more easily visible.

If the stretched rope is set vibrating, for instance, by striking it with a cane, a long, slow wave will rise and fall between the two posts, the to and fro swing being greatest in the middle. Scientists call this middle point the 'loop' or 'anti-node'. If the rope is stretched more tightly, the swings become more rapid because of the closer coupling between the rope particles which transmit motion quicker. The same result is obtained with a shorter rope, since vibrations travel faster through it. If you look closely at the vibrating rope, you will notice not one but several standing waves. This is because the rope vibrates simultaneously in several ways. In the first place, it vibrates as a whole (Figure 1.6a). Then, there are two more waves each half the rope's length, riding the main wave. They are separated by a node – a relatively stationary point – looking like a clamp on the rope (Figure 1.6b). Then, there are three waves each covering a third of the rope's length, also separated by nodes and with a loop or anti-node at the middle of each third (Figure 1.6c). The same is true of the rope's fourths, fifths, etc. (Theoretically, a vibrating rope can be divided into any integral number of equal, or aliquot, parts.) Thus, a long vibrating body is not the smooth arc it appears at first glance. At any moment it is wriggling in intricate turns and is studded with an array of standing waves which are both independent of, and penetrate, one another. The total vibration of the string, therefore, is the sum of all these partial vibrations going on simultaneously.

When a musical string is stretched between two supports attached to a resonator (about which I shall have more to say presently), it behaves exactly the same way as the rope. The only difference is that the rope swings slowly and therefore silently,

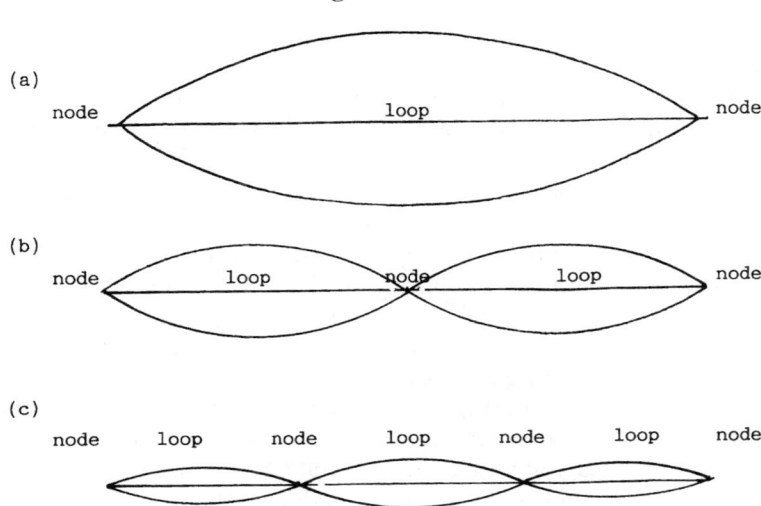

Figure 1.6 Standing waves of a rope
 (a) vibrating as a whole
 (b) vibrating in seconds
 (c) vibrating in thirds

while the rapid vibrations of the string produce an audible tone. In fact, it is not a single tone but a whole series, each part of the string adding its own tone. Thus, it turns out that a single string gives out a combination of tones. When the string is excited by striking, plucking or bowing, the entire length of the string gives the fundamental tone or first harmonic. It is the loudest of all. The string's halves give a tone an octave higher, since they vibrate twice as quickly. Their tone is called the first overtone or the second harmonic. The string's thirds produce the still higher second overtone or third harmonic; its fourths produce the third overtone or fourth harmonic, and so on. When the string is plucked suddenly, rapid and short standing waves are produced in it. When it is pulled gently, the waves are slow and long. Because of this, high overtones can be heard in the former case and low ones, in the latter.

In tubes, such as wind musical instruments, air becomes a long elastic body that behaves like a musical string. For example, when a flute player blows the instrument, an air column is agitated to give out its natural, or fundamental, tone. As the player stops the fingerholes, the length of the air spring changes, and so does the pitch of the flute. If the flutist blows harder, the air spring, instead of vibrating full length, vibrates in its halves, and we hear the first overtone. With a still stronger blast, the air column vibrates in thirds, fourths and so on, so that the second, then the third and the higher overtones appear. Of course, there are some differences between the action of the air and that of a musical string. The air vibrates lengthwise or longitudinally, whereas a string vibrates transversely. Consequently, a column of air is more like a long helical spring than a string. But here, too, there are differences. The air 'spring' is much lighter than one made of steel; it vibrates more rapidly and comes to a stop sooner. Because of this, a single impulse cannot keep it vibrating. On the other hand, it will respond to continuous agitation with steady natural vibrations. In this way the air column reinforces the scarcely audible sound of the vibrator through resonance.

Every musical instrument is a sound vessel, and sound vessels are important because they are resonators, that is, devices which reinforce the sounds produced by vibrators. The sound produced by acoustic vibrators – for example, strings, reeds or a player's lips – is scarcely audible, because their vibrations are weak and excite only a limited volume of air. To transmit their vibrations to larger bodies of air, acoustic vibrators must be fitted to resonators or 'acoustic levers' in the form of wooden or metal cases, bellies, soundboards, tubes and so on which act as devices to reinforce the original vibrations. Not all sound vessels are resonators. For example, woodwinds are not resonators, since they cannot vibrate. Hence, their tubes serve only to contain the resonator, air. In these kinds of instruments, tongues serve as the vibrators. The term 'tongue', however, is misleading, for it does not refer to the human organ in the floor of the mouth and which, in playing wind instruments is used to stop and unstop the stream of air that puts the exciting cause into vibration. Rather, acoustic tongues are the exciting cause; and these tongues may be natural, as, for example, the lips of the flute player, or artificial, as, for example, the reed of the clarinet or oboe.

Unlike woodwind instruments, the tube walls of brass instruments serve as resonators, because they give out their own tones, just as bells do (though bells are percussion, not wind instruments). The most complex resonators, however, are stringed instruments, because the whole of the instrument is made up of numerous separate resonators. For example, the violin's bridge, back, belly and soundpost form an ensemble of resonators, each with a tone of its own. The violin also has numerous vibrators, including the strings on the outside of the body and the numerous air springs on the inside of the body. In short, each type of musical instrument has its own combination of acoustic vibrators and resonators, which are interdependent.

To understand this interdependence, let us return to our example of a musical string, this time adding a soundboard. Before the musical string can function as an acoustic vibrator, it must be drawn so taut as to be virtually unstretchable. In this state any increase of its tension by striking, plucking or bowing will strain the soundboard proportionately: when the string is forcibly bent, the tension increases and the soundboard is overstrained; when the string is released, the soundboard recovers, but recovery is checked as soon as the string is drawn straight at its tuned tension. The tension of a musical string, therefore, will be determined by the elastic resistance of the soundboard strain, so that the soundboard is the mainspring of string tone. But the string controls the frequency of soundboard vibrations by a definite cycle of soundboard reactions which is displayed in each string vibration (and which can be observed directly or indirectly by artificial means).

The cycle is as follows: (1) The tuned string is bent, tension increases, soundboard is overstrained; (2) the string is released, soundboard recovers and draws the string straight; (3) the straightened string checks the soundboard, which therefore recoils and relaxes the tension of the string, allowing it to rebend; (4) the soundboard again recovers and draws the string straight; (5) the string checks recovery of the soundboard as in (3), and the string rebends towards position (1). The string is thus the means by which the elastic energy of the soundboard is made available so that its recovery and recoil may drive the string which controls its frequency, because the check action occurs at the string frequency. The mechanism is analogous to that of a clock which is driven by a powerful mainspring controlled by the frequency of a relatively feeble hairspring.

Every resonator has a natural frequency or normal mode of vibration, so that if a resonating system is given impulses with a frequency approaching the natural frequency, its response, or swings, increases many times as exact synchronism is reached. But when the rhythm of the vibrator coincides with the resonator's natural frequency of vibration, the resonator's movements become too much for its strength and it collapses. In other words, the amount of energy stored up becomes so great that it brings about the destruction or collapse of the structure. This does not often happen with musical instruments, but it does happen with other structures. For example, the biblical story of Joshua (6.10-20) tells how the wall of Jericho fell down flat when the people shouted at the same time that the priests blew their trumpets.[16] Most textbooks, however, cite a much later example, namely, the destruction, in 1940, of the Suspension Bridge in Tacoma, Washington, USA. This occurred when wind supplied the power causing the bridge to vibrate at one of its torsional resonance frequencies without sufficient damping.

2. Human resonance

> *The entrance to the ears is hard and grisly,*
> *with many involutions,*
> *which serve to reflect and amplify the sound,*
> *just as in a lyre tortoiseshell or horn*
> *used to give resonance to the strings.*
> Cicero, *Nature of the Gods* (2.144-146)

2.1. Physiological resonance

In most animals the drum membrane (Figure 1.7:1) covers the cavity of the middle ear and conducts sound as acoustic vibrations through three articulated bones, known as the ossicles (2), to the inner ear (3) deep in the petrous bone. Auditory perception takes place in the *helix* or cochlea (4) of the inner ear, a bony spiral tube of two and three-quarter turns filled with fluid. The fibres of the acoustic nerves enter the petrous bone from above to be distributed throughout the membrane of the cochlea, the true acoustic end-organ. Close to it the labyrinth or vestibule (5) serves only as the organ of equilibrium. Both labyrinth and cochlea are filled with clear fluid; and they become visible only after the

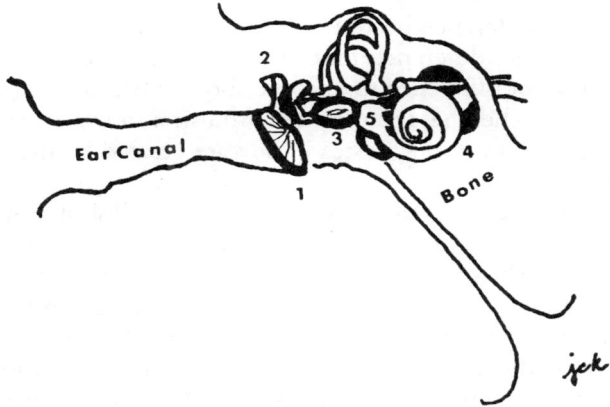

Figure 1.7 The human ear

petrous bone has been cut accurately and carefully across the area of these structures.

Until recently, auditory theories have been pitch theories, of which there are two types. One is the frequency theory, in which pitch perception is related to the waveform of the stimulus; the other is the resonance theory, in which the ear performs a frequency analysis.[17] The latter type of theory was given its first complete form by Hermann von Helmholtz, who conceived the inner ear as a tiny semblance of the piano with twenty thousand 'strings', or nerve terminals, in the form of small hairs differing in length.[18] This live resonator-analyser, hidden in the cochlea, is called 'the basilar membrane'. When the sound wave travels through the fluid of the cochlea across the 'strings' of the 'piano', the hair cells respond at once by resonating and exciting the nerve fibres running to the brain.[19]

Helmholtz's model for auditory resonance was not limited to an internal musical instrument played upon by the external world. To understand the other components of his model, we need to learn how he solved the problem of a 'ghost tone', noticed for the first time in the eighteenth century.[20] This phenomenon occurs when two strings are bowed strongly, thereby producing a third tone, lower in pitch than the two tones actually sounded. Subsequently, it was discovered that the frequency of the third or combination tone was the difference between those bowed on the two strings, hence the name, difference tone. But the puzzle remained, how did this ghost or difference tone come about? Helmholtz answered this question, when he discovered that musical instruments do not produce difference tones. Instead, they are created by the healthy ear itself.

When we listen to music, therefore, we embellish it against our will, since, in addition to its functions as a musical instrument and sound analyser, the ear, in cooperation with the brain, adds to subconscious creativity when we listen to music. This subconscious creativity is fairly extensive, for difference tones are only part of the extras our ear adds to any piece of music we hear. Indeed, Helmholtz also discovered there are less prominent 'summation' combination tones (their frequency, being the sum of the frequencies of the sounded tones). Later on, scientists added others, called 'aural harmonics', with which the ear brightens up sufficiently strong pure single tones. All these sounds may form pairs to produce further tones whose pitch and loudness can be predicted by mathematical analysis.

As we shall see in subsequent chapters, the phenomena added by our ear in cooperation with the brain were unknown to seventeenth-century writers, some of whom nevertheless assumed that the physical process of perception is computational. Such a notion is found in the writings of Hobbes, who is thought to have influenced Gottfried Wilhelm Leibniz, author of the famous remark that music is the soul's unconscious exercise in arithmetic.[21] According to current understanding, the brain and the ear are indeed busy 'doing arithmetic', that is, computing sound frequencies, so that a simple sound, if it is strong enough, may turn into a complex acoustical phenomena in the listener's mind and which, in the final analysis, gives any sound its quality.

You might well ask: Why is it that the ear creates tones that are not sounded? Why is it that the already complex mixture of overtones is complicated still further? The answer to these questions is that human perception of music is greatly enriched and made more flexible and refined, when the ear picks up the overtones of, for example, a plucked string and sets to work combining them. This is where the difference tones come in, for each pair of tones produces a difference tone. Suppose the fundamental tone is of frequency 100, then its overtones are of frequencies 200, 300, 400, 500, 600, etc. Any pair of adjacent overtones will produce a difference tone of frequency 100, or the same as the fundamental tone. As a result, the fundamental tone is fortified many times, and sound information is transmitted with the least expense of energy.

Of course, the physiology of hearing continued to be investigated after Helmholtz's time, so that I omit mention of biopotentials, mechanochemistry, electronics and cybernetics. But my purpose is not to provide an outline of the history of auditory theory; rather, it is to show how a well-known nineteenth-century scientist used a musical model to understand the physiology of hearing. It is worth adding that, afterwards, a similar model was used by an equally well-known twentieth-century scientist, Erwin Schrödinger. According to him, the principal organ of hearing, the cochlea or spiral tube, contains stretched transverse elastic fibres, forming a membrane, the width of which (or the length of the individual fibre) diminishes from 'bottom' to 'top':

> Thus, like the strings of a harp or a piano, the fibres of different length respond mechanically to oscillations of different frequency. To a definite frequency a definite small area of the membrane – not just one fibre – responds, to a higher frequency another area, where the fibres are shorter. A mechanical vibration of definite frequency must set up, in each of that group of nerve fibres, the well-known nerve impulses that are propagated to certain regions of the cerebral cortex. We have the general knowledge that the process of conduction is very much the same in all nerves and changes only with the intensity of excitation; the latter affects the frequency of the pulses, which, of course, must not be confused with the frequency of sound...(the two have nothing to do with each other).[22]

To construct a simpler ear, a scientist would have to model the basilar membrane on a series of resonators, like Helmholtz did, so that each single 'string' across the cochlea would answer to one sharply defined frequency of incoming vibration. But research has shown that the vibrations of the 'strings' are strongly damped, that is, the vibrations are checked or deadened, and this broadens their range of resonance. Without such strong damping, there would be a terrible consequence, as Schrödinger made clear: 'the perception of sound would not cease almost immediately when the producing wave ceases; it would last for some time, until the poorly damped resonator in the cochlea died down.' Hence, the discrimination of pitch would be obtained by sacrificing the discrimination in time between subsequent sounds. Yet, the auditory mechanism manages to reconcile both in a most consummate fashion, though how it does this is a subject of debate.[23]

2.2. Ethical resonance

Physiology is not the only aspect that may be subsumed under the epithet, 'internal character', since, traditionally, that epithet has included ethics. Indeed, Denis Diderot combined both aspects in two philosophical dialogues, written in the second half of the eighteenth century. In each dialogue the respondents, or alternative voices of Diderot, are real people: in the one, *D'Alembert's Dream*, there is Jean Le Rond D'Alembert, a scientist and commentator on the music theories of Jean-Philippe Rameau, a famous composer; and in the other, *Rameau's Nephew*, there is Jean-François Rameau, a musician and nephew of the composer, who was immortalised through Diderot's dialogue.[24]

In the first dialogue Diderot proposes a conception of a 'sentient', whose existence consists of consciousness 'of having been himself from the first instant he reflected until the present moment'.[25] He further proposes that the basis of self-consciousness is memory of one's own actions, for without memory there would be no 'I', no connected 'story' of one's life. Memory enables a sentient to link together the impressions received from the external world; and from these links he constructs a chain or story – that of his life – and so acquires consciousness, for he can affirm, deny, think, conclude. D'Alembert, who agrees with Diderot's conception, asserts that we can think of only one thing at a time. If this assertion is true, the object of our thought would have to remain under the scrutiny of the intellect at the same time that the intellect is affirming or denying certain qualities of the object. How, then, do we remember objects that are not present to the intellect?

Conceiving the Inconceivable

The answer, according to Diderot, is that memory functions like resonance, because 'the fibres of our organs' function like 'sensitive vibrating strings':

> A sensitive vibrating string goes on vibrating and sounding a note long after it has been plucked. It is this oscillation, a kind of necessary resonance, which keeps the object present while the understanding is free to consider whichever of the object's qualities it wishes. But vibrating strings have yet another property, that of making others vibrate, and it is in this way that one idea calls up a second, and the two together a third, and all three a fourth, and so on; you can't set a limit to the ideas called up and linked together by a philosopher meditating or communing with himself in silence and darkness [for he]...can make astonishing leaps, and one idea called up will sometimes start an harmonic at an incomprehensible interval.[26] If this phenomenon can be observed between resonant strings which are inert and separate, why should it not take place between living and connected points, continuous and sensitive fibres?

D'Alembert is unconvinced by the comparison, for he accuses Diderot of turning the intellect into an entity distinct from the instrument, 'a kind of musician listening to vibrating strings and making pronouncements about their harmony or dissonance'. Diderot acknowledges that he may have laid himself open to this objection. But he suggests that D'Alembert would not have raised it if he had considered 'the difference between the instrument called philosopher and the instrument called *clavecin*'.[27]

Clavecin is the French word for harpsichord, a stringed keyboard instrument in the form of an elongated wing, in which the strings are plucked and run from front to back of the instrument, parallel to the individual keys of the keyboard (Figure 1.8). When comparing this instrument to a philosopher, as Diderot points out, we must assume that the *clavecin* has both sensitivity and memory, so that it will know and repeat automatically the tunes played on its keys. Only then may we consider the keys of the *clavecin* as so many senses, 'which are struck by things in nature around us, and often strike themselves'. How the senses strike themselves, Diderot does not say, even though he believes that

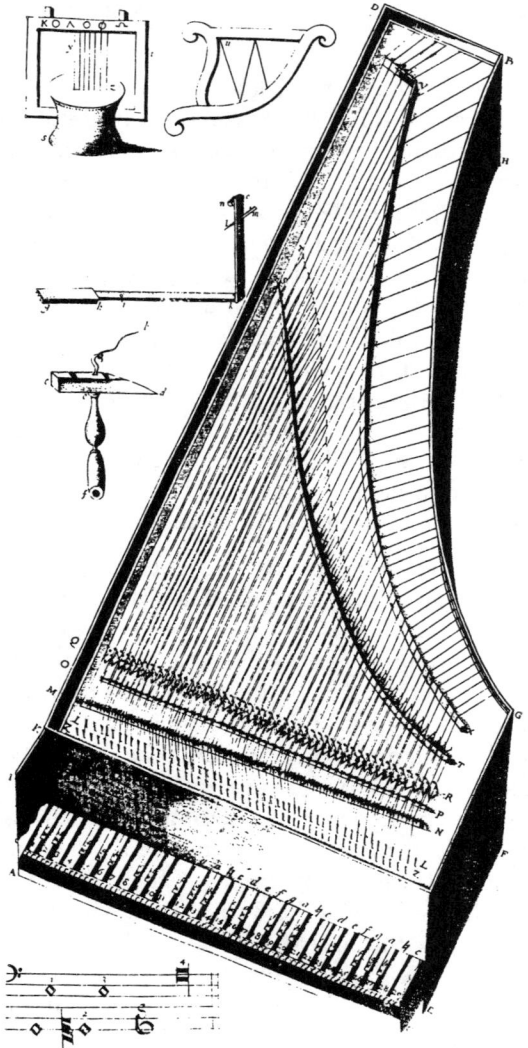

Figure 1.8 The *clavecin*, from M. Mersenne, *Harmonie universelle* (Paris, 1636-37)

...this is all that happens in a *clavecin* organized like you and me. There is an impression which has its cause within the instrument or outside it, and from this impression is born a sensation, and this sensation has duration, for it is impossible to imagine that it is both made and destroyed in a single, indivisible instant. Another impression succeeds the first which also has its cause both inside and outside the animal, then a second sensation, and tones which describe them in natural or conventional sounds.

D'Alembert remains sceptical about the value of comparing natural and artificial instruments, since, in addition to sensitivity and memory, we should have to attribute sexual and other powers to the *clavecin*, so that it may 'engender from itself, or with its female, little *clavecins*, alive and resonant'. Indeed, we should have to assume that *clavecins* communicate one with another.

To overcome this difficulty, Diderot proposes a resonance theory of language, which holds that language (our 'story') originates from a person's innate propensity for associating certain sounds (frequencies/ideas) with certain kinds of objects and actions; that is, a sentient responds to objects and actions in a manner analogous to the way a *clavecin* resonates when struck.[28] Since language consists in having one or more inner experiences or resonances, thought is the same as sub-vocal speech and depends on language, for to think is to 'speak low'. Hence, meaningful communication (understanding) arises only when we press down the homologous key of another person's mental keyboard to establish the same scale of association of things with names to elicit corresponding, not identical, responses (resonances). According to this view, language is excited by an external periodic impulse having a frequency near the natural frequency within each person.

The external world is not the only player on a sensitive instrument, since, according to Diderot, the instrument can play itself. But in this latter kind of playing, 'there can come a moment of madness when a sensitive *clavecin* imagines that it is the only one that has ever existed in the world, and that all the harmony in the universe is being produced by it alone'. The moment of madness is solipsism, when nothing but the self exists, so that the self is the only object of verifiable knowledge. In *D'Alembert's Dream* Diderot does not draw out the implications of solipsism, for after the two interlocutors part, D'Alembert returns home, where he falls asleep and dreams he is a spider at the centre of a web, an image not unlike the *clavecin*.

In *Rameau's Nephew*, however, solipsism and its consequences form an important part of this dialogue.[29] The nephew of the title ('He') is a musician; but he is merely raw material, a near-musician, and an enthusiast of the so-called 'new' music which he contrasts to the 'old' music of his famous uncle. Since Diderot ('I') assumes that every imitative art has a model in nature, he asks the nephew: What is the musician's model when he writes a tune? The nephew answers: 'Speech, if the model is alive and thinking; noise, if the model is inanimate.' But he emphasises the former model to propound a theory of the origin of music from passionate speech: 'The more vigorous and true the speech, which is the basis of the tune, and the more closely the tune fits it and the more points of contact it has with it, the truer that tune will be and the more beautiful. And this is what our younger musicians [composers of new music] have seen so clearly.' He then goes on to speak about the new music; and as he does this, his tone of voice becomes more and more passionate, until, at last, dialogue is no longer possible. Hence, Diderot, as author not interlocutor, resorts to narrative to show the effects on the nephew as he becomes a victim of his overheated imagination.

Diderot's narrative falls into three parts. In the first part, he describes the strange sounds uttered by the nephew, with the corresponding movements:

> With cheeks puffed out and a hoarse, dark tone he did the horns and bassoons, a bright, nasal tone for the oboes, quickening his voice with incredible agility for the stringed instruments to which he tried to get the closest approximation; he whistled the recorders and cooed the flutes, shouting, singing and throwing himself about like a mad thing: a one-man show featuring dancers, male and female, singers of both sexes, a whole orchestra, a complete opera-house, dividing himself into twenty different stage parts, tearing up and down, stomping, like one possessed, with flashing eyes and foaming mouth.

This is the moment of pure solipsism, which Diderot had mentioned in *D'Alembert's Dream*, the 'moment of madness when a sensitive *clavecin* imagines that it is the only one that has ever existed in the world, and that all the harmony in the universe is being produced by it alone'. Instead of speaking, therefore, the nephew lends his voice to imitating singers as well as the entire orchestra, becoming himself a living musical instrument.

In the second part of the narration, the nephew's sounds are interpreted as an expression of passionate interjections – weeping, sighing, laughing, despairing and so on. And in the third part of the narration, Diderot concentrates our attention on the physical state of the nephew: 'Knocked up with fatigue, like a man coming out of a deep sleep or long trance, he stood there motionless, dazed, astonished, looking about him and trying to recognize his surroundings. Waiting for his strength and memory to come back, he mechanically wiped his face'. In this passage Diderot intimates that the nephew's ravings have turned him into an automaton, and so have brought him close to self-annihilation, for without strength and memory we are nothing – there is no continuous story that forms the 'I'. There are two implications to note. First, intensity of passion is not a help but a positive hindrance to a sentient, who is represented here by means of musical activity. Second, to avoid self-annihilation, we must learn to exercise self-control, though how we do this is left unstated.

2.3. Philosophical resonance

In *D'Alembert's Dream* Diderot chose the *clavecin* as a model of internal character, although other keyboard instruments – for example, the organ or pianoforte – would have served equally well. As we shall see, the keyboard model became prominent in the early part of the seventeenth century, and its use since then has been continuous.[30] Since the electronic computer may be considered as a keyboard instrument, let us explore briefly how keyboard instruments might be used to symbolise three different beliefs about mind and body. We may call these beliefs 'dualism', 'materialism' and 'realism', though let us qualify the last, notoriously difficult, term with the adjective 'instrumental'.

The main thesis of dualism is that both incorporeal and corporeal 'substances' exist. Mind is identified with the former and body, with the latter substance. If we recur to a keyboard instrument to symbolise this belief, mind (soul, *animus*) cannot be represented, because mind is immaterial. Hence, mind is like an absent musician, whose mysterious action at a distance plays on the instrument (body), the fingers of the hand (consciousness) being regarded as autonomous. In materialism, the main thesis is that only bodies are substances, so that, using the same keyboard instrument, we may symbolise body in two ways: first, as hands, which represent external objects, and second, as the instrument itself, which represents the sentient subject. Hence, mind (perception) is the simple result of the action of external objects which play on the body. The two different beliefs, therefore, may be represented in the same way – by a keyboard instrument plus hands. But in the one, dualism, the hands are the intermediary between incorporeal mind (the absent musician) and corporeal body (the instrument), whereas in the other, materialism, the hands are the external objects that play on the body of the subject (the instrument).

In *D'Alembert's Dream* Diderot rejected dualism. And he also seems to have rejected materialism, when he insisted that the sensitive instrument is not determined solely by externality – by objects striking its keys. Yet, he provided no insight as to the manner in which a sensitive instrument can strike its own keys. In *Rameau's Nephew*, however, there is an intimation of how this might be possible, because Diderot showed mind in the relationship of reciprocal exchange with the instruments that it uses, rendering to them what it receives from them, and more. Mind manifests itself as the form of the body, because it applies itself to space like a hand to an instrument. But body is more than an instrument or means: it is the nephew's expression in the world, the visible form of his intentions. This conception of mind and body is called 'instrumental realism', which I shall illustrate by 'reading' the painting reproduced at the front of this book.

Starting from the far left, there is a peculiar looking keyboard instrument, which is 'organised', because it combines a number of 'organs' into one whole. One of these organs is a bellows, representing the heart and lungs, the principal organs of the greater and lesser circulation. Connected to the bellows is a manometer, an instrument for determining the pressure of gases, vapours or liquids. As the pressure rises or falls, so too will the tension of the instrument as a whole. The controlling device, therefore, is the adjacent organ, which represents the central nervous system.

But you will note two things about this organ. First, there is a roll of paper with peculiar marks. Like a piano roll that encodes and stores music, we may suppose that the one in the painting encodes and stores experience and, hence, represents memory. Second, there is the structure behind the roll, which forms an extension into the keyboard instrument proper, just as the spinal cord extends from the brain.

Although we do not see inside the box of the instrument, we may speculate that it contains strings, representing the nervous system, and pipes, representing the vascular system. That this reading has some merit is suggested by the metal protrusions on the front left of the instrument box just above the keyboard, for the upper protrusions are like organ stops for pipes, whereas the lower protrusion, suggests a kind of winding device for tensing and relaxing (tuning) the strings. Resting on the instrument, where we would expect to find the music stand, are five articulatory apparatuses, the different tensions of the lips representing the formation of the vowel sounds, A E I O U. We may conclude, therefore, that the instrument is sensitive, has memory and can produce speech. Indeed, the instrument has a name, 'Cecilia'; and its keyboard is fingered by a woman, who we may presume is St. Cecilia, the patroness of music.

According to my reading, mind is partly non-localised, for it extends from the paper roll into the keyboard instrument and beyond to the right hand of the musician, who plays her own instrument, Cecilia. But the extension of mind continues outward as the musician's whole body and particularly her left hand, for it is raised to her mouth in an expression we recognise as 'shh', silence. From this expression we know the musician's intention, as well as what she represents, for in this painting St. Cecilia is not the patroness of sounded music but of silent music, that which 'plays' inside us as our internal character but which, nevertheless, has external manifestations. Hence, St. Cecilia's hands neither represent consciousness, as in the keyboard symbol of dualism, nor the external world, as in the keyboard symbol of materialism. Rather, they signify the extension of mind into the world. On this reading, instrument – internal character – and musician – external demeanour – are inseparable.

What, then, about the combination of objects at the front

and right-hand side of the painting? These are important if we are to avoid the problem of solipsism raised by Diderot, for there are other musicians in the world — we alone do not make the harmony. Let us begin, therefore, with the little dog, who, at first, reminds us of the HMV logo, Nipper. But that dog, you will recall, sits in front of a victrola, listening to music, whereas this dog growls into an instrument that looks like an ear, with its external bell and internal cochlea. Hence, we have a combination of an acoustic vibrator, the dog, and a resonator, the instrument. These two, taken together, represent the external world. But the dog's aspect suggests that the messages, which the world transmits as vibrations, may not sympathise with the natural frequency of the receiver, who, in this painting, is St. Cecilia, so that her gesture, 'shh', takes on dual significance.

Finally, there are the extra rolls of paper hanging on the wall. Like the paper roll on the keyboard instrument, these, too, represent memory stores, where experience is encoded. But the encoding is different on all the rolls, the one on the instrument also. We may assume, therefore, that the rolls hanging on the wall represent the 'stories' not of St. Cecilia but of other identities. We may make the further assumption that these identities are no longer living, because their memory stores are no longer connected to organised body.

II. MUSICAL ETHOS

> *Man's character is his daimon.*
> Heraclitus (Frag. 247)

Introduction
The ancient Greeks employed musical concepts to develop theories of ethos, which is rendered inadequately by the English term 'character'. Ethos, however, was always associated with the cultural and ethical experience called 'paideia' and, particularly, with musical paideia, for music has a double power of representing and also influencing moral character.[31] This double power may be illustrated from a fragment of Aristophanes, who pictured the once popular poet, Cratinus, in his dotage, with the electrum pegs falling out, the tuning no longer present and the modes showing yawning

holes. Rendered into somewhat whimsical English, the fragment is as follows:

> And then he remembered Cratinus, who
> in a spate of applause one day
> Tore through the broad leas and swept the great trees,
> with his rivals, root-upwards away;
> No song was sung then at the tables of men
> but his *'Bribery, fig-slippered Dame'*,
> And his *'Masters of musical graftsmanship'*
> was the work of a man with a name.
> But now, when you meet this poor *lyre* in the street,
> the bowels of compassion are shut;
> He must needs drivel on with his pegs half-gone
> and with gaps both in gamut and gut;
> Like Connas forgotten he shuffles about
> in a wreath as dried up as his throttle,
> Though you owe him, methinks, everlasting free-drinks
> and a seat by the Lord of the Bottle.[32]

The meaning of this fragment applies not to Cratinus' musical technique but to the man himself: He is an old, battered lyre that will no longer stay in tune; his pegs have come loose and are slipping from their sockets; as a result, string tension or tuning cannot be maintained and the intervals of the mode, relaxed beyond proper bounds, 'gape open'. According to Warren D. Anderson, this is 'a typically Aristophanic treatment of the Pythagorean doctrine which views the soul as a Harmonia, to be slackened or tightened by musical paideia'.[33]

It has been suggested that there actually were two theories of the soul that went under the name 'Pythagorean' – the one, put forward by Plato's mouthpiece, Simmias, a pupil of the Pythagorean, Philolaus; the other, held by Dicaearchus and the musician, Aristoxenus, both pupils of Aristotle. According to the first theory, the soul is a harmony of abstract numbers, and the relation of soul to body is envisaged as an organisation by a pre-existing harmony of numbers which outlasts the body.[34] According to the second theory, the soul is a harmony of the body, like the attunement of the strings of a lyre.[35] Scholarly opinion notwithstanding, there is evidence that the theory of the soul as a harmony developed in three distinct ways, each of which was indebted to a different theory of world harmony.

3. Ancient harmony theories

> ...*the body of the universe was created to be at unity owing to proportion; in consequence it acquired concord....*
> Plato, *Timaeus* (32)

3.1. The cosmos as a harmony

The hypothesis of an harmoniously conceived universe is very ancient, but it was expounded in the West by three pre-Socratic philosophers, who flourished from about the sixth to about the fourth centuries B.C. First, there was Pythagoras, who left no writings. But he inspired his followers with an harmonious vision that was founded on reverence for certain numbers in their roles in music and cosmology.[36] For the early Pythagoreans, the basic facts of music were derived from speculation and everything else stemmed from operations in arithmetic. In their calculations of the scale of music, this school employed ratios based only on the prime factors of 2 and 3, thereby restricting the consonant intervals in music to the octave, with the proportion 2:1, the fifth, with the proportion 3:2; and the fourth, with the proportion 4:3; or to compounds of these – for example, the octave plus fifth, with the proportion 3:1.

In addition to the ratios of integers corresponding to pitch or tuning, harmony also was an operation of placing a third term, or mean, between two terms of a given ratio. But the characteristic construction of Pythagorean harmony consisted of an application of all three means – the arithmetic, geometric and harmonic proportions – to produce a numerical system bound together by interlocking ratios, externally limited by the octave and internally by the means (Figure 1.9). It was this particular combination of species of proportion that was the model for Pythagorean cosmic harmony, because it was believed to be useful not only for all progress in music but also for the theory of the nature of the universe.[37]

Next, there was Heraclitus, who expounded his theory of cosmic harmony in aphorisms, or terse statements, only fragments

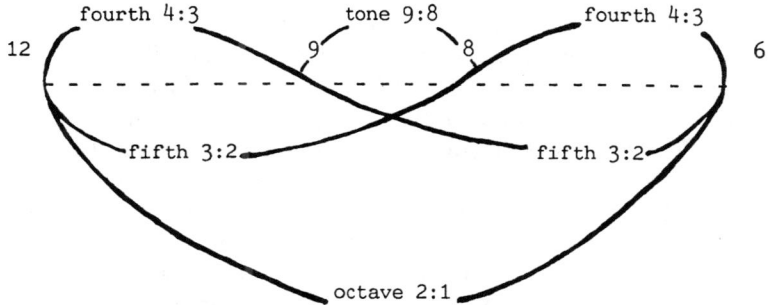

In this combination of proportions one series (12, 8, 6) preserves the harmonic; a second series (12, 9, 6) preserves the arithmetic; and the four terms taken together (12, 9, 8, 6) show in their disposition the geometric proportion (12: 9 = 4:3, 12:8 = 3:2). Moreover, the product of the means is equal to the product of the extremes (12 × 6 = 72; 9 × 8 = 72).

Figure 1.9 Pythagorean harmony of numbers

of which have come down to us.[38] According to this philosopher, wisdom consists in understanding cosmic fire (*logos*), the common element in things. Fire embodies measure (proportion) and, by dryness, ensures that change does not produce chaos. By fire the universe came into being, and by fire its order as a whole is maintained, for cosmic fire is 'an ever living fire, kindling in measures and going out in measures'. The sun, like everything else in the universe, partakes of this cosmic fire, for the 'Sun will not overstep his measures; otherwise the Erinyes, ministers of Justice, will find him out'. This is true of the soul also – a dry (fiery) soul is best. Because all nature has this common element, there is universal kinship. People's lives, therefore, are bound up with their whole surroundings, whereas in sleep this kinship is partly sundered.

Although cosmic fire is ethereal and invisible, it is like everyday fire in its movement by opposite tensions. The observable world is harmonious in the same way, for 'being at variance it agrees with itself': there is a 'back-stretched' connection, as in the bow that is strung and the lyre that is tuned.[39] Coherence is maintained by these opposing forces, for if the tension in one direction of the string does not produce an equivalent tension in the other direction, the system (e.g., bow or lyre) collapses. The implication is that apparent rest or equilibrium, may conceal an underlying tension, so that an unapparent connection is stronger than an apparent one.

Finally, there was Empedocles, whose theory of cosmic harmony may be gleaned from his poem, *On Nature*.[40] According to this philosopher, the world is made not of number but of four substances: earth and air, fire and water. From these substances all things are fitted and fixed together, and by means of these people think and feel both joy and sorrow. Number represents the substances, which come together proportionately, the ideal ratio being 1:1:1:1. This ideal determines the two tissues – flesh and blood – on whose composition man's intellectual excellence, his reason and skill, are predicated. Every departure from the ideal ratio entails some kind of shortcoming or lack of perfection, as in the case of sinews, which contain fire, earth and water in the ratio 1:1:2 (or 2:2:4).

Flesh and blood form composite 'mortal' things. And these things arise, when earth, air, fire and water mix through Love, a universal power of attraction which is in harmony with the eternal substances. In addition to Love, there is Strife, a universal power of separation, so that the attunement of the four substances implies more than the sexual principle of affinity. Rather, harmony consists of an equal balance, apportionment or mixture between polar and distinct powers, Love and Strife, whereby every natural blend is an embodiment of harmony.

From this brief summary, it is clear that Pythagorean cosmic harmony is the source for the theory of the soul as a harmony of abstract numbers, as scholars now hold. This theory, however, propounds a dualism of incorporeal and corporeal entities and, accordingly, cannot provide a model for mind/body interaction. Hence, we are left with the cosmic harmonies of Heraclitus and Empedocles as sources for the theory of the soul as a harmony of the body. But the cosmic harmonies of these pre-Socratics are different and lead to different soul theories. According to Heraclitus, the soul is a harmony when it is tense (dry, fiery), like a taut bow or lyre string. Here we have an easily grasped model of mind/body interaction.

Less easily grasped is Empedocles' model, according to which the soul is a harmony, when substances mix in an equal balance. You might ask, therefore, how music could symbolise this conception. The answer is that the system of Greek music, like the mixture theory of Empedocles, was based on a doctrine of four 'substances' – four contiguous strings or tones constituting a tetrachord. The extreme tones of the tetrachord were called 'immovable' and the inner ones, 'movable', because they changed, that is, required different tunings, thus producing different classes of tetrachords. Hence, music could symbolise the Empedoclean doctrine of mixture, because, on the theory of proportions of the tones in tuning, it was supposed that two consonant tones constitute a single blend, whereas two dissonant tones do not.[41]

3.2. Health as a harmony

In the second century the physician, Galen, emphasised the direct causal connection between bodily constitution and character, for he based his method on the doctrine that the passions and errors of the soul are linked to the errors of the body and should not be treated separately. This doctrine was not contradicted by Galen's inclusion of a set of practical ethics and education as part of his medical therapy, since ethical and philosophical training, combined with instruction in hygienic measures, represented a joint effort toward health, namely, toward wisdom, moderation and balance.[42] It is not surprising, therefore, that Galen defined health as 'a sort of harmony'.[43] But Galen utilised this term in two different ways to denote either the mixture of opposites in perfect balance or the cohesion of parts of any whole.

The first usage stems from Aristotle, who accepted from Plato's *Timaeus* the four Empedoclean substances of air, fire, water and earth but systematised these by means of a formula:

earth is dry and cold
water is   cold and moist
air is   moist and hot
fire is   hot and dry.[44]

According to this formula, the contrarieties – hot, cold, wet and dry

– were the primitive qualities of matter which cannot exist in isolation, whereas fire, air, water and earth were the simplest substances and were transformable, one into another, by a process of mixture. Transformation implied a passage between two opposing attributes, for example, 'tunedness' into 'untunedness'.[45] And mixtures were of two kinds: a chemical compound (Gk.: *krasis*; Lat.: *temperare*) and a mechanical compound (Gk.: *mixis*; Lat.: *miscere*).[46]

Both transformation and mixture were thought to result in a compound containing all the four substances, the essences of each compound being expressed by the ratio of the four qualities. However, in a chemical mixture the constituents reciprocally altered one another, whereas in a mechanical mixture the constituents could be detected lying side by side. The passage of opposites in either kind of mixture was between two extremes, for Aristotle held that all natural things are composed of a dynamic equilibrium of opposites and that these opposites are blended in a mean. Moreover, his evaluation of natural things was in accordance with their maintenance or restoration of the mean.[47]

By extending this doctrine, the so-called 'humoral physicians' not only established four humors – blood, yellow bile, black bile and phlegm – by analogy to the four substances, but also accepted the four qualities of matter – heat, dryness, moisture and cold – consisting of two pairs of opposites. They then ascribed all material existence to the various mixtures of the four substances and qualities, thereby accounting for climate and temperature (caused by a mixture of the four basic qualities), as well as for different temperaments of people – sanguinic, choleric, melancholic and phlegmatic (caused by a mixture of the four humors that make up the body and the four qualities that make up the climate). It was this doctrine that provided Galen with a definition of health as a harmony, in which the various substances and qualities blend in an equilibrium.

But he also defined health as a harmony of similar parts, the functions of which occur naturally.[48] By similar parts he denoted those organs constituting either the vascular system or the nervous system, both of which were instrumental to life.[49] But these systems were related, because their principal organs, the heart and the brain, were related: the brain exerted a cooling influence in opposition to the heating influence of the heart. Hence, there were two different relations that may form a harmony. Under one relation it was the constituents of a particular structure – the vascular or nervous systems, whereas under another relation, it was the entire constitution of the organism. The harmony of the separate systems, as well as their unification as one optimal harmony, took place because of a sympathy (Gk. *sympatheia*; Lat. *consensus*) amongst the parts.

For example, in treating the nervous system, Galen distinguished between two kinds of pathological conditions – the one, 'idiopathic', as originating in the same part where the disease or injury is felt; the other, 'sympathetic', where a condition arising in one part has an effect which is felt in another. He regarded the vascular and nervous structures as pathways of sympathetic transmission which was accomplished by means of *pneuma*. This concept had appeared in the late writings of Aristotle, for whom *pneuma* was an instrument of the soul.[50] But Zeno, the Stoic philosopher, conceived the cosmic soul as an Heraclitean fire and the human soul as *pneuma*. And his successor, Cleanthes, by emphasising heat, conceived the human soul as hot *pneuma*, thereby assimilating the human soul to the soul of the cosmos rather than the other way round.[51]

Galen continued Cleanthes' emphasis on the role of heat, for he believed that *pneuma* was an exhalation of the blood under the influence of innate heat.[52] Before exhalation could occur, however, *pneuma* must first become hot. This happened through a chemical process of 'circulation'.[53] On inspiration the *pneuma* was drawn into the lungs with the air and passed, with the air, to the right ventricle of the heart. There, the blood underwent its first transformation as innate heat – hot *pneuma*, when breath was exhaled from the blood as natural spirit. In passing to the left ventricle and subsequently to the brain, two further transformations of the pneumatised blood occurred, during which breath was exhaled, respectively, as vital and animal spirit. Thus, life consisted of blood, because blood contained soul.

Since Galen likened the pneumaticised blood to fire in its requirements, he believed that respiration was carried on for the sake of the pneumaticised blood, providing it with nourishment as well as ventilation.[54] But he also believed that cosmic as well as inward fire moved in opposite directions, thereby exerting an inward pull (cold) and an outward push (hot). In this way the transformations of the pneumaticised blood established balance not as mixture but as pneumatic pressure, the opposing forces of pull/push. In so doing, the pneumatised blood enabled the organs to function naturally, because its pressure maintained cohesion – the sympathy or consent between different parts of any whole.

4. Toward new harmony theories

> *'Harmonizing' theory and facts is not easy.*
> Aristotle, De anima (408a)

4.1. The self as musical activity

In the early part of the seventeenth century, two crucial questions came to the forefront of philosophical debate: what holds matter together? what is the source of movement? Both questions, however, were closely related to the allocation of power. Hence, in addition to their importance for philosophy, the two questions had religious and political ramifications.[55] Indeed, it is tempting to believe that the problem of power, with its related questions concerning matter and motion, gave rise to the explorations of mind/body interaction that proliferated in that century, since, traditionally, theories of the person had provided models for political order or 'body' politic, for church hierarchy or 'body' of Christ and for the Trinity or 'body' of the three-in-one deity. Whatever the reason, there is overwhelming evidence that the technology of music and its semantic field guided many seventeenth-century explorations into the nature of body.

For example, in his lectures on male and female anatomy, read in c.1616, William Harvey divided the human body into musical ratios, for he stated that the 'proportion of the chest to the belly' is an interval of the fourth 4:3; that of the chest to the head, a fifth 2:3; and that of the chest to the stomach, 'a whole octave' 2:1.[56] He also compared various parts of the body to musical instruments, when he observed, for example, that the shape of the stomach is like a horn or a bagpipe, since the stomach 'is rounded in order to be more capacious'; the windpipe is like a reed-pipe; and the uvula is like a plectrum, since it plucks the tongue just as the plectrum plucks the lyre.[57] Then, in his 1627 lectures on the motion of animals, he resorted to a more important musical analogy, when he assigned the role of 'choir-master' to the brain.

Harvey first used this analogy in connection with voluntary movements, as in the following passage, where 'WH' indicates Harvey's own interjections upon the usual authorities (especially Aristotle) which had to be surveyed in medical lectures:

> WH it is fit that some movements should be carried on incessantly and should not be regulated by free will, as the movement of the heart and the intestines, etc.
>
> Other movements can be regulated according to their speed, fast or slow, to their degree of motion or quiet, to their timing, with this, after this, before this, etc. In these kinds of movements there is need of nerves by whose intermediacy sensation is purveyed and by whose communication with the brain understanding is brought. The brain is therefore the *mester del choro*, the choir-master. WH is nerve like the intervention of a judge? Are its works performed through rhythm and harmony?[58]

Although Harvey followed Aristotle in assigning movement as the characteristic of that 'which is itself sensitive', he noted that animals whose heads have been cut off and people who are drunk or in a delirium move 'with a disorderly action and not with the harmony and rhythm necessary for work'. Indeed, even at this early stage Harvey was certain that 'Nature performs her works in animals by the power of the muscles and attains her end by means of rhythm and harmony', which he conceived as the 'silent music'.[59] He then added his own observation about the 'motor faculty': 'WH muscles are...like separate living creatures which when they are in action pulsate' like the heart; and, repeating the musical analogy, Harvey asserted that the brain regulates the muscles, because it 'is like the *mester del choro*, the choir-master'.[60]

At the conclusion of the lectures, Harvey explored various other analogies – military, political, architectural and navigational. All these, however, depict two different kinds of order, one in which the brain is the chief regulator, the other where the heart has an important role:

> ...is the brain the choir-master? The nerves, the time-keepers and prompters, dancers. The muscles, the actors, singers, dancers....
>
> Or is the heart the musician [i.e, composer] or the architect? The brain, the choir-master, surveyor. The nerves, clerks. The little nerves, controllers, prompters, directors. The muscles, singers, workmen, etc.[61]

In his 1627 lectures Harvey drew no conclusion about the allocation of power, for he continued to explore the issue in later writings, as we shall see in Chapter 2.

A few years later Harvey's friend and colleague, the physician, Robert Fludd, symbolised aspects of his mystical philosophy by recourse to musical analogies of mind/body interaction.[62] One symbol to which he frequently recurred was the monochord, a measuring device used in antiquity and still in use today for the investigation and demonstration of musical ratios. This instrument consists of a single string stretched over a long wooden resonator to which a movable bridge is attached so that the vibrating length of the string can be varied (Figure 1.10). In Fludd's use, however, the monochord's wooden box (resonator) represents mind, the formal principle, whereas the monochord's string (vibrator) represents body, the material principle.

But the mind/box has two regions, between which the tense body/string is stretched in a double octave (Figure 1.11). The upper region (above the heart) represents the 'spiritual octave' which allows man to rise spiritually to heaven and eternal life. The lower region (below the heart) stands for the 'material octave' which is transitory because subject to temptations of the flesh. Life (movement), whether transitory or eternal, is given by God as the 'pulsator' of, or player on, the cosmic monochord (Figure 1.12). But God also functions as the inner principle (the sun/bridge) which, from the centre of the whole, creates consonant effects in life. Hence, power resides solely in God, who gives life or movement by tensing or relaxing the string, thereby controlling the pulses, which spread concordant effects as pitches and rhythms of love. On this view, the mind/box functions merely as a

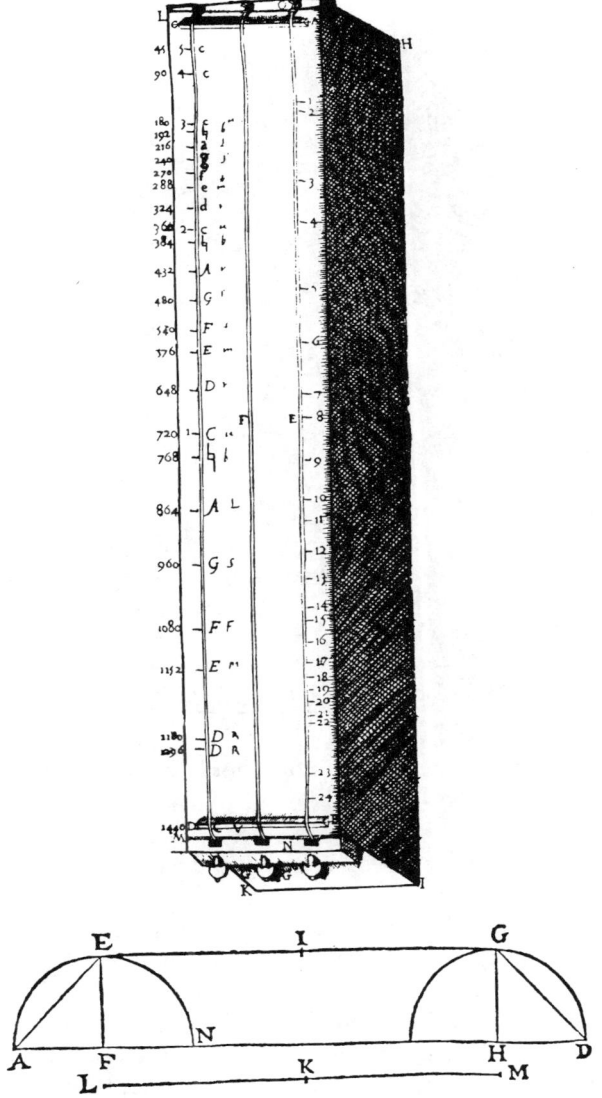

Figure 1.10 The monochord and its geometrical representation, from M. Mersenne, *Harmonie universelle* (Paris, 1636-37)

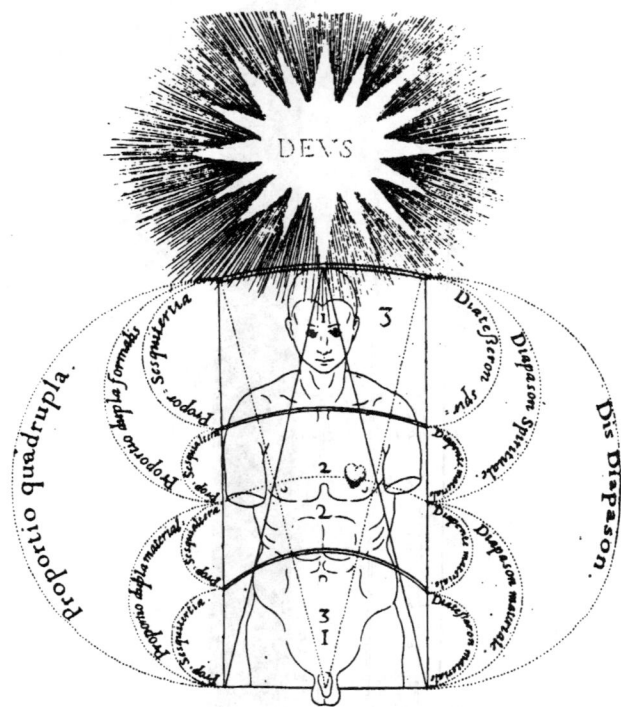

Figure 1.11 The sentient as a monochord, from R. Fludd, *Utrius cosmi...historia*, II (Oppenheim, 1619)

resonator for the purpose of echoing the concordant effects of the body/string.[63]

That evil exists in Fludd's model is clear from his representation of lust, the temptation of the flesh, as the lower octave, materiality. But where does evil come from? According to traditional accounts, mankind was trapped between the world, the flesh and the devil (or the devil's agents, intervening demons); lust was characterised as the 'music of the flesh'; and musical instruments were symbols of erotic images (Figure 1.13).[64] In Fludd's symbol, however, the devil does not appear, for the emphasis is on God's goodness as the source of concord. Yet, as a physician, Fludd could not be ignorant

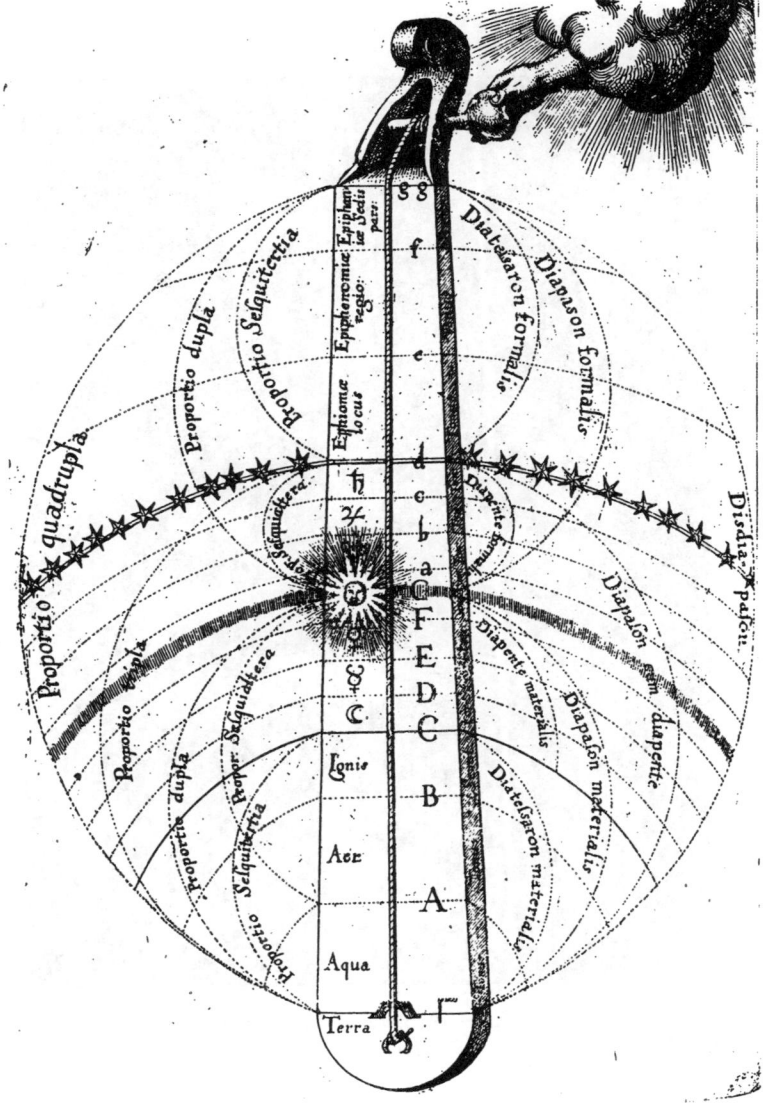

Figure 1.12 The cosmic monochord, from R. Fludd, *Utrius cosmi... historia*, I (Oppenheim, 1617)

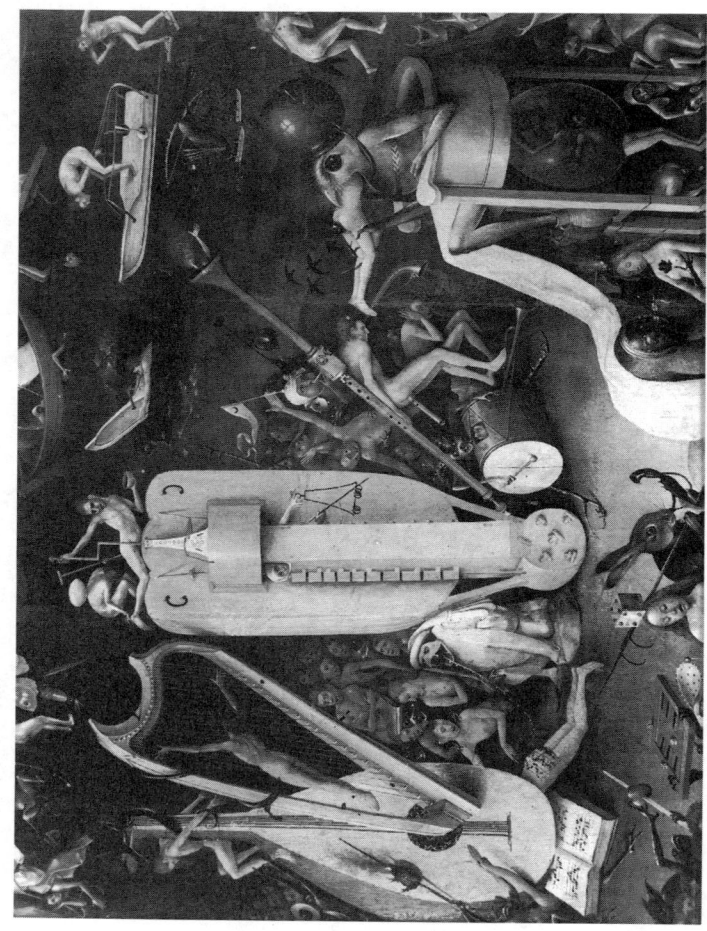

Figure 1.13 The damned tortured on musical instruments, detail from H. Bosch, *Garden of Earthly Delights* (Prado, Madrid)

of discord (to retain the analogy). Where does this come from? On this point he is silent.

4.2. The body as an instrument

The problem of evil was avoided in a different way by the French philosopher, René Descartes, who sought to demonstrate the independence and distinctness of mind and body in order to prove that the human soul is immortal.[65] Hence, he turned mind into an immaterial 'substance' located in the pineal gland (*conarian*) at the base of the brain. In so doing, he assigned the operative principle to the brain and nervous system, for he proposed an explanation of how the brain can receive impressions of external objects through the mediation of the nerves. Although aspects of this explanation may be found in a number of Descartes' writings, its most systematic expression was given in *De homine figuris*, drafted in 1632.[66] In that and subsequent writings Descartes reduced sensation and movement to three principles: 'the objects, the internal organs which receive the impulses of these objects, and the external organs which dispose these impulses to be received as they ought'.[67] But he developed these principles by a doctrine of automatism, according to which the concealed motive power in animals is controlled by laws that govern machines.

To model the animal machine, Descartes chose the pneumatic organ, for he wrote:

> If you have ever had the curiosity to look closely at the organs in our churches, you know how their bellows push air into certain receptacles called − for this reason, presumably − wind trunks. [You know] also how from there the air enters the pipes, now one, now another, as the organist moves his fingers on the keyboard. And you can think of the heart and arteries of our machine (which push animal spirits into the cavities of its brain) as similar to the bellows (which push air into the wind trunks of organs): and of external objects (which, by displacing certain nerves, make spirits from the brain cavities enter certain pores) as similar to the organist's fingers (which, by pressing certain keys, make air from the wind trunks enter certain pipes).[68]

According to this explanatory analogy, the animal machine operates on the same principle as the pneumatic organ: instead of bellows, wind trunks, pipes and air, there is the heart (plus arteries), brain, hollow nerves and animal spirits. But 'harmony', the normal mode of performance, does not depend on 'the externally visible arrangement of the pipes nor on the shape of the wind trunks or other parts', but only on three things: '[a] the air that comes from the bellows, [b] the pipes that sound, and [c] the distribution of this air to those pipes'. The same is true for vascular function, which depends 'only [a] on the spirits that come from the heart, [b] on the pores of the brain through which they pass, and [c] on the way in which these spirits are distributed to these pores'.

Since the organ analogy did not account for nervous function, Descartes resorted to a carillon, which is a set of tuned bells hung dead (i.e., stationary) in a tower and played from a keyboard. According to this second analogy, sensation (nervous function) is explained by the action of delicate filaments that compose the marrow of the nerve/pipes. These filaments, which function like bell pulls, are attached to the sensory organs at one end and to the 'bells' or orifices of certain pores which exist on the internal surface of the brain at the other. When the sensory organs are excited by external stimuli, they cause a slight pull on the filaments which, at the same instant, open the orifices in the brain and permit the animal spirits to flow through the hollow nerve pipes toward the muscles.[69] There is thus a twofold function of the animal spirits. First, they enable the mind (*animus*, soul) to interact with the body; then, they inflate the muscles to which the spirits are carried by the nerves.

The combination of pneumatic organ and carillon served Descartes' purpose of reducing all motion to impact and pressure. For example, in the case of hearing, he supposed that the filaments in the nerves are so arranged at the 'back of the ear cavities' that 'they can be easily moved, together and in the same manner, by the little blows with which the outside air pushes a certain very thin [drum] membrane stretched at the entrance to these cavities'.[70] The membrane, once pressed, transmits the blows to the air 'under' it, and the air, in turn, transmits the blows to the brain through the medium of the nerve filaments, thereby opening a pore or pores in the brain and causing the mind to conceive 'the idea of sound'. A single blow, however, would cause nothing but a dull noise; but

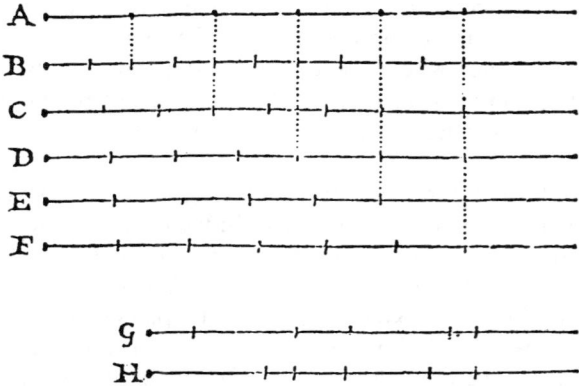

Figure 1.14 Mental representation as line lengths, from R. Descartes, *De homine figuris* (Leyden, 1662)

when many blows succeed one another, they compose one sound which

> ...[a] the soul will judge equal to one another, and which [b] it will judge [to be] higher or lower according as they succeed one another more promptly or tardily, so that if they are a half or a third or a fourth or a fifth more the soul will judge to be higher by an octave, a fifth a fourth, or perhaps a major third, and so on. And finally, several sounds mixed together will be harmonious or discordant according as more or less equal intervals occur between the little blows that compose them.[71]

To form judgments, the mind must read certain images transmitted by external objects to the brain. In the case of hearing, the images are line lengths (Figure 1.14); but Descartes believed there were many other things besides 'which can stimulate our thought, such as, for example, signs and words, which do not in any way resemble the things which they signify'.[72] Yet, 'in order to depart as little as possible from currently acceptable beliefs', he maintained 'that the objects which we perceive truly transmit their images to the inside of our brain', for just as a blind man touching some object with his cane and moving it in different ways according to the object's inherent qualities, so too external objects move the nerves of his hand and, afterwards, the places in his brain where these nerves originate. 'Thus the mind is caused to perceive as many different qualities in these bodies, as there are varieties in the movements that they cause in the brain.'[73]

Although the mind has power to form judgments, we are never told how this power is exercised. Indeed, we cannot be told, because mind is immaterial. At most, we may conclude that neuro-muscular function involves a two-way process (Figure 1.15), for, first, an external object (1) plays on the external senses (2), whereby the internal nerves (3) transmit messages to the pineal gland (4) at the base of the brain (5). There, the immaterial mind (6) reads the messages, although how it does this is left unexplained. The process is then reversed, for the mind (6) plays on the brain (5), (4), thereby transmitting messages via the nerves (3) to the muscles (2), so that the sentient may perform some action (1). Hence, neuro-muscular function consists of an automatic response to a stimulus – once there is a 'ding', there must be a 'dong'. Today, we call this conception by the term 'reflex'.

The essentials of this concept are that a specific external stimulus activates the sensory peripheral neural pathways to the central nervous system, where the reflex is initiated via a neural path back to the appropriate muscles to give rise to a characteristic motor response to that particular stimulus. Human behaviour is then defined as consisting of neuro-muscular movements which may be accomplished 'via the agency of some kind of machine, that the type of machine required is one that also has means of communicating information, that it works by elementary switching [logical] operations, and that the movements produced are appropriate to external events'.[74] In Descartes' theory, the reflex is characteristic of all neuro-muscular action, and the nature of the reflex is involuntary, aimless (machine-like) and due to a fixed mechanical arrangement. The implication is that the brain, like the rest of the animal machine, is a passive instrument – it does not generate functions. Moreover, it matters not whether the model of neuro-muscular function is a pneumatic

Conceiving the Inconceivable 47

Stimulus		Response
Object	(1) Fingers	Subject
External senses	(2) Keyboard	Muscles
Nerves	(3) Strings	Nerves
Pineal gland	(4) Clappers	Pineal gland
Brain	(5) Bells	Brain
Mind	(6) Musician	Mind

Figure 1.15 Neuro-muscular function, after R. Descartes, *Discours de la méthode* (Leyden, 1636), from M. Mersenne, *Harmonie universelle* (Paris, 1636-37)

organ, carillon or some other instrument, because, for Descartes, the reflex is a type of action qualitatively distinct from willed reactions. Such reactions, the products of consciousness, cannot be explained, because mind, being immaterial, is not part of nature.

Chapter 2
The Paradoxes of Power

INTRODUCTION

> *The soul attains her perfectly rounded form*
> *when she is neither straining out after something*
> *nor shrinking back into herself....*
> Marcus Aurelius, *Meditations* (11.12)

About a decade before Descartes' death, one writer began to develop a systematic theory of mind/body interaction that could account for morality. This writer is the controversial English philosopher Thomas Hobbes, who argued that we are intentional creatures, not aimless machines, because we are born with complex internal tensions. This is our first nature. But we form our second nature in the same way that we acquire the skill of music, by a process of learning to exercise tension against resistance. If we learn this exercise well, we shall cultivate moral goodness, namely, wisdom, temperance and justice. Wisdom is the *skill* of distinguishing truth from falsity; temperance, the *skill* of restraining the passions and making them congruent to reason; and justice, the *skill* of behaving sympathetically with other people. While the goodness of the Creator has given us the potential for developing moral goodness, the responsibility for this development resides with us. Since there is a developmental continuity of reactions from instinct to willed actions, mind is not separate from nature but develops from nature.

This summary of Hobbes's philosophy differs from received opinion, which gives currency to a brief passage at the beginning of his most well-known tract, *Leviathan*, where he wrote about 'artificial life' by comparing the heart to a spring, the nerves to strings and the joints to wheels.[1] From this comparison some commentators believe that Hobbes regarded living creatures as automata, and from this model constructed his body politic. Other commentators, perhaps the majority, suppose that Hobbes's mechanism implies egoistic individualism, because it is based on materialistic atomism of the Epicurean variety. When consideration is paid to the original cause of the motion of automata, commentators are widely divergent, some holding that Hobbes is an atheist and others, that Hobbes's God is the same as Aristotle's prime mover.[2]

The Peripatetics had developed the physical aspects of Aristotle's philosophy by means of a species theory. But in 1650 Hobbes clearly distanced himself from such a theory, for he asserted: the 'opinion' that sound and noise are the qualities of the bell or the air 'hath been so long received, that the *contrary* must needs appear a great paradox; and yet the introduction of *species*...(which is necessary for the maintenance of that opinion) passing to and fro from the *object*, is *worse* than any paradox, as being a plain *impossibility*'.[3] The Epicureans had adopted a similar theory, according to which 'qualities', little material atoms, are actually transmitted. But Hobbes rejected this emission theory, when, from c.1639, he began to develop a continuum theory, according to which transmission is that of a state (for Hobbes, always a motion) through an intervening medium, just as, in the classic Stoic analogy, ripples are effected when a stone is thrown into a still pond.[4]

In Stoic cosmology, the universe is a filled with an all-pervading *pneuma*, which serves to generate sympathy as the cohesion of matter and contact between all parts of the cosmos. But cohesion – the interaction and affinity of different parts of a unified structure – is maintained by *tonos* (Lat.: *intentio*), a dynamic property of the all-pervading *pneuma*. Since modifications of *pneuma* take place in body as modifications of tension, cohesion refers to a chain of efficient causes on a cosmic scale.[5] A musical meaning was given to this theory by Cleanthes, who called the sun 'the pick' (blow of fire), because 'in rising it implants its rays and, as if plucking the cosmos, leads it into its harmonious course'.[6] And Cleanthes' successor, Chrysippus, went farther, when he compared the universe to a lyre which coheres and is harmonious, because it is bound together by *neura* (Lat.: *nerva*; i.e., sinew). Like lyre strings, these *neura* function as a binding agent when they possess tension.

But if they lack tension, the universe, no longer bound up, begins to dissolve.[7]

There are a number of points to note about Stoicism, as developed by Chrysippus. First, the all-pervading *pneuma* necessitates circular motion of bodies. This is the ideal motion, a mark of totality and perfection. Second, circular motion may be altered by modifications of *pneuma*. But, and this is the third point, for motion to take place at all, there must be contact between bodies and *pneuma*. Fourth, this contact is achieved by *tonike kinesis*, tensional motion, the propagation of an impulse through a fluid medium in a state of tension. Fifth, *pneuma* is the cause of tension, because *pneuma* is seed, and the character of this seed is heat and, hence, active force. And, lastly, regulatory power is given to the seed and not, as in the Aristotelian cosmos, to the circular movements of celestial bodies.[8]

If some of Hobbes's writings are understood as neo-Stoic, the problematic nature of the original cause comes quickly into focus, since 'the Stoic conceived of the divine in terms that tended strongly towards monotheism [but]...found it difficult to posit the existence of a God who was not in every way identical with the universe'.[9] As we shall see, Hobbes attempted to circumvent this problem by interpreting the universal cause as God's *will*, conceived as *a physical law* of tension, immanent in everything and directing events by expansion and contraction to achieve worthy ends. God, therefore, is not the cause of evil; rather, evil arises from our failure to hear the immanent *logos*. In *Leviathan* Hobbes encoded the consequences of this failure by drawing on a biblical source, the story of Job (40.15-24, 41.1-34), in which two beasts, Behemoth and Leviathan, symbolise nature's crude forces or instincts. The latter beast, for example, can make 'the deep to boil like a pot', thus unleashing the 'sea' or tidal wave that destroys all in its wake. In humans this instinct translates into uncontrolled desire, for it raises people above themselves, whence they become 'king over all the children of pride' (Figure 2.1). How, then, do we develop moral goodness?

My story proper begins with this chapter, in which I tell how Hobbes conceived internal character as a bundle of musical strings to be slackened and tightened by paideia. There are three parts to my story. In the first part I analyse his solution to a classical

Figure 2.1 King over all the children of pride, from T. Hobbes, *Leviathan* (London, 1651)

problem – the paradox of freedom and determinism, in which he reconceptualised Stoic naturalism, the fundamental tenet of which is the fiat: *live in harmony with nature*. In the second and third parts I analyse his solution to two further classical problems, in which he proposed a method for learning to live in harmony with nature. Since Hobbes reconceptualised Stoic naturalism by recourse to the new science of music, it is necessary to introduce you to some aspects of that new science which emerged toward the end of the sixteenth century.

In Hobbes's youth the universities still taught the ancient science of *musica speculativa*, which was a university subject, because it was used to explain concordant relationships of all kinds, not just musical relationships.[10] But the fundamental relationships, those which belonged to the nature of all being, were measure or geometric proportion, number or arithmetic proportion and weight or harmonic proportion.[11] Measure fixed the mode of being, number gave it its form, and weight provided the order of rest and stability. But measure, number and weight also symbolised the values of unity, truth and goodness, each of which is the effect, respectively, of an efficient, an exemplary and a final cause. Since ancient *musica speculativa* believed that proportionate numbers were the cause of all concord, it was this science that continued the Pythagorean tradition, in which the soul was conceived as an incorporeal harmony of numbers and in which numbers (special ratios) were made the cause of string length, the placement of wind holes and the like.

By the time Hobbes had completed university, however, a new science of music was emerging. According to this new science, concord was not related directly to numbers but to rates of vibration – frequencies – of the source of sound.[12] These frequencies could be increased or decreased by tensing or relaxing a musical string. In addition, it was supposed that when air waves produced by different tones coincided frequently in agreement, concord occurred (and was heard); but when the waves coincided infrequently or broke in on one another, the result was discord.[13] According to this supposition, strings vibrating in the ratio 2:1 would coincide on every other vibration; in the ratio 3:2, on every sixth vibration, and so on. The direct cause of concord was thus related to a physical phenomenon, which in turn bore a relation to certain numbers. But – and this is important – the numbers as such were not regarded as the cause of the phenomenon of concord; they were merely a means of representing the physical phenomenon.

Why is this point important? There are two reasons. First, ancient *musica speculativa* was a mathematical science, whereas the new science of music began a movement toward physico-mathematics, the achievement of Newton. Second, according to the new science, by multiplying together the terms of the ratio, it would be possible to establish degrees of concord – that is, some concords would be more and others less perfect. The smaller the product, the greater the concord. In this way concord and discord could be classed not as two separate and contradictory qualities but rather as terms in a continuous series without sharp divisions. As we shall see, Hobbes applied this notion of a scale as a continuous series without sharp divisions to many kinds of physical phenomena.

In the first part of the seventeenth century, two men, both of whom Hobbes knew personally, did more than anyone to popularise this new science of music. These men were Galileo Galilei and Marin Mersenne, whose writings became 'the starting point of all subsequent musico-scientific inquiry for at least half a century'.[14] Mersenne's work spans the period 1623 to 1651, when he published several encyclopedic expositions on the science of music.[15] But it was his great compilation of 1636-37, *Harmonie universelle*, for which he is most well known, because this work presented the results of his efforts to determine the actual number of vibrations per second made by a string when it sounded in unison with a particular musical tone. Mersenne had scaled down the frequency by working with long strings that would vibrate slowly enough to enable him to count the vibrations. By this means he was able to establish the chief laws of the stretched string: that the frequency of the string is directly proportional (a) to its length, (b) to the square root of the weight which stretches it, (c) to the square root of the weight of the string itself, (d) to the reciprocal of its diameter, and (e) to the reciprocal of its specific gravity.[16] Here, then, was a new approach to measure, number and weight.

Galileo's presentation of the new science of music was, by contrast, extremely short and succinct. But it occurred in a pioneering work, published in 1638 as *Discorsi e dimostrazioni matematiche, intorno a due nuove scienze*.[17] The two new sciences of the title are those of elasticity and the study of pure motion that we now call 'kinematics'. In its broadest sense, a body has elasticity when it has the power of recovery. Hence, the study of elastic bodies involves not only their strength or resistance to fracture but also the motion of such bodies when they are displaced from their position of equilibrium. You will recall that acoustic vibrators are elastic bodies. But there are other elastic bodies that are non-acoustic. The pendulum, for example, is such a body, and it figures prominently in Galileo's work. In this place, therefore, I wish to draw particular attention to that work not only because of its importance for the new science of music but also because of its implications for Hobbes's last philosophical treatise, even though, in that treatise, Hobbes never mentioned the word 'pendulum'.[18]

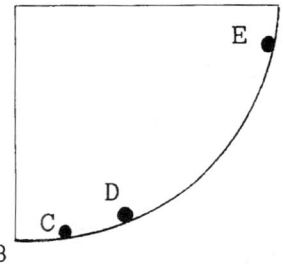

Figure 2.2   The hoop or rigid pendulum

As is well known, Galileo used the pendulum to refute the Aristotelian doctrine of contrary motions, which denied that oscillations are or can be continuous and regular.[19] But Galileo's work on the pendulum was sufficiently extensive that it has been regarded as a piece of research in its own right. In the course of this research, he discovered the quasi-isochronism of the simple pendulum and the law of variation of its period with length; he also formulated the brachistochrone thesis – that in a circular pendulum the curve of quickest descent is a cycloid.[20] To produce these results, Galileo worked with three distinct types of pendula: non-rigid, rigid and ideal pendula. The non-rigid and rigid types were physical pendula, the former of which consisted of a string with a weighted bob (e.g., cork or lead) and the latter of a ball which was free to roll down the inside surface of a vertical hoop – Galileo suggested the rim of a sieve (Figure 2.2). The third type, as its name implies, was ideal, in which the thread of the pendulum became the radius of the circle and the bob, a moving point. In this way Galileo was able to eliminate disturbing influences such as damping, in which the amplitude of pendula oscillations decreases continuously. Hence, he could represent the motions of the ideal pendulum geometrically, in the same way Hobbes later attempted to solve the quadrature of the circle – 'by rule and compass only'.[21]

It has been assumed that Hobbes adopted circular motion as a fundamental cosmological hypothesis and as a kind of 'panacea' to understanding.[22] It is true that he made frequent reference

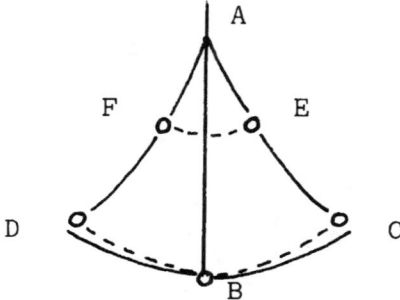

Figure 2.3 The compound pendulum

to circular motion, of which he supposed there were two kinds. But these kinds invite comparison with two kinds of non-rigid circular pendula used by Galileo: the simple and the compound pendula. When the simple (physical) pendulum is removed from the perpendicular and left free, it will oscillate to and fro about the point of suspension with a continuous and regular motion. The period of oscillation of such a pendulum is constant; that is, successive oscillations of the same pendulum are isochronous – equal timed – or nearly so. But this is not the case with the compound pendulum (Figure 2.3). In the compound (physical) pendulum, every particle is a pendulum with its own period, so that each particle will persist in its period at the cost of obstructing the oscillations of all other particles. Thus, according to Galileo, the pendulum will decrease the amplitude of its oscillations and finally stop.[23]

If these two pendula are idealised, we have two different ways of conceiving motion. In the simple (ideal) pendulum the descending and ascending arcs of the pendular path are movements compounded of equally natural motions; and because they are symmetrical with respect to the perpendicular, the oscillation from A to C and back to A may be dealt with as a whole or unit. The bob then becomes a moving point, and its path is described as traversing equal arcs in equal times. In a compound (ideal) pendulum the whole is conceived as divisible into any number of parts, each part having a relationship to the other parts with respect to the axis of oscillation. I suggest this is how Hobbes conceived motion, for, first, there is his 'simple circular motion' or that in which 'the several points of a moved body in equal times describe equal arches'.[24] Then, there is his 'compound circular motion', or that in which 'all the parts of the moved body do at once describe circumferences, some greater, others less, according to the proportion of their several distances from the common centre, carries about with it such bodies, as being not fluid, adhere to the body so moved: and such as do not adhere, it casteth forwards in a strait line which is a tangent to the point from which they are cast off'.[25] In other words, compound circular motion occurs when the several points of a body revolving upon its own axis do not in equal times describe equal arches but arches that are greater or less according to the greater or shorter distance of points from the common axis.

Hobbes's two definitions of circular motion thus refer to the 'pendulum condition',[26] that is, to systems ('bodies') having equilibrium configurations along axes, since his motions have the properties of isochronism and simultaneous crossing of the axis. From the time of Galileo, it was assumed that isochronism meant the restriction to the case of small vibrations and that isochronism and simultaneous crossing of the axis meant that each element of the system would move as a simple pendulum.[27] Although the vibrating string provides a counterexample, it was supposed that musical strings exemplified the 'pendulum condition' until mid-eighteenth century. In Hobbes's day, however, theories of vibrating pendula and strings were still closely connected. Indeed, Galileo's work on the pendulum led to an analysis of vibrating strings, in which he explained the relation of pitch to frequency, consonance and dissonance and the frequency ratios corresponding to musical intervals, vibratory resonance, sympathetic vibrations and the quantitative dependence of the frequency of vibration of a string on its length and tension.[28]

In a demonstration of the law of length, Galileo also used pendula to make visible to the eye why 'certain pairs of notes, differing in pitch produce a pleasing sensation, others a less pleasant effect, and still others a disagreeable sensation'.[29] His demonstration consisted of taking three simple pendula of the non-rigid string kind, the strings each having different lengths: $16 (= 4^2)$, $9 (= 3^2)$,

4 (= 2²). The bobs are then given a push so that they swing simultaneously through arbitrary arcs, their vibrations coinciding at every fourth vibration of the longest string. When 'produced on [tuned] strings', this 'combination of vibrations...yields [to the hearing] the interval of the octave and the intermediate fifth'.[30] By varying the lengths of the string-pendula, all sorts of combinations of musical intervals may be made visible. In this way Galileo confirmed that when the ratios are incommensurable (and therefore never coincide) or when the vibrations coincide only after long intervals of time, 'then the eye is confused by the disorderly succession of crossed threads', just as 'the ear is pained by an irregular sequence of air waves [i.e., pulses] which strike the tympanum without any fixed order'.[31]

In this simple demonstration, we have an incipient theory of pleasure and pain, since, according to Galileo, the drum membrane is a deformable body, subject to stress and strain. Hence, agreeable consonances are 'pairs of tones which strike the ear with a certain regularity; this regularity consists in the fact that the pulses delivered by the two tones, in the same interval of time, shall be commensurable in number, so as not to keep the ear drum in perpetual torment, bending in two different directions in order to yield to the ever-discordant impulses'. Whereas when the impacts are incommensurable, they produce 'a harsh effect upon the recipient ear which interprets them as dissonances'.[32] Finally, although Galileo expressed his conclusions about the isochrony of the simple pendulum, the law of length, and the brachistochrone thesis in terms of ratios, he also expressed his findings discursively – in his treatment of music.

The study of pendular or other harmonic motion in the abstract forms part of kinematics. But there is another phenomenon that has been idealised and taught as a science of pure harmonic motion, and this science is counterpoint, which teaches the art of contrary motion in music. In Hobbes's day, counterpoint was studied by most educated gentlemen, so that we might ask: did Hobbes have any experience in this branch of music? The answer to this question is almost certainly 'yes', although the evidence is chiefly circumstantial. It is known that Hobbes had an abiding love of music and played on his own bass viol.[33] But he also had other musical skills, the most direct evidence for which comes from two sources. First, there is the report of John Aubrey that Hobbes 'had alwayes bookes of prick-song lyeing on his table: which at night, when he was abed, and the dores made fast, and was sure nobody heard him, he sang aloud (not that he had a very good voice) but for his health's Sake: he did beleeve it did his Lunges good, and conduced much to prolong his life'.[34] Then, there are the lists of Hobbes's library to c.1631,[35] which include music, as well as two treatises on music — the one on singing and the use of the monochord, the other on all aspects of practical music, including musical counterpoint.[36]

Less direct evidence comes from Hobbes's life-long connections with the Cavendish family, which began in 1608, when he became tutor to the son of William Cavendish, Baron Hardwicke and afterwards (1626) second Earl of Devonshire. The first Earl (also William) maintained one of the most important musical households in England, in which there was 'a genuine concern for the finest musical education, for the most recent musical publications and for a resident corpus of musicians and teachers'.[37] The household musicians were chiefly lutenists, and, not surprisingly, the bulk of music owned by Hobbes was for the lute.[38] This instrument, a chordophone, has a neck that serves as string bearer and as handle, with the plane of the strings running parallel to the belly or soundboard (Figure 2.4). Although the lute may be used as a solo instrument, or to accompany a singer, it could also function in 'consort', the seventeenth-century term that denoted (1) to sound in harmony, and (2) a group of instruments, usually lutes and viols, that produce such a sound. If Hobbes's skill on the lute was adequate to the music he owned, we may assume that he was one of the performers in the consort of lutes maintained by Cavendish.

The work of Mersenne and Galileo, the household activities of the Cavendish family, and the musical skills of Hobbes do not provide direct evidence for Hobbes's theory of internal character. In the argument that follows, therefore, I have drawn my evidence from a number of Hobbes's writings and, especially, the text which I call *Body*. Hobbes began work on this text in the 1640s, but it was not published until the mid-1650s (1655 in Latin, 1656 in English). *Body*, however, is not an isolated text, for it forms the first of three parts.[39] The second part is a continuation of the argument in *Body*,

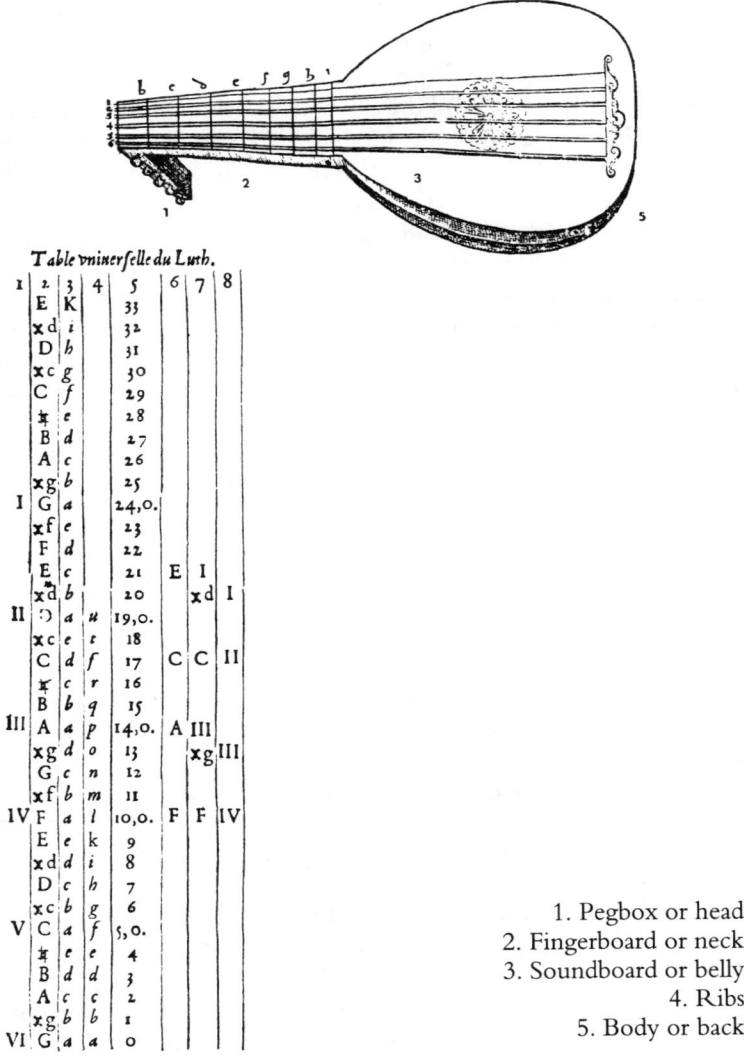

Figure 2.4 Seventeenth-century lute, from M. Mersenne, *Harmonie universelle* (Paris, 1636-37)

whereas the third part is a conclusion drawn from the premisses laid down in the first two parts. Since the standard edition of the second and third parts is problematic, I have cited them infrequently. Nevertheless, in constructing my argument, I have tried to avoid the criticism which Hobbes levelled at biblical interpreters, that

> ...it is not the bare Words, but the Scope of the writer that giveth the true light, by which any writing is to bee interpreted; and they that insist upon single Texts, without considering the main Designe, can derive no thing from them cleerly; but rather by casting atomes of Scripture, as dust before mens eyes, make every thing more obscure than it is; an ordinary artifice of those that seek not the truth, but their own advantage.[40]

I. NATURE'S FIAT

> ...live...in harmony with nature.
> Marcus Aurelius, *Meditations* (7.56)

Introduction

In the debate about liberty, necessity and chance, begun prior to 1646 in Paris, John Bramhall charged Hobbes with adumbrating the Stoic conception of fate.[41] When Hobbes answered Bramhall's charge, he drew on the work of Justus Lipsius, who, in asserting the congruence of Stoicism with Christianity,[42] had divided destiny into four kinds: mathematical or astrological destiny, natural destiny, Stoic or violent destiny and the godly destiny of the Christians.[43] And Hobbes himself pointed out that Lipsius defined the last kind of destiny 'just as T.H. doth his destiny', as 'a series or order of causes depending upon the divine counsel'.[44] Lipsius' third kind of destiny, the Stoic or violent destiny, was a doctrine of conflagrations and regenerations of the universe, not a doctrine of fate. Rather, the Stoic doctrine of fate was that which Lipsius described, and Hobbes assented to, as the godly destiny of the Christians and which was conceived as a 'chain' of necessary causes.

This Stoic doctrine of causes provoked a great deal of controversy in its own time; and the most violent objectors were those who felt that determinism did away with human freedom and, hence, with human responsibility. Hobbes's philosophy provoked similar controversy; indeed, Bramhall's charge focused specifically on the problem of freedom. The Stoics were not unaware of what a doctrine of fate could mean for morality, since Chrysippus tried to work out a deterministic doctrine and at the same time make a place for human responsibility.[45] His solution was to distinguish between things that are in our power and things that are not. Since he also recognised that maintaining both these strands at the same time was a logical impossibility, he appears to have held them successively or alternately.

In adopting a determinist position, Hobbes, too, had to confront the problem of human responsibility. Like Chrysippus, he distinguished between things that are in our power and things that are not. But he developed this distinction by acknowledging that what we will is determined not merely by external situations but also by our internal character. In the course of his treatment of determinism and responsibility, Hobbes adopted a new definition of freedom. The customary definition of freedom was a privilege held by grant or prescription by which men enjoy some benefit beyond the ordinary subject, whereas Hobbes understood freedom in the Stoic sense as the power to do as one thinks fit unless restrained by law.[46] According to this definition, we have the possibility of determining our own actions by acquiring knowledge of what is permitted and what is not.[47] But a problem remained, as Hobbes indicated when he wrote: 'that which is chiefly wanting…is a true and certain rule of our actions, by which we might know whether that we undertake be just or unjust'.[48] This rule is what Hobbes set out to achieve.

1. *Not in our power*

> *The sun is seen to pour down*
> *and expend itself in all directions,*
> *yet is never exhausted.*
> *For this downpouring is but a self-extension.*
> *…thought should be the counterpart of this….*
> Marcus Aurelius, *Meditations* (8.57)

1.1. Nature's government: motion inward

Hobbes's cosmic determinism is best understood from the perspective of his theory of light, a version of which was published in

1644 and presented as the seventh book of Mersenne's *Universae geometriae, mixtaque, synopsis et bini refractionum demonstratum tractatus*. This version is now referred to as *Tractatus opticus*, a title assigned when it was reprinted in Molesworth's edition of Hobbes's Latin writings.[49] Although almost every optical writer of note in the seventeenth century was aware of the theory, some writers did not realise the book was by Hobbes, since it was attributed to him in a *monitum* on p. 548. In 1973 Alan E. Shapiro provided a seminal analysis of Hobbes's 1644 theory, at the same time placing it within the context of seventeenth-century optics, thereby demonstrating for the first time that Hobbes began the kinematic tradition in the continuum theory of light.[50]

The operative word here is 'kinematic', for it is well known that Descartes also developed a continuum theory, when he reduced all attributes of matter to extension. From this identification, two things follow. First, there is a conception of matter as homogeneous, incompressible, filling all space and allowing no void. Second, since there is no void, all motions must be in a circle or ring, because if one body moves, then another must simultaneously occupy the space it left, and a third must occupy the space left by the second, and so on in succession, forming a closed ring of motion.[51] For this concept, which is called '*antiperistasis*', Descartes was indebted to the continuum theory of Aristotle.

The Aristotelian and Cartesian approach to a continuum theory was based on the analogy of the motion of a body. For example, to explain the motion of a stone rotated circularly in a sling, Descartes would analyse the motion of the stone merely and ignore any motion along the string, even though the stone is restrained by the tension of the string.[52] Hobbes rejected this approach in favour of that of Galileo, who sought to give a kinematic description of a pulse. Hobbes, therefore, distinguished between the motion of a body, the stone in the above example, and that of a pulse, the pendular motions along the taut string. If focus is directed to that part of the stone's motion that is restrained by the string, Descartes as well as Hobbes would have said that the stone endeavours to recede from the centre radially outwards along a straight line. But the operative word here is *endeavour*, which, in Descartes' theory is a tendency to motion and not, as in Hobbes's theory, an actual motion.

With these points in mind, we may now move on to Hobbes's 1644 theory, in which he argued that the sensation of light is produced by a vibratory motion propagated through an all-pervading medium of uniform density. There are two points to note about Hobbes's argument. First, we have the Stoic tension conceived as vibratory motion, that is, as a real but insensibly small (infinitesimal) expansion and contraction. Hobbes compared this motion to that of the heart: like the systole and diastole of the heart, the entire body of the sun expands and contracts together, so that all the rays of light emanate radially from the center of the sun. This analogy, however, implies a regularity but not a strict periodicity in the oscillations.[53]

Second, we have the Stoic goodness conceived as relief from ignorance ('darkness'), for the all-pervading medium, which Hobbes introduced as a 'crucial, unstated hypothesis', enables sensation to take place.[54] This is so, because not only the luminous source but also the medium vibrates, that is, expands and contracts. In this way light is propagated through the medium by a vibratory motion to the retina and through the optic nerve to the brain, which by its reaction transmits the motion back again towards the sun. Only the motion propagated outwards by the reaction of the brain is called light, but it consists of a representation conceived in the brain. For conception to take place, therefore, two things are required: sensation, which is a motion directed from the external world inward to the sentient, and representation, which is a motion directed from within the sentient outward.[55]

In *Body* Hobbes introduced three significant modifications to the 1644 theory. First, he explained light by a 'simple circular motion' and not by expansion and contraction. Then, he altered the all-pervading medium (now a stated hypothesis) into a scale of degrees of density, the most rare being the ether. Finally, he made the heart the 'fountain of sense' and the source of the reaction outwards. Let me take each of these modifications in turn and, first, the introduction of simple circular motion in which every line in a body is always moved parallel to itself. The problems of this modification for Hobbes's theory of light have been noted by Shapiro, who points out that such a motion cannot account for the sun's radiation, since light would only be radiated in directions normal to the axis of rotation and not in all directions. Even though

Hobbes was aware of this problem, he seems to have dropped the theory of expansion and contraction, because he thought it demanded the existence of a vacuum,[56] and in *Body* Hobbes denied the existence of a vacuum.[57]

But if Hobbes restricted the sun's external motion to simple circular motion, does the ambient medium also move in a circular fashion? Hobbes's answer to this question is somewhat obscure and must be teased out by the few clues he provided as to the nature of the ambient medium. These clues indicate that it is the same in all bodies; that it has no weight ('gravity'); that it fills up the universe so as to leave no empty space; that it is fluid in consistency; and that this fluid has no motion at all but what it receives from little bodies, that is, 'particles' or 'atoms' of different sizes that float in it and which are not themselves fluid.[58] These atoms, which have different degrees of hardness, are moved by the sun so that they perpetually change places one with another. But the sun does not effect this by its simple circular motion alone, for Hobbes pointed out that there also is a 'motive power' *in* the sun.[59] By means of the sun's compounded motions, then, homogeneous atoms are attracted ('congregated') and heterogeneous atoms are repulsed ('dissipated'), a process Hobbes called 'fermentation', from the Latin *ferveo*, meaning to boil, seethe, steam; to foam; to swarm; to be busy, bustle about; and, figuratively, to burn, glow, rage, rave.[60]

But Hobbes also indicated that 'the generation of the light of the sun is accompanied with the generation of heat',[61] and that 'when a body hath its parts so moved, that it sensibly both heats and shines at the same time, then it is that we say fire is generated'.[62] Both of these statements occur within the context of the theory of light, where Hobbes asserted that he who could account for 'whence, and from what action, both the *shining* and *heating* proceed, may be thought to have given a possible cause of the generation of *fire*'.[63] In proposing such a cause Hobbes argued that heat and pain are not in the fire but within us, for 'when we grow hot, we find that our spirits and blood, and whatsoever is fluid within us, is called out from the internal to the external parts of our bodies, more or less, according to the degree of heat; and that our skin swelleth'.[64]

We now have the grounds for Hobbes's third modification, by which he made the heart the 'fountain' of sense. Initially, Hobbes identified sense as the usual five – seeing, hearing, smelling, tasting and touching, the common organ of which is the brain.[65] But he afterwards identified pleasure and pain as 'another kind of sense', namely, a temperature sense, since '*our* heat is *pleasure* or *pain*, according as it is *great* or *moderate*'.[66] The temperature sense proceeds

> ...not from the reaction of the heart outwards, but from the continual action from the outermost part of the organ towards the heart. For the original of life being in the heart, that motion in the sentient, which is propagated to the heart, must necessarily make some alteration or diversion of vital motion, namely, by quickening or slackening, helping or hindering the same. Now when it helpeth, it is pleasure; and when it hindereth, it is pain.[67]

In this context vital motion is the motion of the blood 'perpetually circulating...in the veins and arteries'.[68] When its circulation is helped, we feel pleasure; when it is hindered, we feel pain. But the common organ of this kind of sense is the heart.[69]

Hobbes, therefore, established a clear-cut separation between the function of heart and brain.[70] But these organs are merely instruments of the blood, the source and centre of life, for the blood ministers to, indeed, activates, the motions of the heart and the brain, both of which have a propensity to vibrate.[71] Even the blood is an instrument, for it performs its functions because of the ether, which, in humans, is a spirit in the blood.[72] In circulating with the blood, these spirits pass through the veins to the heart, where they are 'purified' and driven from the heart through the arteries. Upon reaching the brain, the spirits are impelled into, and retracted out of, the roots of the nerves at the base of the brain.[73]

1.2. The natural life: Hobbes and Harvey

All three modifications are illuminated by recourse to the work of Harvey, whose major achievement, as Hobbes recognised, was the discovery of the circulation of the blood.[74] Harvey announced this discovery in *De motu cordis*, where he compared the blood's circulation to the water cycle: transformed by distillation (a chemical concept), the blood becomes an example of the Aristotelian *antiperistasis* – whereby all movement in space is circular thrust – in which substances succeed departing substances, thereby preventing the formation of a vacuum.[75] In that same work Harvey argued that the source of life is heat, namely, the heart as a unit of flesh, fibre, blood and spirit. Accordingly, he assigned to the heart the chief function in the body.[76] In other writings he likened the action of the heart to a pump, the force of which drives the blood round in a circle.[77]

Since Harvey regarded the heart as a muscle and, hence, passive, the pump analogy did not settle the question of how, in the embryo, the heart first beats. In addressing this question, he changed his mind about the role of the heart, arguing, in *De generatione animalium*, that the blood, not the heart, is the source of life and co-extensive with spirit – innate heat.[78] But heat is not a substance in the blood, for Harvey consistently denied the particulate nature of living blood: it became so only as gore.[79] Rather, the blood is the hottest part of the body because of its motion; hence, it imparts heat to the heart rather than receives heat from the heart. According to this modification, Harvey supposed that, in the embryo, the heart's first diastole is a 'fermentation', the origin of which is heat in the embryonic blood.[80]

If fermentation serves only to ignite the heartbeat, what is responsible for the continued beating of the heart throughout life? An answer to this question may be found in Harvey's comments about an 'obscure' pulsating motion inherent in the blood.[81] Since the blood is the 'first born', he supposed that 'in it and from it pulsation begins'.[82] But he also stated that when the heart ceases beating in a dying animal, 'you will perceive in the blood itself a kind of undulation and vague fluttering or palpitation, the last token of life'.[83] On the basis of this internal motion, Harvey inferred that the blood is a living creature and, therefore, sentient, for from variations in the blood's pulsations, it was plain 'how sensitive it is to harm done to it by things that are hurtful and to the comfort of things that cherish it'.[84]

That sensation and movement exist before the brain develops in the embyro is a paradox, which Harvey solved in two ways. First, he added to the usual five senses the feeling of pleasure and pain.[85] Then, he distinguished different functions for heart and brain: the heart governs all natural motions and actions which 'go on whether we will or no', whereas the brain governs all animal motions.[86]

But these 'instruments' perform their 'public offices' because of the circulation of the blood. When circulation is helped, heart and brain function normally, according to their inherent 'harmony and rhythm'.[87] But when the circulation is hindered, neither heart nor brain function properly, since variations in the blood's pulsation bring disorder and, consequently, disease.[88] Harvey, therefore, centralised all physiological functions in the blood: the blood flows round the whole body, imparting heat and life continually to all its parts.

Here, then, we have the source of all three modifications which Hobbes made to his 1644 theory of light. But in converting Harvey's natural animal into cosmic animal, Hobbes had to provide a solution to a problem that had puzzled Harvey. In *De generatione animalium* and against prevailing opinion (another paradox), Harvey reintroduced Aristotle's doctrine of epigenesis: all animals have a uniform pattern of generation which begins when the male semen activates the egg by exerting some vital influence. Lacking a microscope, Harvey was prevented from seeing the male spermatozoa, so he was unable to point to a contribution from both sexes.[89] Consequently, he supposed that fertilisation could be explained by the analogy of contagion, that is, by 'some kind of contact' or 'touch'.[90]

But Harvey went farther, for he compared the 'fecundating contagion or first conception' to conception of the brain, 'so that fecundity be acquired in the same way as knowledge (for there is no lack of arguments to prove it), and whether, like the movements and animal operations which take their origin from the conception of the brain and we call appetites, natural movements also and the operations of the vegetative faculty (especially generation) depend upon the conception of the womb'.[91] Although he never settled on an explanation of contagion, he suggested that the problem would be 'rightly and piously' investigated by one 'who deduces the generation of all creatures from that same eternal and omnipotent Deity upon whose nod the whole universe itself depends'.[92] On this assumption, an explanation of contagion would have to account for how, in a chain of efficient causes, the 'final' efficient cause acts at a distance.

At the conclusion of *Body* Hobbes provided an hypothesis of how this action might take place, when he wrote about magnetism as follows: 'It is...certain, that the attractive power of the loadstone is nothing else but some motion of the smallest particles thereof and that this motion is 'reciprocal motion in a line too short to be seen'.[93] Hobbes then continued: 'Now in what manner and in what order of working this cause produceth the effect of attraction, is the thing to be enquired. And first we know, that when the string of a lute or viol is stricken, the vibration, that is, the reciprocal motion of that string in the same strait line, causeth like vibration in another string which hath like tension.'[94] For both Hobbes and Harvey, therefore, the first link in the chain of causes is touch; for both men, a fluid substance is the instrument of touch, since it transmits the creative power of nature. While Harvey remained puzzled about the manner in which this power was transmitted, Hobbes provided an hypothesis in his analogy to sympathetic resonance. The implications of this analogy are twofold: first, that the ambient medium has a dynamic property similar to a tense string; second, that affinity is a precondition of vibration.

2. In our power

> ...avoid forming opinions
> that are at variance with nature and
> with the constitution of a reasonable being.
> Marcus Aurelius, *Meditations* (3.9)

2.1. Self-government: motion outward

It is highly probable that Hobbes's emendations to the 1644 theory of light were due principally to his more global aims in *Body*. According to the cosmic determinism elaborated there, the world is a plenum filled with matter of different degrees of density. But matter has two principles, a passive and an active principle. The manifold variety in the world is explained by reference to these two features. The passive principle is unqualified body – the ambient fluid ether; the active principle is the pulsating *aggregate* motion of the constituent atoms or smallest bodies. This aggregate motion, however, is not random, like the atomic motion of the Epicureans. Rather, it has different *rates* of pulsation, and these rates, in turn, generate different degrees of heat in, and thus density of, the ambient medium.[95] Hobbes's aggregate motion, therefore, is like the Stoic seeds, for it is innate spirit – the motion of heat. Hence, it constitutes the dynamic property or tension of the ether.

We may conclude, therefore, that Hobbes's plenum behaves like bundles of musical strings, possessing different lengths and tensions, and which expand and contract with temperature changes. At the highest conceivable energy – the fermentation in the sun – the universe exhibits the full consequences of this stringiness in all its subtlety; but as the temperature falls, the tension shrinks the strings so that they become more and more point-like.[96] For convenience, I shall call Hobbes's aggregate motion by the name 'impulse', because the kinetic energy of this motion functions as a stimulus to excite ('help', heat up) or inhibit ('hinder', cool down) other, grosser motion in the universe – for example, the circulation of the blood and planets, the ebb and flow of the tides, the water and isothermal cycle, even illumination (expansion) and gravity (contraction).[97] Like Harvey, therefore, Hobbes conceived two kinds of motions, one of which is a natural rhythm or periodicity, the other a natural tempo or impulse. But it is the latter kind of motion that tempers string-like phenomena, thereby causing them to expand and contract. Hence, impulse is the source for all activity, change and variety and, therefore, for knowing.

In humans, impulse is the stimulus for exciting or inhibiting vital and animal motion. Vital motion, being natural, is not in our power, for it is born with us and continues until death. Such are the cyclic motions of the blood, breathing, concoction, nutrition and excretion.[98] At a certain level of biological organisation, impulse also generates animal motions, the first appearance of which Hobbes identified with 'the Interiour Beginnings of Voluntary Motions':

> ...if vital motion be helped by motion made by sense, then the parts of the organ will be disposed to guide the spirits in such manner as conduceth most to the preservation and augmentation of that motion, by the help of the nerves. And in animal motion this is the very first endeavour, and found even in the embryo; which while it is in the womb, moveth its limbs with voluntary motion, for the avoiding of whatsoever troubleth it, or for the pursuing of what pleaseth it.[99]

Animal motions grow with us, for they are acquired in the same way as a musician acquires musical skills, by habituation.[100] Such motions, therefore, are artificial, and so are in our power.

Now, animal motions involve not only the use of our limbs but also those deliberative processes that Hobbes called 'reckoning',[101] for the *product* of animal motions are the passions, the object of which is some sensible good. But sensible good and virtue are not the same, for only the right use of the will entails the virtuous life. Unlike the passions, the object of the will is that good which reason leads us to seek. It is not in our power not to be stirred mentally by our passions; but it is in our power to translate them or not to translate them into action.[102] Thus,

> Neither is the freedom of willing or not willing, greater in man, than in other living creatures. For where there is appetite, the entire cause of appetite hath preceded; and, consequently, the act of appetite could not chose but follow, that is, hath of necessity followed....And therefore such a liberty as is free from necessity, is not to be found in the will either of men or beasts. But if by liberty we understand the faculty or power, not of willing, but of doing what they will, then certainly that liberty is to be allowed to both, and both may equally have it, whensoever it is to be had.[103]

Passion, then, is the will's mainspring, whereas the will is passion's controller. But it is only by being thoroughly enlightened by reason that the will can be victorious. Though it is possible to make a wrong choice through an error of judgment – what Hobbes called 'misreckoning', it is also possible for the will to be so corrupt as to go against the evidence of reason.[104]

In Hobbes's account of cognition, the lowest form of reason concerns our immediate acts only. Will, in this context, is practical reason, for it is the outcome of prudential calculations and generalisations concerning the utility of a given act.[105] But practical reason is an attribute we share with other animals.[106] To become fully human, therefore, we must aspire to higher forms of knowledge. One form is knowledge of God's will, and this is the same as knowledge of nature; the other form is self-knowledge, that is, knowledge of one's own will. Thus, Hobbes argued:

> ...there is a saying much usurped of late, That *Wisedome* is acquired, not by reading of *Books*, but of *Men*. Consequently whereunto, those persons, that for the most part can give no other proof of being wise, take great delight to shew what they think they have read in men, by uncharitable censures of one another behind their backs. But there is another saying not of late understood, by which they might learn truly to read one another, if they would take the pains; and that is, *Nosce teipsum,* Read thy self.[107]

Accordingly, self-knowledge is not egoism; rather, it is the beginning of all virtue.

To account for virtue, Hobbes had recourse to the phenomenon of tension, whereby virtue or its opposite arises from the strength or weakness, tautness or slackness, of the self. The precondition for virtue, therefore, is affinity of the various parts of the self, all of which together form a unity.[108] If there is no cohesion of the self, we behave as if asleep or as in a dream or as if distempered with sickness.[109] The self, therefore, requires tempering in the same way that the strings of a musical instrument require adjustment to bring them into agreement. Indeed, in matters pertaining to the will, the chief virtue is temperance, that habit in choice and avoidance which preserves the judgments of reason.[110] Temperance, therefore, may be defined as the exercise of tension in matters of choice. But to live temperately, we must consider the role of the passions in moral action.

Although passion is consubstantial with nature, the individual has an identity in his own right, since human nature possesses many passions, differing with the individual.[111] What, then, is the best condition of the self? Hobbes's answer to this question is completely different from that of Aristotle, whose model of the self was the lever, the fulcrum being the fixed centre (the prime mover/heart), the unmoving point from which opposite motions arise.[112] For Hobbes, however, the model is a bundle of strings, extended in three dimensions with resistance: if the strings are too tense, they will break; if they are too slack, there will be no 'passion'. The best condition of the self, therefore, is that degree of inner tension which checks the strings and brings them into harmony. Failing this, the self will be overcome by the power of excessive passion and pushed toward vice or madness, both of which are contrary to reason. To be properly free, and therefore wise, a man must liberate himself from the vices that derive from excessive passion.

2.2. The happy life: Hobbes and Cowley

That human freedom consists in self-restraint was asserted by Hobbes's friend, Abraham Cowley, who wrote: 'THE Liberty of a people consists in being governed by Laws which they have made themselves, under whatsoever form it be of Government. The Liberty of a private man in being Master of his own Time and Actions, as far as may consist with the Laws of God and of his Country.'[113] That assertion was printed in Cowley's collection, entitled *Several Discourses by Way of Essays, in Verse and Prose*,[114] where he offered a sustained philosophic argument that centres on the Stoic paradox concerning the Great Man and the Happy Man: while the former, in having all, has nothing, the latter, in having nothing, has all. Against the Puritan creed of a highly emotional conversion and subsequent daily exposure in the eternal battle between good and evil, Cowley pitted the Stoic exhortation never to give in to passion or fanaticism but always to preserve a soundly balanced spirit untouched by the vicissitudes of life. Happiness is a question of internal peace: the Happy Man is he who, having nothing, yet has all, because he is completely self-possessed and serene.[115]

The passions that enslave Great Men are outward signs of vexation of spirit, so that Cowley only 'slightly' touched upon 'particulars of the slavery of Greatness': 'I shake but a few of their outward Chains; their Anger, Hatred, Jealousie, Fear, Envy, Grief, and all the *Etcaetera* of their Passions, which are the secret, but constant Tyrants and Torturers of their life, I omit here, because though they be symptoms most frequent and violent in this Disease; yet they are common too in some degree to the Epidemical Disease of Life it self'.[116] In developing the notion of freedom as self-restraint, Cowley employed a symbol that may be traced back to Hellenic times.

> Why, I'le tell you who is that true Freeman...; Not he who blindly follows all his pleasures (the very name of Follower is servile) but he who rationally guides them, and is not hindred by outward impediments in the conduct and enjoyment of them. If I want skill or force to restrain the Beast that I ride upon though I bought it, and call it my own, yet in truth of the matter I am at that time rather his Man, then he my Horse.[117]

Here, the unruly horse represents Cowley's own passions, or what he called 'his Man'.

But we also are enslaved by other men, as well as by 'Custom, Business, Crowds, and formal Decency'.[118] To symbolise this more inclusive tyrant, Cowley replaced the horse with a beast drawn from Scriptures, when he outlined the wretched existence of a Great Man, 'guarded with Crowds and shackled with Formalities'.

> The half hat, the whole hat, the half smile, the whole smile, the nod, the embrace, the Positive parting with a little Bow, the Comparative at the middle of the room, the Superlative at the door; and if the person be *Pan huper sebastus*, there's a *Hupersuperlative* ceremony then of conducting him to the bottom of the stairs, or to the very gate: as if there were such Rules set to these *Leviathans* as are to the Sea, *Hitherto shalt thou go, and no further*....Thus wretchedly the precious day is lost.[119]

In this passage the over-elaborate social code is the Leviathan, because its rules fetter not merely the Great Man but also his suitors. Thus, according to Cowley, happiness cannot be found in the kind of servitude that court life requires. And in an essay, 'Of My self', he intimated that contentment – internal peace – is unobtainable, since 'God laughs at a Man, who says to his Soul, *Take thy ease*'.[120] Nevertheless, by nature we have a tendency to seek internal peace, and our endeavour to obtain this unobtainable goal is what Cowley called 'the Epidemical Disease of Life'.[121]

Cowley's words echo the Stoic belief that all life is a striving, a belief clearly stated by Hobbes, when he wrote: 'there is no such thing as perpetuall Tranquillity of mind, while we live here; because Life it selfe is but Motion, and can never be without Desire, nor without Feare, no more than without Sense'.[122] Yet, even if Hobbes's own writings exemplify this striving in their developments and emendations, they also exhibit a consistent belief that the chief object of human striving is relief from ignorance. This *goal* is Hobbes's highest good; and it derives from his principle that the evident is true: since falsehood is the evil of the intellect, the complete goodness of the universe would have to be denied if the human desire to know were eternally thwarted.[123] Thus, 'neither things, nor imaginations of things, can be said to be false, seeing they are truly what they are; nor do they, as signs, promise any thing which they do not perform; for they indeed do not promise at all, but we from them'.[124]

In this extraordinary statement Hobbes did not reaffirm the classical view that nature manifests itself; rather, he maintained that knowledge of nature is conditioned by thought and mediated by speech or by writing. This, too, was the view of the Stoics, who regarded speech as a symbol involving not only a sign and a thing signified but also a perceiver who makes a connection between the two.[125] Or, to put it in Hobbes's terms, speech or writing involves external reality, conceptions and propositions and arguments, opposites and paradoxes. Significant speech always implies a linking between word and reality, so that through language can be shown how people re-arrange, combine and contrast their conceptions.[126] On these assumptions Hobbes could identify two sources of error. The first source, 'affirming and denying', is an error of speech or of writing, in which error arises from misnomers as well as from hasty inference. The second source, 'perception and silent cogitation', is an error of thought, in which errors are tacit and are made in three ways:

> ...by passing from one imagination to the imagination of another different thing; or by feigning that to be past, or future, which never was, nor ever shall be;...lastly, when from any sign we vainly imagine something to be signified, which is sense; and yet the deception proceeds neither from our senses, nor from the things we perceive; but from ourselves while we feign such things as are but mere images to be something more than images.[127]

Hobbes's two sources of error, then, are either false propositions or false conceptions (inferences), both of which he called by the name 'passions'. Hence, the passions, *ratio* as well as *oratio*, are false opinions or beliefs, for they rest on grounds insufficient to produce certainty. Reason, therefore, must supervene on the passions, as Hobbes suggested, when he wrote: 'The best way...to free ourselves from such errors as arise from natural signs, is first of all, before we begin to reason concerning such conjectural things, to suppose ourselves ignorant, and then to make use of our ratiocination; whereas, errors which consist in affirmation and negation (that is, the falsity of propositions) proceed only from reasoning amiss.'[128] The implication is that we need an appropriate method which may guide us in our generalisations and interpretations of nature's signs. As we shall see, Hobbes provided an exemplar of this method, which constitutes his own personal striving to reach a rational, that is, causal, understanding of the universe by viewing the parts in light of the whole and, so, grasping the underlying principle.

II. NATURE'S LAW

> ...*reason speaks no less universally to us all with its 'thou shalt' and 'thou shalt not'. So then there is a world-law....*
> Marcus Aurelius, *Meditations* (4.4)

Introduction
The Stoic fiat, live in harmony with nature – or in Hobbes's version, live temperately – is an imperative command to action. Moreover, for the Stoics, as well as for Hobbes, the principle underlying all action is tension, for this principle governs natural events, and this same principle guides people. Hence, tension is a natural law. If one obeys this law, then one's actions will be in harmony with events as they unfold.[129] But what is this law of tension, and how does it operate? To answer this question, it will be necessary to examine Hobbes's solution to another classical problem – body going through body. This problem is a paradox, because it presents a scientific idea contrary to general opinion not only in antiquity but also in Hobbes's own day.

In antiquity the paradox arose because Zeno, the first of the Stoics, assumed that two bodies – substance and *pneuma* – are thoroughly mixed, that is, interpenetrate so completely that both bodies are present in the same place. How, then, could *pneuma* spread through substance? A solution to this problem was offered by Chrysippus, who argued that body could combine in three ways: (1) by juxtaposition, whereby the ingredients maintain their own qualities and individuality; (2) by confusion, whereby the ingredients are destroyed and a new body arises from their combination; and (3) by blending, whereby the ingredients completely interpenetrate one another in such a way that each preserves its own substance and qualities.[130]

The first two types of combination were conventional Aristotelian doctrine; but the third type, blending, was new with Chrysippus, who introduced it in order to explain the way in which *pneuma* penetrates bodies, providing them with cohesive force and generating properties in them. More importantly, the Chrysippian penetration was a superposition principle, because, in blending, every component retains its special properties and can be separated out again from the mixture. Thus, blending is not comparable to the juxtaposition of two musical strings drawn side by side – which would mean an increase in area – but to the superposition of the two strings whereby no increase occurs. The physical structure of a body, therefore, is 'nothing else but the superposition of all the mixtures of *pneuma* corresponding to the various qualities of the body', all the mixtures together permeating the body as tensional motions, thus making it a dynamic entity.[131] In short, Chrysippus posited continuous forces of tension within body.

The Chrysippian doctrine of blending was criticised and subverted by the Peripatetics, who treated body going through body as a paradoxical relation occurring between three-dimensional solids.[132] When early in the 1640s Hobbes re-introduced this classical problem, his solution presented a major criticism not only of the Peripatetics but also of the new mechanical theories of matter and motion.[133] As is well known, the new theories began with Descartes, who in 1644 announced and elaborated upon his influential proposition regarding the conservation of total motion in the universe, from which he deduced that hard bodies rebound. According to Descartes, God created and supported a perfectly mechanical universe that never runs down of itself, because an unchanging quantity of motion is conserved through His laws in every impact of the material particles. The material particles crack and may be pulverised, because they are brittle ('hard'). Indeed, since the particles have no elasticity, they are divisible indefinitely.

Since Descartes conceived the universe as a plenum, he explained the motion of matter by rotation of smooth particles, like bearings on an axle, and by the subdivision or aggregation of others into smaller or larger sizes to fit the lacunae being created along the path. Motion is exerted by external pressures between all physical parts, which crumble, because all their parts are at rest (inert). Not being bound by any imaginary glue, cement or force, the parts separate whenever a force is sufficient to overcome their inertia. Hence, the Cartesian universe is like a great mill in which various particles are continually ground by a divine force, acting without friction or slippage.[134]

Besides Descartes' mechanical theory, there was the theory of Pierre Gassendi, who revived Epicureanism and argued that the world consists of very small spaces not filled by any body and very small bodies that have within them no empty space.[135] According to Gassendi, the very small bodies are real entities of minute size, whose surfaces are rough. Because they are also absolutely hard, he called them 'atoms', regarding them as the first matter – indivisible, indestructible and solid. Gassendi attributed degrees of hardness to the varying spaces between these solid atoms and considered that the universe was everywhere intermingled with atoms and spaces. At creation God impressed motion upon an atom, and this motion remained in the atom as a 'moving urge'. Atoms then act upon one another only by impact, and they change course only by the direction in which their moving urges are free to develop.

Despite the different approaches of Descartes and Gassendi, whereby one argued for a plenum and the other for a void, their general conceptual scheme of matter in motion differed very little, as Richard Westfall points out.[136] First, their mechanical theories were restricted to the mechanics of simple machines and did not include kinematics. Second, both men assumed that God, as the first cause of motion, always conserves an equal quantity of it in the universe. By this proposition they meant conservation of an unchanging quantity of motion for every instant of time, so that no motion is lost upon collision of material particles. Third, since both men regarded material substance as absolutely homogeneous, they accounted for apparent variety by the mere differences of shape, size, position and arrangement. According to this approach, even fluids are 'corpuscular', that is, composed of particles and 'pores' which are filled with some subtle matter (Descartes) or empty of matter (Gassendi). Fourth and finally, both men adopted the metaphysic of absolute hardness or impenetrability, according to which two bodies cannot be in the same place at the same time.

In offering a competing theory, Hobbes eliminated coming-into-being and the derivation of plurality from unity (i.e., homogeneous substance) by positing an indefinitely continuous scale of degrees of length and tension.[137] Empty space, therefore, is not empty but filled with kinetic energy, an energy that may be likened to the zero-point jiggling of a pendulum caused by the mote of energy remaining in the system when nothing is left. From this potential energy (infinitesimal vibratory motion), nature creates something from apparent nothing. Hobbes then addressed the most important question of seventeenth-century cosmology: what holds the universe together? For Descartes and Gassendi, the answer was an immutable, transcendental God; for Newton, it was the law of gravity. By outlining Hobbes's solution to the paradox, body moves through body, I shall show that, for Hobbes, the universe coheres, because God's will is an immanent conserving principle which has the regularity of a physical law.

3. Body as a deformable system

> *Matter in the universe*
> *is supple and compliant,*
> *and the Reason which controls it*
> *has no motive for ill-doing.*
> Marcus Aurelius, *Meditations* (6.1)

3.1. Matter as endeavour to cohere

In the very first section of *Body*, Hobbes introduced the classical problem as follows:

From...consideration of what is produced by simple motion, we are to pass to the consideration of what effects one body moved *worketh upon* another; and because there may be motion *in* all the several parts of a body, yet so as that the whole body remain still in the same place, we must enquire first, what motion causeth such and such motion in the whole, that is, when one body *invades* another body which is either at rest or in motion, what way, and with what swiftness, the *invaded body* shall move; and again, what motion this second body will generate *in* a third, and so forwards. From which contemplation shall be drawn that part of philosophy which treats of [compound] motion.[138]

In this passage Hobbes asserted the Stoic paradox that body moves through ('invades') body.[139] And, in scattered parts of his treatise, he provided a physical solution to this classical problem, which is based on three hypotheses. According to the first hypothesis, there are three kinds of body: fluid, consistent and mixed of both. '*Fluid* are those, whose parts may by very weak endeavour be separated from one another; and *consistent* those for the separation of whose parts greater force is to be applied.'[140] According to the second hypothesis, there are no absolutely consistent bodies. Instead, bodies may be distinguished by degrees of consistency, according as their parts have more or less degrees of cohesion. These degrees, 'by comparison with more or less consistent, have the names of *hardness* or *softness*',[141] so that 'some bodies will be harder, others softer through all the several degrees of *tenacity*'.[142] According to the third hypothesis, more or less cohesion derives from a fluid plenum that surrounds and penetrates bodies, giving them cohesive force.[143]

On these hypotheses, Hobbes could explain cohesion as an internal resistance to separation.[144] But separation is not the same as vacuum, as Hobbes made clear in his criticism of the ancient Epicureans. Their spokesman, Lucretius, had argued that '*if two flat bodies be suddenly pulled asunder, of necessity the air must come between them to fill up the space they left empty. But with what celerity soever the air flow in, yet it cannot in one instant of time fill the whole space, but first one part of it, then successively all*'. Hobbes conceded that 'if two bodies were of infinite [absolute] hardness, and were joined together by their superficies which were most exactly plane, it would be impossible to pull them asunder, in regard it could not be done but by motion in an instant'.[145] But he pointed out that since 'the greatest of all magnitudes cannot be given, nor the swiftest of all motions, so neither the hardest of all bodies'.[146]

Hobbes, therefore, rejected the metaphysic of impenetrability. Instead, he argued that all bodies are more or less deformable – that is, change shape or dimensions due to stress or strain.[147] Moreover, this argument enabled him to reject separation as vacuum, because, if body is deformable, separation is a successive process, as in the example of what he termed 'all flexion', which

> ...supposes necessarily that the internal parts of the body bowed do either come nearer to the external parts, or go further from them. For though *flexion* be considered only in the length of a body, yet when that body is bowed, the line which is made on one side will be convex, and the line on the other side will be concave; of which the concave, being the interior line, will, unless something be taken from it and added to the convex line, be the more crooked, that is, the greater of the two. But they are equal; and, therefore, in flexion there is an accession made from the interior to the exterior parts; and on the contrary, in tension, from the exterior to the interior parts.[148]

Thus, if a body is bent, 'the first separation will necessarily be in the convex superficies of the bowed part of the body, and afterwards in the concave superficies. For in all bowing there is in the convex superficies an endeavour in the parts to go one from another, and in the concave superficies to penetrate one another'.[149]

The problems of cohesion and strength of materials had been studied by Galileo, who described an experiment of two cohering polished marble surfaces as an example of the aversion of nature for empty space. But he added another cause in the form of a gluey or viscous substance which binds firmly together the component parts of a body.[150] Galileo did not elaborate on this second cause and later withdrew it, so that he seemed to have accepted the notion of a resistance to vacuum as the cause of cohesion. Galileo's theory of resistance to vacuum, however, is not the same as Hobbes's theory of resistance to separation (breaking), for Galileo allowed for dimensionless interstitial point-voids, whereas Hobbes seems to have rejected microscopic as well as macroscopic voids.[151]

It is probable, nevertheless, that Hobbes's theory of cohesion owes a debt to Galileo's investigations into the resistance that solid bodies offer to fracture. As part of those investigations Galileo considered a rope, the strength of which 'is derived from a multitude of hemp threads which compose it'.[152] Although Galileo's entire treatment of the nature of the rope is illuminating, I shall merely state his conclusion: that the resistance which one meets with in the case of a thick hemp rope derives from 'the fibres which form thousands and thousands of...spirals...indeed, the binding effect of these turns is so great that a few short rushes woven together into a few interlacing spirals form one of the strongest of ropes which I believe they call pack rope'.[153]

According to this model, it is the intertwining fibres which bind together the whole rope and make it cohere, just as the intertwining ether binds together the whole universe and makes it cohere. Hobbes's universe, however, is filled with different degrees of tensile strength, which depend, in turn, on the different degrees of tensional motion, for the fluid plenum itself is passive and derives its tension from the innate activity I have called 'impulse'. Hence, we may describe body as elastic, remembering that, for Hobbes, there are always degrees of more and less.

3.2. Motion as virtual power and actual work

In *Body* Hobbes never utilised the word 'elasticity'[154] but his conception of this phenomenon may be teased out by an examination of one of the most important terms in his entire philosophy: endeavour. Fortunately, an investigation of this term has been made by H.R. Bernstein, who enumerates the following five points about Hobbes's 'rational mechanics'.[155] First, endeavour is a kinematical, as well as a dynamical or force-related idea.[156] Second, the notion of resistance is (tacitly) involved in Hobbes's concept of endeavour,[157] since equilibrium conceals an internal or dynamic tension of competing 'forces' and apparent rest is thoroughly kinetic.[158] Third, endeavour and impetus both are reducible to the same idea of instantaneous velocity (i.e., they share a common infinitesimal status); but endeavour applies only to initial moments and the term is restricted to the phenomena of impact and collision,[159] whereas impetus is acquired and does not partake of a dynamical connotation.[160] Fourth, endeavour, impetus and velocity may be related to one another in terms of what later would be called 'orders of smallness'. Fifth and finally, endeavour may be related (vaguely) to the modern idea of momentum, for while Hobbes did not use the phrase, 'quantity of motion', he does invoke a force (*vis*).[161]

Bernstein claims (point 5) that Hobbes did not use the phrase, 'quantity of motion'; but in *Body* he wrote that '*velocity is the quantity of motion determined by time and line*',[162] and he also stated that the 'velocity of any body, in whatsoever time it be moved, has its quantity determined by the sum of all the several quicknesses or impetus, which it hath in several points of the time of the body's motion'.[163] Moreover, a careful reading of *Body* indicates that in a number of places Hobbes signified quantity of motion, though he may not have expressed it precisely in those terms.[164] Hence, there is considerable support for Bernstein's supposition (point 4) about the relation of endeavour, impetus and velocity.

If we return to the context of Hobbes's cosmic determinism, we may now conclude that the universe vibrates with endeavours working from within and which consist of an equalisation of action and reaction.[165] Action is 'force' — kinetic motion or change, whereas reaction is 'power' — dynamic tension or cause of change. Indeed, Hobbes wrote: 'although endeavour...perpetually propagated do[es] not always appear to the senses as motion, yet it appears as action, or as the efficient cause of some mutation'.[166] Reaction, therefore, respects the future ('to which'), whereas action respects the past ('from which'), as Hobbes made perfectly clear in a chapter treating 'power and act':

> 1. CORRESPONDENT to *cause* and *effect*, are POWER and ACT; nay, those and these are the same things; though, for divers considerations, they have divers names. For whensoever any agent has all those accidents which are necessarily requisite for the production of some effect in the patient, then we say that the agent has power to produce that effect, if it be applied to a patient....Wherefore the *power of the agent* and the *efficient cause* are the same thing. But they are considered with this difference, that *cause* is so called in respect of the effect already produced, and power in respect of the same effect to be produced hereafter; so that *cause* respects the past, *power* the future time.[167]

If we take both action and reaction into account, the total endeavour in the universe may be defined as the capacity to act or to do work,[168] for, according to Hobbes, 'whensoever the cause is entire [i.e., consists of both power and act], the effect is produced *in the same instant*, it is manifest that causation and the production of effects consist in a certain *continual progress*; so that as there is a *continual mutation* in the agent or agents, by *the working* of other agents upon them, so also the patient, upon which they work, is *continually altered and changed*'.[169] The phrase, 'in the same instant', occurs frequently in Hobbes's text and, like all his key terms, has a number of meanings, depending on the perspective taken. When understood in the context of processes that are perfectly inverse, the phrase signifies that point when the conclusion of one movement is identical with the beginning of the opposite and conversely.[170] For example, in continuous processes, such as oscillatory systems, 'in the same instant' is that point when action (kinetic motion) and reaction (dynamic tension) conjoin, thereby producing the 'entire cause' or turning point, in which motion is reversed.[171] Hence, elastic processes drive the universe, since action and reaction cause all the manifold occurrences in the world.

Like a musical instrument, deformable bodies may be 'played upon' by external forces such as percussion (striking), pressure (squeezing, as of an air sack), friction (bowing) or wind (blowing). Impact would then consist of a contest of forces in opposite directions, since, according to Hobbes, 'such things as are removed from their places by forcible compression or extension, and, as soon as the force is taken away, do presently return and restore themselves to their former situation, have the beginning of their restitution *within themselves*, namely, a certain motion *in their internal parts*, which was there, when, before the taking way of the force, they were compressed, or extended'.[172]

Since restitution is motion, Hobbes's model of impact is an elastic process entailing deformation ('action') and restitution ('reaction') through continuous intervals to and through the infinitesimal motion that constitutes rest:

> In hard bodies...which are compressed or extended, if, that which compresseth or extendeth them being taken away, they

restore themselves to their former place or situation, it must needs be that that endeavour or motion of their internal parts, by which they were able to recover their former places or situations, was not extinguished when the force by which they were compressed or extended was taken away. Therefore, when the lath of a cross-bow bent doth, as soon as it is at liberty, restore itself, though to him that judges by sense, both it and all its parts seem to be at rest; yet he, that judging by reason doth not account the taking away of impediment for an efficient cause, nor conceives that without an efficient cause any thing can pass from rest to motion, will conclude that the parts were already in motion before they began to restore themselves.[173]

Upon impact, inelastic ('soft') bodies do not lose motion; rather, motion is transferred to submicroscopic orders in the fluid plenum and conserved. This solution is completely different from that of Descartes and Gassendi, for whom God must intervene to conserve motion in the universe.

3.3. Matter as a point, motion as a way

In *Body* Hobbes made two assumptions about parts and wholes: first, that 'nothing can rightly be called a whole, that is not conceived to be compounded of parts, and that it may be divided into parts; so that if we deny that a thing has parts, we deny the same to be a whole'; and, second, that 'nothing has parts till it be divided; and when a thing is divided, the parts are only so many as the division makes them'.[174] But computations such as dividing are acts of the mind, so that quantity (extension) is divisible into divisibles 'perpetually', wherefore 'there is no impossible smallness of bodies'.[175] According to his own computations, Hobbes conceived parts in three ways.

Under one conception, part denotes that which may be quantified (numbered, weighed or measured).[176] To signify this conception, Hobbes used the term 'part' to refer to that which has dimensions and must always be capable of being divided. For example, when considering 'the immense space, which we call the world',[177] he assumed that some parts ('bodies') are 'greater, others less, and many unspeakably little',[178] although he pointed out that 'how little soever some bodies may be, yet I will not suppose their quantity to be less than is requisite for the salving of the phenomena'.[179] Accordingly, we need not assume the existence of infinitely small quantitites; it is sufficient for the purpose of mathematics to be able to reach a magnitude as small as we please by continued division of a given magnitude.[180]

Under a second conception, part signifies that which is incapable of physical division without transformation into something else (e.g., fire, light). The change involved here is not mechanical alteration ('mutation') but chemical transformation ('fermentation') that reveals itself as heat. To signify this conception, Hobbes usually (but not always) employed the term 'particle' and its cognates ('small bodies', 'smallest bodies', 'atoms', etc.) since, according to his theory of mechanical and chemical change, 'greater and less degree of hardness depends upon the quantity and velocity of those small bodies [fluid and consistent], and upon the narrowness of the place both together'.[181]

Under a third conception, part is not a physical entity but a mathematical point. According to this conception, mathematical points cannot be counted, weighed or measured, for although a point is a quantity, it is either more or less than any quantity that can possibly be named.[182] Thus,

> ...by a point is not to be understood that which has no quantity, or which cannot by any means be divided; for there is no such thing in nature; but that, whose quantity is not at all considered, that is, whereof neither quantity nor any part is computed in demonstration; so that a point is not to be taken for an indivisible, but for an undivided thing; as also an instant is to be taken for an undivided, and not for an indivisible time.[183]

Although actual bodies have magnitude, we may describe dimensions by considering them as if they are points alone, that is, as if they have no magnitude.

Although Hobbes used the word 'describe' as an equivalent word for the science of geometry (the process of drawing or generating 'a line, figure, or magnitude by supposing that a selected motion causes it'[184]), he also adopted an approach in which lines are conceived as points in motion. For example, in treating simple circular motion, he asserted that such motion is the most common in nature: 'being the same which is used by all men when they turn anything round with their arms, as they do in grinding or sifting. For all the points of the thing moved describe lines which are like and equal to one another. So that if a man had a ruler, in which many pens' points of equal length were fastened, he might with this one motion write many lines at once'.[185] In this passage there is a hint, perhaps gleaned from Galileo, that oscillatory motion may be represented graphically in a manner similar to modern displacement diagrams of the vibrating point.[186]

But Hobbes definitely followed Galileo in defining the spiral as the locus of a point which moves with uniform radial velocity along a line, while the line in turn revolves uniformly about one of its end points which is kept fixed.[187] According to this procedure, Hobbes demonstrated that it is possible to construct a semiparabolical line equal to the length of the Archimedean spiral of the first revolution;[188] and he took the argument one step further to deal with the quadrature of the semiparabola.[189] On the basis of this approach, Hobbes argued that 'any ordinary man may much sooner and more accurately find a strait line equal to the perimeter of a circle, and consequently square the circle, by winding a small thread about a given cylinder'.[190]

In eliminating magnitude from bodies, motion becomes a 'way' – a dimension subject to both determination and calculation.[191] Thus: 'Though there be no body which has not some magnitude, yet if, when any body is moved, the magnitude of it be not at all considered, the way it makes is called a *line*, or one single dimension; and the space, through which it passeth, is called *length*; and the body itself, a *point*'.[192] A point, then, may be said to 'pass through' or move through superficies (surfaces), which are generated by the motions of lines, and likewise through solids, which are generated by the motion of surfaces.[193] In this way, therefore, Hobbes provided a mathematical, as well as a physical, solution to the paradox of body moving through body.

4. Body as a habit

> ...do not remain out of tune
> longer than you can help.
> Habitual recurrence to the harmony
> will increase your mastery of it.
> Marcus Aurelius, *Meditations* (6.11)

4.1. Nature's habit: what is given at birth

From the foregoing account, we may conclude that Hobbes conceived body as a physical system of units that may be represented mathematically. He defined 'work' as a change in the configuration of such a system in opposition to the forces resisting it, and he treated energy as the capacity to do work. In passing through any cycle of changes of configuration, a physical system ('body') does the same quantity of external work which is done upon it, so that the energy derived from systems without is compensated for by an equal amount of energy communicated to external systems. When forces are in disequilibrium, action continues until equilibrium is reached, as in the examples of an oscillating pendulum or a vibrating musical string. Physical systems, therefore, are conserved by the law of tension, which, for Hobbes, is an equalisation of action and reaction.

Although the equalisation of action and reaction is not established by dint of repetition, it is nevertheless a regular tendency (*conatus*, endeavour). As such, it constitutes a way that is nature's habit. To live temperately in conformity with the law of tension, therefore, means learning to imitate nature's habit. But what does this imitation entail? To answer this question, we must refer briefly to Hobbes's solution of yet another classical problem: the identity of indiscernibles. This problem arose in antiquity because the Epicureans supposed that information is conveyed by the actual transmission of indiscernible atoms, whereas the Stoics believed that information is conveyed by the propagation of an impulse through an indiscernible but elastic medium in a state of tension.

When these two physical doctrines were revived as seventeenth-century emission and continuum physics, so, too, were their different solutions to the problem of the identity of indiscernibles. You will recall that Descartes had propounded a continuum physics. But

The Paradoxes of Power

his continuum is completely different from that of Hobbes, for it is based on a discrete, corpuscular model – continuous atomism, in which even fluids are particulate. Hence, his solution to the problem of the identity of indiscernibles was the same as that of Gassendi and the emission physicists who emphasised the complete equality of all indiscernible atoms of the same kind. This view was shared also by the Peripatetics, who, in other respects, were opponents of the emission physicists. In antiquity the Stoics alone had argued that the complete indistinguishability of bodies would mean that they are identical. Hence, they insisted that nothing is the same as that which some other thing is.[194]

In alluding to the problem of the identity of indiscernibles, or 'in what sense it may be conceived that a body is at one time the same, at another time not the same it was formerly',[195] Hobbes identified three solutions, one of which placed individuality in the unity of matter, a second, in the unity of form, and a third, in the unity of the aggregate of all the accidents together. Hobbes's own solution is to be found in what he called 'the *beginning of individuation*', for if

> ...the name be given for such form as is the beginning of motion, then, as long as that motion remains, it will be the same *individual* thing; as that man will be always the same, whose actions and thoughts proceed all from the same beginning of motion, namely, that which was in his generation; and that will be the same river which flows from one and the same fountain, whether the same water, or other water, or something else than water, flow from thence; and that the same city, whose acts proceed continually from the same institution, whether the men be the same or no. Lastly, if the name be given for some accident, then the *identity* of the thing will depend upon the matter; for, by the taking away and supplying of matter, the accidents that were, are destroyed, and other new ones are generated, which cannot be the same numerically; so that a ship, which signifies matter so figured, will be the same as long as the matter remains the same; but if no part of the matter be the same, then it is numerically another ship; and if part of the matter remain and part be changed, then the ship will be partly the same, and partly not the same.[196]

An accident of matter may suggest the name 'man', because the matter is so figured. And we may give the matter called 'man' various other names, depending on its changing attributes (e.g., old or young man, bad or good man). But names (utterances) and other external actions, which symbolise thoughts, spring from 'first beginnings' of motion. In Hobbes's philosophy, there are many first beginnings. For example, there are the beginnings of animal motion, and there are also the beginnings of knowledge.[197] In the first part of this chapter I referred to these beginnings as 'impulse'. In this second part closer scrutiny revealed that impulse is the physical law of tension. I shall now refer to this law as 'primary impulse', because primary impulse is nature's habit – that which is given at birth. Hence, primary impulse is a basic fact of nature in terms of which other and more complex impulses (behaviour patterns) may be explained.[198]

In physiological terms, primary impulse is the effort (*conatus*) by which each living thing strives to conserve its own being. Hence, it is the characteristic attribute (identity) of the living thing, as well as the very definition of life. But endeavour is more than self-conservation, for it includes also developmental drive or drive towards completion – a movement toward fulfillment of the normal life cycle. Although self-conservation is there for the sake of completing the life cycle, it is also a means for actualising potentialities. This actualisation is the perfect realisation of all that any creature or power is capable of becoming. Accordingly, life processes are fundamentally directive and creative; directiveness and creativeness are properties of living things and only of living things.[199]

In psychological terms, endeavour is a state of consciousness; but it is a relative state which cannot exist without a subject. Moreover, consciousness in all its states has two components – awareness and reactivity, what I earlier called 'sensation' and 'representation'.[200] Awareness constitutes the sensory component and reactivity, the motor component of consciousness. But there is also a scale of degrees of consciousness between sleeping and waking, when thoughts are either unguided or guided. Thus, when there is

> ...no Passionate Thought, to govern and direct those that follow, to it self, as the end and scope of some desire, or other passion: In which case the thoughts are said to wander, and seem

impertinent one to another, as in a Dream. Such are Commonly the thoughts of men, that are not onely without company, but also without care of any thing; though even then their Thoughts are as busie as at other times, but without harmony; as the sound which a Lute out of tune would yeeld to any man; or in tune, to one that could not play. And yet in this wild ranging of the mind, a man may oft-times perceive the way of it, and the dependance of one thought upon another....[But the] second [kind of thought, or mental discourse] is more constant; as being *regulated* by some desire, and designe.[201]

When awareness and/or reactivity are diminished, consciousness is distempered. For example, if awareness is distempered, as it is in sleep, our mental discourse (dream) lacks coherence.[202] Or if reactivity is distempered, stupor (akinesis and mutism) results.[203]

4.2. Our habit: things to be done and known

Although primary impulse is the source, or first beginning, of all compounded impulses in the universe, two additional factors are requisite for the full development of humans. These two factors are experience and study, for by means of these we develop 'natural' and 'acquired wit'. By 'natural' Hobbes did not mean 'that which a man hath from his Birth; for that is nothing else but Sense; wherein men differ so little one from another, and from brute Beasts, as it is not to be reckoned amongst Vertues'. Rather, natural wit is that 'which is gotten by Use onely, and Experience; without Method, Culture, or Instruction' and which 'consisteth principally in two things: *Celerity of Imagining,* (that is, swift succession of one thought to another;) and *steddy direction* to some approved end'.[204] He then added that the other kind of wit, that which is 'acquired by method and instruction', is nothing else 'but Reason; which is grounded on the right use of Speech; and produceth the Sciences'.[205]

All varieties of human character are to be sought in the compounded or complex impulses which Hobbes called 'passions'; and these in turn are owing partly to the different constitution of human bodies ('temperament', 'complexion') and partly to different habits (use and experience) and education (method and instruction) of people. In short, he accounted for differences of character on the basis both of nature and nurture; but he placed great emphasis on the latter aspect, for by habit and study we acquire our second nature, that which we make ourselves.

In *Body*, Hobbes defined habit as:

> ...a generation of motion, not of motion simply, but an easy conducting of the moved body in a certain and designed way. And seeing it is attained by the weakening of such endeavours as divert its motion, therefore such endeavours are to be weakened by little and little. But this cannot be done but by the long continuance of action, or by actions often repeated; and therefore custom begets that facility, which is commonly and rightly called *habit*; and it may be defined thus: HABIT *is motion made more easy and ready by custom; that is to say, by perpetual endeavour, or by iterated endeavours in a way differing from that in which the motion proceeded from the beginning, and opposing such endeavours as resist.*[206]

To make this definition 'more perspicuous', Hobbes provided two examples. In one example he described how the lath of a crossbow will become bent by the constant restraint of the string. According to this example, the tension of the string is responsible for restraining the lath. When that tension is maintained over a long period of time, the lath will not restore itself to its original or natural position but will remain bent in its artificial one even when the string is loosed. In a second example he described how an aspiring musician learns to finger a musical instrument:

> ...when one that has no skill in music first puts his hand to an instrument, he cannot after the first stroke carry his hand to the place where he would make the second stroke, without taking it back by a new endeavour, and, as it were beginning again, pass from the first to the second. Nor will he be able to go on to the third place without another new endeavour; but he will be forced to draw back his hand again, and so successively, by renewing his endeavour at every stroke; till at the last, by doing this often, and by compounding many interrupted motions or endeavours into one equal endeavour, he be able to make his hand go readily on from stroke to stroke in that order and way which was at the first designed.[207]

According to this example, skill is acquired by a method of trial and error which takes time and must be often repeated until the skill is mastered.

In both examples the concept involved is plasticity, not elasticity. But body must possess both properties, the one property, plasticity, being called upon in forming body, the other property, elasticity, in using body.[208] When the two properties are conjoined, the exercise of tension leads to learning by experience. Thus, art – natural wit – is understood as a habit with reference to things to be done. In attaining art, rules of performance are internalised as skills and in this way become second nature. For Hobbes, however, science alone – acquired wit – is the basis of the ethical life, a life lived temperately in conformity with law. How, then, do we acquire science? Since Hobbes defined self-determination with respect to action, the corollary is that on the same terms as art is attained, so all science is acquired, for science is a habit with reference to things to be known.

III. NATURE'S GUIDE

> *Where, then, can man find the power to guide his steps?*
> *In one thing and one thing alone:*
> *Philosophy.*
> Marcus Aurelius, *Meditations* (2.17)

Introduction
The first beginnings of science occur when we 'bend' our mind to the enquiry of truth.[209] But the goal of such bending is to temper our passions, which Hobbes defined as untested beliefs. If untempered, our passions may become excessive and lead to madness, an internal condition that is manifested externally by loud screams, wild motions and other inharmonious actions.[210] Hobbes assigned two causes of madness: one from the diseased constitution of the instruments of the body, the other from a vehement and too long continued passion. In both cases 'the Madness is of one and the same nature', for, whatever the cause, all madness is contrary to reason.[211] Although a physician and a teacher may help in the cure, we alone are responsible for learning how to exercise the appropriate tension in matters of choice, resistance, equity and strength. Practice, therefore, leads to the virtues of prudence, temperance, justice and endurance, all four of which are both

science and art, because the chief object of natural wit is to contemplate and put into practice what must be chosen, done, awarded, avoided.

Although tempering the passions involves both voluntary motive and cognitive 'powers', these powers can be 'encreased by study and industry; and...learned by instruction, and discipline'. But Hobbes singled out 'Speech, and Method' as the chief means of improving the motive and cognitive faculties 'to such a height, as to distinguish men from all other living creatures'.[212] To achieve this improvement, however, we must resort to philosophical education, which Hobbes conceived as a 'way' or 'method of study'.[213] By this method we learn to recognise the law of tension, which then becomes a measure or model of true knowledge. According to this conception, philosophy serves as a medium between things themselves about which certain truths must be known and manifest and the habit of mind acquired concerning them. Philosophical education is not abstruse contemplation but the development of each human being's capacities for active, practical reasoning. Since the active use of practical reason is the common and universal possession of all healthy people, cultivation of practical reason is a central human need. Teaching, therefore, must be flexible and responsive to individuality.

This conception of philosophy derives from the Stoics, whose moral ideal of humanity is a value-attribute that refers to the complete development of ethical character. According to them, ethical character alone differentiates humanity from the beasts. The concept of humanity in this moral sense is not to be found among the virtues discussed in the writings of Plato or Aristotle. It was formed by the Stoics as a demand for a certain kind of life – a life in harmony with nature. The Stoic fiat had many levels of meaning and included conformity with one's own nature, with one's family, with larger social groups and with God. Hence, living in harmony with nature necessarily entailed recognising and acting upon the bond that exists between things human and things divine.

Through later writers such as Cicero and Seneca, humanity, as a moral ideal, became firmly established in Roman philosophy and Latin literature, passing into medieval and modern European culture as the study of the 'humanities'. By denying any irrational function of the soul, the Stoics regarded reason as the essential function of mind. The idea that there is a community of reason in all people implies the notion of a community of people. The intellect is regarded as the universal bond of agreement that makes it possible for people, as rational beings, to live in harmony with themselves, with others and with the rest of nature. Before the all-comprehending unity can be reached, however, the secondary unities of knowledge must be grasped.

5. *Philosophy as method*
5.1. Teaching by example
In Stoic philosophy the secondary unities of knowledge are logic (including grammar, linguistics, semantics), physics and ethics.[214] On first glance, this does not seem to be the structure of Hobbes's last treatise on philosophy, which consists of three separate volumes: *Body, Human Nature* and *De corpore politico; or the Elements of Law*. It is to be noted, however, that of the three volumes, only the first is sub-divided. If we list the sub-divisions, we have the following sequence of six parts:

1 Logic or Computation (*Body*)
2 The First Grounds of Philosophy (*Body*)
3 Proportions of Motions and Magnitudes (*Body*)
4 Physics, or the Phenomena of Nature (*Body*)
5 Human Nature
6 Elements of Law

The subject matter of this sequence has been differently described by different commentators, most of whom give the sequence as logic, first philosophy, geometry, physics, psychology and politics. Against this received opinion, I shall argue that Parts 1 and 2 constitute Hobbes's logic, Parts 3 and 4, his natural philosophy, and Parts 5 and 6, his practical philosophy.

That logic is the subject of Part 1 is clear from Hobbes's title. This part begins with an introductory chapter, 'Of Philosophy', in which Hobbes distinguished the two kinds of wit, now named 'natural reason' and 'right reason'. Natural reason comes into the world and develops with us; but right reason is cultivated by 'sowing and planting', for only thus is natural reason improved. In the same introductory chapter Hobbes stated that his aim was 'to lay open the few and first Elements of Philosophy in general, as so many seeds from which pure and true Philosophy may hereafter spring up by little and little'.[215] The first 'seeds' of philosophy are sown in the subsequent chapters of Part 1 which treat names, propositions, syllogisms of various kinds, the sources of error, and method.[216] But the chapter on method is incompletely understood without taking into consideration a sub-section in Part 3, where Hobbes treated 'logistica'.[217] The enlarged method then becomes a pair of 'perfectly inverse' methods, analytic and synthetic, which together form the 'ways' of philosophy. Although the two methods may be conjoined in various fashions and in reference to various subject matters, 'the preeminent and most successful one is an inclusive employment of both'.[218]

In Part 1 Hobbes intimated that the most important was yet to come, for he wrote: 'such things as I have said are to be taught last, cannot be demonstrated, till such as are propounded to be first treated of, be fully understood. Of which method no other example can be given, but that treatise of the elements of philosophy, which I shall begin in the next chapter, and continue to the end of the work'.[219] By 'the next chapter' he denoted the opening of Part 2, in the very first sentence of which he enters as a teacher of natural philosophy.[220] In this Part Hobbes adumbrated, first, a Stoic conception of place and time as the defining characteristics of particular things which are extended and endure. According to this conception, space and duration are absolute, but place and time are relative to the observer, since in thinking 'we compute nothing but our own phantasms'.[221] He then set out his own version of the four Stoic categories (predicaments) that guide enquiry into the status of particular things. The four categories are body, accident, disposition and relative disposition.[222]

To be admitted into each category, a thing must be an existing thing. For example, under the first category, body, an existing thing may be matter – the sum total of existence, which is everlasting and which neither grows nor diminishes. To use Hobbes words: 'matter cannot by any endeavour of ours be either made or destroyed, or increased, or diminished, or moved out of its place'.[223] Or an existing thing may be particular things or 'parts' of matter, which are qualified in particular ways. Hence, an analysis of matter (the whole) will be an analysis of particular bodies, so that the next enquiry will focus on the second category, accident, whereby particular bodies are differentiated according to qualities which are common to all particular bodies (disposition) or according to qualities which are particular to some bodies only (relative disposition).[224]

Parts 1 and 2, therefore, may be designated as logic. But these parts deviate from Peripatetic logic, for Hobbes argued that knowledge consists of the necessary connectivity of events rather than the necessary relation of genus and species. The Stoics argued similarly, for they replaced the Aristotelian categories, which are classes of predicates constructed on the model of genus and species, with a set of four categories which were intended to illustrate the enchainment of things in that each succeeding category presupposes the preceding. The Aristotelian categories were standard features of textbooks on logic from the time of Porphyry, and Hobbes described them in Part 1. But he concluded his treatment by confessing:

> ...I have not yet seen any great use of the predicaments in philosophy. I believe *Aristotle* when he saw he could not digest the things themselves into such orders, might nevertheless desire out of his own authority to reduce words to such forms, as I have done; but I do it only for this end, that it may be understood what this ordination of words is, and not to have it received for true, till it be demonstrated by good reason to be so.[225]

Hobbes did not ignore genera and species or categorical propositions; but he followed the Stoics in subordinating them to hypothetical propositions and syllogisms (if..., then...) which, he argued, have equal force.[226]

In antiquity, the Stoic interest in hypothetical syllogisms compelled thinkers to address the problem of logical inference. For example, the Stoics held that predetermined events unfolded in the course of time. As certain combinations and constellations of events repeat themselves continually (i.e., cyclically), careful study of their nexus can furnish the means of knowing the future. For the Stoics, such knowledge formed inductive divination, that is, divination from inference based on signs of events in the physical surroundings. And Cicero described this process as an art of those who follow up new things by inference, having learned old ones by observation. Accordingly, logic can be described as a computation of signs; and this is indeed how Hobbes defined it, for he followed the Stoics in holding that signs, which are presented for us to read and cogitate upon, represent phantasms in the mind; and it is these which we compute (add and substract) in order to calculate the possibilities.[227]

Parts 1 and 2, therefore, are propaedeutic or introductory to natural philosophy, the particular subject matter of which constitutes Parts 3 and 4.[228] Commentators usually describe Part 3 as pertaining to geometry; but Hobbes himself regarded it as 'conducing to natural philosophy', as he declared at the opening of this section:

> The next things in order to be treated of are MOTION and MAGNITUDE, which are the most common accidents of all bodies. This place therefore most properly belongs to the elements of geometry. But because this part of philosophy, having been improved by the best wits of all ages, has afforded greater plenty of matter than can well be thrust together within the narrow limits of this discourse, I thought fit to admonish the reader that...the little...that I shall say concerning geometry in some of the following chapters, shall be such only as is new, and conducing to natural philosophy.[229]

Part 3, on 'Proportions of Motions and Magnitudes', tends to natural philosophy, because it considers multiple relations 'in the abstract'.[230] But Part 4, on 'Physics, or the Phenomena of Nature', likewise tends to natural philosophy, because it considers multiple relations of particular things. Unlike Part 3, therefore, this part 'hath its principles in the appearances of nature, and endeth in the attaining of some knowledge of natural causes'.[231] Moreover, it is at the very beginning of this part that Hobbes outlined his physiology.

Parts 1 through 4, then, are not restricted to the observation of natural phenomena and the scientific investigation of nature and nature's laws, for they also present a particular system or doctrine of nature. Hence, the grounds of Hobbes's ethics must be sought here and not in his so-called psychology. Modern interpreters who employ this term do so anachronistically, for Hobbes's psychology is physiology, whereas his ethics covers the whole range of practical philosophy, the subject of Parts 5 and 6. In these parts Hobbes treated five principal topics, though not as a sequence. These topics are character, the passions, conduct, casuistry – consideration of cases of conscience when different duties conflict, and natural theology – knowledge of God, including a determination of the relations between God and man. He repeated these concerns in *Leviathan*.

5.2. Finding the image

In treating the secondary unities of knowledge, Hobbes presented a system – a coordinated body of methods or complex plan of procedure.[232] And he announced this plan at the very outset of the first volume, where he wrote:

> Philosophy...the child of the world and your own mind, is within yourself; perhaps not fashioned yet, but like the world its father, as it was in the beginning, a thing confused. Do, therefore, as the statuaries do, who, by hewing off that which is superfluous, do not make but find the image. Or imitate the [order of] creation:...*light, distinction of day and night, the firmament, the luminaries, sensible creatures, man;* and, after the creation, the *commandment*. Therefore the order of contemplation will be, *reason, definition, space, the stars, sensible quality, man;* and after man is grown up, *subjection to command*.[233]

Hobbes then added: 'This is the method I followed; and if it like you, you may use the same; for I do not propound, nor commend to you anything of mine'. There are two implications to note. First, philosophy is a method for the acquisition of science, defined as knowledge. Second, this method is not authoritative but historical, so that knowledge is not *science made* but *science to be made*.

Before science can be made, however, we must first 'find the image'. In this chapter I have argued that Hobbes's 'image' is a musical string extended in three dimensions (length, breadth, thickness) with resistance (tension). I shall now make the further claim that this image is also the controlling metaphor of his last philosophy. According to this metaphor, contrary ('reciprocal') motions can and do exist in the same body,[234] for when plucked, or otherwise impacted upon, a taut string is bent violently in one direction and returns swiftly to its normal straight position. But because of the impetus, it crosses the normal straight position in the contrary direction and then returns again in the opposite direction. A vibrating string performs this action many times, and it stops vibrating after percussion only when the impetus it acquired is exhausted through friction.

The taut string is a demonstration of Hobbes's tension law: the equalisation of action and reaction. When applied to people, this law becomes a condition of physiological equilibrium which is always associated with the presence of life. But in Hobbes's system equilibrium is not static, for internal tension is a constant infinitesimal motion that changes with time. Thus, any disturbance of this constancy, resulting in an excess of tension (e.g., restlessness, activity, goal-seeking behaviour) and leading to the attainment of goal and quiescence, can be said to exhibit the operation of dynamic equilibrium. A recurrence of the same disturbance leads to the perception of cues, to tension (understood today as cortical tension) and to appropriate action; or, in other words, repeated disequilibrium leads to learning by experience, as in Hobbes's example of a musician learning to finger an instrument.

The mechanisms of equilibrium ensure that the sentient, so long as it remains alive, will tend toward optimal functioning; when optima are attained, so too is equilibrium. For example, the simplest mechanism of equilibrium is what we call 'reflex action', a mechanism first identified (but not named) by Descartes. According to this concept, a stimulus constitutes a disturbance of our internal equilibrium, thereby setting off a reflex mechanism. But in Descartes' version, there is no temporal sequence, because the stimulus ('ding') produces an instantaneous response ('dong'). In Hobbes's version, however, there is a temporal sequence, because the reaction of the organism 'aims' at restoring the equilibrium; and as partial restoration occurs, the activating force of the reaction wanes, just as the amplitude of a vibrating string decreases through damping.

Another mechanism of equilibrium is the regulation of body temperature, where internal temperature is maintained by the regulation of heat production and of heat losses. In the case of reflex action, the 'information' about the degree of success in restoring the balance is 'fed back' to a controlling power, so that its reactivity is regulated. In the case of temperature, the 'information' about the degree of heat necessitated for internal equilibrium is 'fed back' to the same controlling power. The two actions are complete when advantageous adjustment or the necessary protection of the body is achieved.

In both cases, reflex and temperature, the controlling power is primary impulse, the aggregate, infinitesimal vibratory motion of the constituent atoms or smallest particles of body, the 'fermentation' of which reveals itself as heat. On this view hot and cold are not opposites; rather, the different degrees on the temperature scale are different rates of infinitesimal vibration: as the rates increase or decrease, the volume of body expands or contracts, just as a taut string expands and contracts with atmospheric changes.[235] Because Hobbes associated pleasure and pain with heat, different rates of infinitesimal vibration thus become the source for degrees of feeling tone. And in these different rates, too, we will find the source of our social (sympathetic) passions, for when the infinitesimal motion is communicated by sympathetic resonance from the atomic particles of one body to those of another, the first loses heat and the latter gains it.

In Hobbes's philosophy there is no simple reflex, because our internal character is not simple, like one taut string, but complex, like bundles of strings of different lengths and tensions. Nevertheless, the single string demonstrates that the same controlling mechanism is manifested in all cases of physiological equilibrium, including the deliberative processes which Hobbes conceived as operations of arithmetic ('reckoning' and 'misreckoning'). For the taut string is a rudimentary servomechanism: the output of the string is made to control its operation with a view to not allowing the output at any time to exceed or to be less than a certain value. This value may be called 'plus' or 'minus', although today we refer to it as positive and negative feedback. Under such a conception there is a physical limit, for if the tension of the string exceeds a certain value, it is likely to break, whereas if it is less than a certain value, there will be no reactivity.

Still other aspects of internal character may be represented by a taut string. First, there is vibration, the action and reaction or 'reciprocal' motions of the string. This vibration is twofold, for it is the infinitesimal primary impulse when the string is in equilibrium (potential energy), as well as the compound or complex impulse when the string is played upon by the external world (actual or kinetic energy). Second, there is resonance, the reverberation or echoing of the original vibrations. And third, there are the impulses received and transmitted as plus and minus signals. We may call these things 'life' or subconsciousness (infinitesimal vibration), 'consciousness' or awareness and reactivity (sensible vibration), 'remembrance' or recall (reverberation), 'imagination' or fading remembrance (decaying reverberation)[236] and 'deliberation' or affirming and denying (signal encoding and decoding).

None of these activities are aimless and machinelike, because all our endeavours are motivational, that is, consist of appetites and aversions, attractions and repulsions.[237] These terms, however, are merely shorthand for the acceleration of the velocity of approach and the acceleration of the velocity of recession, in which each degree of acceleration is a different value or degree of tension in the string. Hence, as Hobbes's friend and colleague, Mersenne, pointed out, 'one can compare all these motives [appetites and aversions] to the tones which accompany the movement of the string and say, as well, that the intention which is the strongest…is comparable to the…natural tone of the string'.[238]

Contrary motion, therefore, is the basis of our common nature (the infinitesimal primary impulse), as well as our particular nature (compound, secondary impulse) which we cultivate by an exercise of tension. At first, this exercise derives from experience, which is a method of trial and error, according to which practice makes perfect. To live in harmony with nature requires another kind of method, one that begins with self-reflection. This activity, too, may be represented by a taut string, for when the string is fixed at both ends (as between heart and brain), any disturbance runs along it, backwards and forwards. That is, any disturbance of a stretched string gives rise to two series of waves propagated in opposite directions with equal speeds. Every portion of a wave is reflected, with simple reversal of the displacement, as soon as it reaches the fixed end. This is the reflected wave of the string, and the interval between the periodic shocks at either end is the time taken by the disturbance in running from end to end of the string and back again.

5.3. Learning by making

Once we find the image, we may begin to make science. In Hobbes's version of this making, geometry plays an important role, because he regarded geometry as 'the onely Science that it hath pleased God hitherto to bestow on mankind'.[239] It is not surprising, therefore, that one particularly acute commentator, William Sacksteder, devotes close attention to Hobbes's treatment of geometry in a series of illuminating articles.[240] Nevertheless, I believe Hobbes's conception of geometry requires some additional qualification on the basis of his concept of endeavour, which includes both a kinematical and a dynamical component. To illustrate this, let us reconsider the Galilean pendulum.

In the case of a simple (string) pendulum, it is possible to determine the tension from the relative position of the bob: the bob changes velocity at every point, but the velocities at points equidistant from its point of maximum velocity are equal. This kind of consideration is an extension of geometry by the introduction of the idea of time and the consequent idea of velocity. It constitutes Hobbes's kinematics, or laws of pure motion. But if the pendulum is compound, and we have two or more connected particles, or two particles attracting or repelling one another, we need the additional consideration of matter (Hobbes's 'magnitude', later called 'mass') and force. By endowing geometrical figures with elastic properties, Hobbes physicalised geometry, and it is this physicalisation that constitutes his dynamics. The Stoics had taken a similar approach, which followed necessarily from their conception of the continuum as dynamic. Hence, their geometrical figures exhibited tensions, and this applied also to the interval between points.[241]

The Galilean pendulum and its supposed equivalent, the musical string, are not the only phenomena that may be studied from a kinematic or dynamic point of view. The same procedures may be applied to that kind of harmonic motion called 'counterpoint', the study of which was distinguished into simple ('plain') and compound ('figurate') motion. In plain counterpoint, each note is considered as a point, being of 'equal time and number', moving 'jointly together'. Occasionally, because of syncopation ('Binding and Disjoyning'), the notes do not move jointly together, though they are presently 'made even again'.[242] Simple counterpoint, therefore, is the study of pure motion. But in figurate counterpoint the point becomes a mass, that is, 'a certain number and order of observable Notes in any one Part, iterated in the same or in divers Parts'.[243] Thus, 'Integral Notes of longer time in one Part, are sung equivalent Particles, or Notes of shorter time,... the Parts following one another in Melodious Points, Reported, or Reverted, or both; (with other Harmony interposed) until at the last they meet all together in the Close'.[244]

The art of arts, in counterpoint, is fugue, for this is both a measure and a method of composing.[245] In the making of fugue, the chief skill of a composer resides in 'maintaining of the Air, or Tone of the Song', whereby 'the Parts are sweetly conformed one to another, and each of them to itself: and without which, not only the other Ornaments [accidents] lose their vertue and cease to bee Ornaments; but also both Melody and Harmony themselves, lose their Grace, and will be neither good Melody nor good Harmony, the whole Song being nothing else, but a Form-less *Chaos* of confused sounds'.[246] Science is made in the same way, for it consists not of single words but of connected propositions, a 'chain' of which must be internally consistent, that is, coherent or in harmony one with another. Counterpoint and science, therefore, are similar to, but more complex than, the art of tuning. Before playing a lute, for example, a musician, after tensing or relaxing one string, regulates and adjusts the tones of all the other strings, until all strings together produce the desired harmony and no dissonance is heard in any. Before making music, therefore, the musician begins by tuning the strings of his own instrument. Where, then, does science begin?

Hobbes's answer is that it begins in the same way, with 'what is past',[247] namely, 'sense' and accumulated associations. To these we add uses recalled or anticipated, seeking the mutual relationship which harmonises them all. The results thus obtained by correct inference we compare with the propositions of others. Having made a careful examination of these propositions, we may find that geometrical proof requires the acceptance of some and the rejection of others.[248] We may then invent different propositions;

and by applying mathematics, we may geometrically establish the conclusions which can be drawn from them by correct inference. We may then harmonise the propositions of others with the propositions adopted. And after performing all these operations we may finally write down the laws found out. But our task does not end here, for science is always becoming, because we are always interacting with other people's speech acts, and this interaction requires continual revision of the laws we have made. Like the composers, therefore, we are always making anew.[249]

We may now remember what is perhaps Hobbes's most famous phrase, that the 'end of knowledge is power'. The full quote is as follows: 'The end of knowledge is power; and the use of theorems (which, among geometricians, serve for the finding out of properties) is for the construction of problems; and, lastly, the scope of all speculation is the performing of some action, or thing to be done'.[250] According to the interpretation given in this chapter, we may now understand power as referring to the virtual power of the mind (science) and the actual work of the hand (art) which, by the 'power of lines' and other geometrical methods, tests the generalisations we make from experience. These two powers, when united, constitute the entire power, which is conscience, that is, true knowledge or right reason.

CONCLUSION: THE VIRTUOUS LIFE

> *O world,*
> *I am in tune with every note of thy great harmony.*
> Marcus Aurelius, *Meditations* (4.23)

According to the argument in this chapter, Hobbes's solution to the paradox of determinism and responsibility involves a complex of ideas relating virtue to knowledge and to imitation of the divine will. This complex of ideas begins with the dynamic power of nature which operates immanently by means of primary impulse. All conative states in the cosmos, including in humans, are impulses, that is, movements toward or away from some thing. By these means natural phenomena are generated as well as corrupted ('dissolved'). But it is nature's innate power of primary impulse that binds together every particular reality and event and assigns to them their unchanging measure.

Impulse is not brought in from outside the biological realm but at a certain level of organisation arises spontaneously within it; and the form taken by impulse below this level is not irrational but prior to the rational.[251] People alone have the power of regulating this kind of impulse in accordance with the law of tension; but when they fail to exercise this power, impulse is liable to become incommensurate and, thus, contravene the law of universal nature, which impulse cannot do in any other creature. Hobbes's digressions about bees and ants must be understood in this context, for the impulses of these creatures do not, indeed, cannot, contravene universal nature.[252] The law of tension, therefore, is God's will; and it is here that we find Hobbes's moral imperative, because 'God knoweth the heart'.[253]

But God does not compel us to follow universal nature, for we have the possibility of determining our own actions by self-restraint. How do we accomplish this? Hobbes's answer is that our complex internal tensions need to be slackened or tightened by philosophical education.[254] This is so, because in human society the deliberative process Hobbes called 'natural reason' produces a clash of wills and leads to social discord. For social concord another kind of deliberative process is necessary, one that involves counsel and study methodically pursued.[255] By this method we may cultivate our true self, one that is in sympathy not only with our own latent powers but also with the active powers of nature. By this method also we may achieve 'right reason' or 'evidence of truth',[256] the only kind of knowledge that entails the virtuous life.

When considering human actions, which are our will, the law of tension becomes a norm – a measure or model – in conformity with which people ought to mould their lives. From this norm Hobbes derived a set of natural laws which in *Leviathan* he treated as 'dictates of Reason'. These dictates, he wrote: 'men use to call by the name of Lawes; but improperly: for they are Conclusions, or Theoremes concerning what conduceth to the conservation and defence of themselves; whereas Law, properly is the word of him, that by right hath command over others. But yet if we consider the same Theoremes, as delivered in the word of God, that by right commandeth all things; then are they properly called Lawes.'[257] Conformity to law 'binds' people together, cohesively, just as the law of tension binds the universe together, cohesively. The virtuous life, therefore, is truly in our power, for it is a striving to live in conformity with laws we have made ourselves in imitation of divine law.[258]

Chapter 3
Calling to Mind

I. MEMORY AS A PLACE

> *Of all the gods*
> *he [Hermes] first honoured Memory with his song,*
> *Memory, mother of the Muses....*
> Homer, *Hymn to Hermes* (416)

Introduction

In 1661 Joseph Glanvill published a tract on the ancient and the new, modern philosophies that included an attack on Hobbes. When, in 1665, the tract was reissued with a dedicatory address to the Royal Society, Glanvill announced that

> ...*the ingenious World being grown quite weary of* [the Scholastic] Qualities *and* Formes, *and declaring in favour of the* Mechanical Hypothesis, (to which a person that is not very fond of Religion is a great pretender) *divers of the brisker Geniusses, who desire rather to be accounted* Witts, *then endeavour to be so, have been willing to accept* Mechanism *upon* Hobbian *conditions, and many others were in danger of following them into the* precipice. *So that 'tis not conceivable how a more suitable* remedy *could have been provided against the* deadly influence *of that* Contagion, *then your Honourable* Society, *by which the meanest intellects may perceive, that* Mechanick Philosophy *yields no security to* irreligion, *and that those that would be* gentilely *learned and ingenious need not purchase it, at the* dear *rate of being* Atheists.[1]

The chief danger from Hobbes was to be found in his concept of a '*material Reaction*'. Against this 'Mechanism *upon* Hobbian *conditions*', Glanvill promoted Cartesian mechanism, since he shared Descartes' belief that the immaterial soul alone constitutes our true self.[2] But Glanvill also preferred Cartesian mechanism, because it derived 'all *sensitive perception* from *Motion,* and corporeal impress'.[3]

To save dualism, Glanvill adopted the stance of a dogmatic sceptic by stressing the fallibility of our cognitive powers and the imperfection of 'science'. Nevertheless, his tract is of considerable interest in setting out, point by point, the subjects of contention and, especially, those that tended to undermine supernaturalism. These subjects are the soul; its nature and origin; how it moves the body; how it is united to the body; how it directs the spirits; how the soul perceives; the nature of sensation; the 'instruments' of perception; how the soul reads an image or a stroke; the nature of memory; and, lastly, body – its composition, parts and coherence.[4]

You will recall that Hobbes conceived the internal structure of body like a bundle of taut strings, extended in three dimensions with resistance. In so doing, he provided a model for mind/body interaction that brought mentation and computation into one consistent explanation. Glanvill, however, could not assent to such a model, for he could see no 'affinity betwixt *length, breadth* and *thickness*; and *apprehension, judgement* and *discourse*: The former of which are the most immediate results (if not essentials) of *Matter,* the latter of *Spirit*'.[5] Nor could Glanvill conceive how the soul could move the body through intermediary spirits, since such spirits are also bodies, 'though of a purer mould'.[6] For what would be the 'regulating efficiency'; how would it be managed? Glanvill could not accept that the agency of direction was a mere mechanism, because he believed that 'our *spontaneous* motions are under the *Imperium* of our *will*',[7] at least in the first instance, since 'an Artist will play a Lesson on an Instrument without minding a stroke; and our tongues will run divisions in a tune not missing a note, even when our thoughts are totally engaged elsewhere: which effects are to be attributed to some secret *Art* of the Soul, which to us is utterly occult, and without the ken of our Intellects'.[8]

Glanvill also wondered how the soul could be excited to action 'by mutation made in *matter*[,] a substance of another kind', and 'how bodily alterations and motions should concern *that* which is subject to neither', for '*body* cannot act on any thing but by *motion*; motion cannot be received but by *quantity* and *matter*; [and] the *Soul* is a stranger to such gross *substantiality,* and ownes nothing of these'.[9] Although it might be possible to perceive motions that result in figures, distances and the like by simple sense, yet 'without some *implicit inference*', the soul could not apprehend the archetypes of figures, distances and the like. Even Descartes' theory of mental representation was inadequate to the purpose, since representations, for example, of distance or magnitude, could not result from objects striking the various filaments or 'strings' of the brain.

If internal character is conceived as a bundle of strings, possessing different lengths and tensions, the soul, extended throughout the body, will compute frequencies of vibration. Hence, it will measure vibrations not geometrically, as line lengths (Descartes' procedure), but arithmetically, in time. Glanvill's criticisms suggest that he did not understand this aspect of Hobbes's theory. But he did grasp the centrality of another aspect, since, in his attack on Hobbes, Glanvill focused on memory. From what has been said in the foregoing chapter, it is now possible to understand Hobbes's conception of memory as an aspect of the conserving principle in the universe which is extended throughout nature. Like that conserving principle, memory is twofold: on the one hand, it is a tendency (virtual power) which belongs to a person, whether awake or asleep; on the other hand, it is a remembrance (actual work) that follows perceiving, apprehending, experiencing or learning. In both of its functions, it is the state (*hexis, pathos*) of the strings – their degrees of tension – that keep memory/remembrance (vibration/reverberation) alive.[10]

In his attack on Hobbes, Glanvill's main strategy was to argue against the possibility that a material substance could conserve motion for any considerable period of time. To sustain this argument, he singled out the consistency of the material and the nature of its motion, concluding on both accounts that conservation was impossible, for, first, the brain, like a quagmire, was too clammy, and the spirits, like fluid media, were too liquid. And second, the motion of memory would be damped by countermotions, so that we could not remember anything till the next sensory impression. Since Glanvill himself believed that the functions of our bodies are carried on 'by such a multitude of *parts* and *motions*, which neither interfere, nor impede one another in their operations; but by an *harmonious Sympathy* promote the perfection and good of the whole',[11] he failed to grasp how, in Hobbes's theory,

...such an abundance of motions should orderly succeed one another, as things do in our *memories*: And to remember a *song* or *tune*, it will be required, that our Souls be an *Harmony* more then in a *metaphor*, continually running over in a silent whisper those *Musical accents* which our retentive faculty is preserver of. Which could we suppose in a single Instance; yet a multitude of *Musical Consonancies* would be impossible, as to play a thousand tunes on a *Lute* at once. One motion would cross and destroy another; all would be clashing and discord: And the *Musicians Soul* would be the most *disharmonious: For according to the tenour of this opinion, our memories* will be stored with infinite variety of divers, yea contrary motions, which must needs interfere, thwart, and obstruct one another: and there would be nothing within us, but *Ataxy* and disorder.[12]

The importance of this passage resides in the two problems raised by Glanvill and which we now call 'superposition' and 'interference'. In its geometrical meaning superposition denotes the placement of one figure ideally in the space occupied by another, so that the two figures coincide throughout their whole extent. In its physical meaning superposition signifies that, given a complex motion, one can calculate its future trajectory by adding the components that comprise it under the assumption that each of them acts as if the others do not exist. Both meanings of superposition were known to Galileo, who employed a thought experiment to justify the principle in its physical sense.[13] Both also appear in Hobbes's reinterpretation of the Stoic concept, total mixture. As we have seen, this concept is not comparable to juxtaposition of, for example, two vibrating strings side by side. Rather, for Hobbes, total mixture is both a geometrical and a physical superposition of the two strings, whereby no increase in either magnitude or motion occurs.

Afterwards, the principle of superposition became important within the context of theories of the propagation of waves in elastic media, a direction of research inaugurated by Hobbes. In the case of a musical string, for example, any number of the different modes (patterns) of vibration of which a string is susceptible may be going on simultaneously, that is, may be superposed on each other. For example, the phenomenon of beats, recognised by Mersenne, consists of periodic fluctuations of loudness produced by the superposition of tones of close but not identical frequencies. This phenomenon is a consequence of the principle of the superposition of small motions: when the excursions of the parts of a system from their places of rest are infinitely small, this principle admits all the motions to go on at once without interfering with or disturbing each other.

Interference is a direct consequence of the principle of superposition. In the context of elastic media, two or more wave trains passing through a given point exert their effect independently of the other. Hence, when sound waves act on an air particle, the resultant displacement, velocity and pressure produced will be the sum of the effects due to the separate waves. If the combined effect produces a distribution of energy which is quite different from that due to the separate wave train, then interference is said to have taken place. In the language of seventeenth-century musical science, we may say that the general wave is broken up into a multitude of non-coincident waves, emanating from different origins and crossing and interfering with each other in all directions. Whenever this takes place, a mutual destruction of the waves, to a greater or less extent, arises, so that, to use Glanvill's examples, both sound and recall are stifled or obstructed.

Hobbian as well as non-Hobbian theories of memory would have to address the two problems raised by Glanvill, and these in turn would involve a reconsideration of the material nature of the memory store and the motions involved in remembrance. The purpose of this chapter is to outline how the two problems were treated by those whose theories competed with Hobbes and, afterwards, to illustrate how one investigator developed aspects of Hobbes's theory. It should be noted, however, that the philosophy of Hobbes precipitated a crisis in English intellectual life, for reasons that have yet to be fully scrutinised and understood. The dominant reception of Hobbes's work was hostile – indeed, his books were burned at Oxford.[14] Consequently, those who became Hobbians, even in a modified form, seldom mentioned Hobbes's name or owned up to their indebtedness to him. Instead, they preferred to proceed cautiously so as to avoid charges of atheism.

1. Discordant theories

> *Now which [theory] do you prefer,*
> *that knowledge is recollection or*
> *that the soul is a harmony?*
> Plato, *Phaedo* (92c)

1.1. Localisers vs. non-localisers

Until the seventeenth century there seems to have been little interest in theoretical problems relating to memory, since prior to that time attention was devoted chiefly to practical problems of memorisation and to mnemonic aids for assisting the memory.[15] In the sixteenth century sceptical currents of thought contributed to bringing about a change from practical to theoretical investigations as ancient doctrines concerning the soul were re-examined, often ironically.[16] But the new theoretical investigations continued to adumbrate two ancient, opposing beliefs. According to one belief, that of the localisers, the soul is 'seated' somewhere in the body – for example, the liver, heart, stomach, or a ventricle of the brain. According to the other belief, that of the partly non-localisers, the soul is extended throughout the body. Plato is the source for the first belief and Aristotle, for the second.

Although Plato continued the Pythagorean tradition of an immaterial soul, he developed three models of memory as its material substitute.[17] In one model, the wax tablet, Plato represented memory traces as impressions in wax, for he directed us (through his mouthpiece, Socrates) to imagine 'for the sake of argument, that our minds contain a block of wax, which in this or that individual may be larger or smaller, and composed of wax that is comparatively pure or muddy, and harder in some, softer in others, and sometimes of just the right consistency'. According to this model, whatever is imprinted on the wax we remember and know so long as the image remains. In another model, the aviary model, Plato represented each memory as a bird of a different species. And in yet another model, the one Plato seems to have preferred, he represented memory as a record of experience written down according to the whims of the scribe. When memory writes the truth, we form true beliefs, and vice versa.

Aristotle improved on Plato's wax tablet model by introducing a number of modifications.[18] First, he used stamping of impressions on a wax tablet to suggest that the faculty of memory depends on the quality of a specific sense organ. Then, he made reference to projectiles and the transmission of heat to suggest how impressions may persist even when what originally caused them is no longer present. And third, he employed the image of eddies that occur in rivers to suggest how impressions may become disrupted by objects that obstruct them and how they may become confused when the movements causing them are too violent. These modifications led to a partly non-localised approach, which Aristotle summarised as follows:

> Though *sense perception* is innate in all animals, in some the sense impression comes to *persist*...and when such persistence is frequently repeated a further distinction arises between those animals which out of the persistence of such sense impressions develop a power of systematizing them and those which do not. So out of sense perception comes to be what we call *memory*, and out of frequently repeated memories of the same thing develops *experience*. From experience again, i.e. from the *universal* now stabilized in its entirety within the soul, the one beside the many which is a single identity within them all, originate the *skill* of the craftsman and the *knowledge* of the man of science, skill in the sphere of coming to be and science in the sphere of being.[19]

Since the intellect produces science and art from sense experience, and experience is produced from memory, memory is important in all intellectual activity. Yet, memory is entirely a function of the central sense power which, for Aristotle, is in the heart.[20] This sense power produces a phantasm that is identical with the faculty of memory, a faculty shared by animals as well as people. But people alone have the power of deliberate recollection, which is closely associated with the intellect and operates through a chain of phantasms linked in memory. According to Aristotle, the intellect depends upon the phantasm, both in the initial formation of universals and in their retention and recall. But a disturbance of passion or a disease can hinder the central sense faculty from producing accurate perceptions and phantasms, from remembering and recollecting, so that the operations of the intellect will be impaired.

The different beliefs of the localisers and the partly non-localisers continued to be elaborated as perennials not only in philosophy but also in the specialised sciences of internal character that developed from the seventeenth century. Indeed, in the modern neurosciences, as Walther Riese observes: 'Any attempt to find an intelligible and workable formula for the interrelation of nervous function and nervous structure presupposes the recognition, avowed or not, of a difference between function and structure, mind and body, and in this respect the apologist of cerebral localization is bound to remain Platonic and Cartesian'.[21]

1.2. The soul as a recollection

We may now better understand Glanvill's attack on Hobbes and his support of Descartes, for the latter continued the Platonic tradition in which the soul is a reminiscence. Plato had argued that knowledge is acquired, not through the senses or as information conveyed from one mind to another by teaching, but by recollection in this life of truths seen and known by the soul before its incarnation.[22] Seeking and learning, therefore, is recollection, that is, the recovery of latent knowledge which is one's own and is within oneself. In the seventeenth century this doctrine was reiterated by Glanvill's friend and supporter, Henry More, who devoted much energy to writing against Hobbes. According to More, the active 'sagacity in the Soul, or quick recollection' is like

> ...a skilfull *Musician* fallen asleep in the field upon the grasse, during which time he shall not so much as dream any thing concerning his Musicall faculty, so that in one sense there is no *actuall Skill* or Notion, nor representation of any thing musicall in him; but his friend sitting by him, that cannot sing at all himself, jogs him and awakes him, and desires him to sing this or the other Song, telling him two or three words of the beginning of the Song, whereupon he presently takes it out of his mouth, and sings the whole Song upon so slight and slender intimation.[23]

The soul, being 'jogg'd and awakened by the impulses of outward Objects, is stirred up into a more full and clear conception of what was but imperfectly hinted to her from externall occasions'; and it is this faculty that More called '*actuall Knowledge*', just as the sleeping musician's skill could be called '*actuall Skill*' when he thought nothing of it.

In More's use of Plato's doctrine, a distinction is made between remembering and recollecting. Remembering starts with almost no gap, for once the musician's knowledge is awakened by the first three tones sung by his friend, the musician completes the song. But recollecting involves a gap, during which knowledge is lost, as in sleep. What, then, 'jogs' the soul to awaken and recollect? One of Plato's answers was that recollection involves an association of ideas, just as learning sometimes involves an association. Indeed, he pointed out that learning of something can be preceded by, and also made possible by, earlier knowledge of that same thing. But if one is learning something anew, one's earlier knowledge must have been temporarily lost in the interim. Implicit in these ideas is the notion of action at a distance, since association is not synonymous with habit or reiterated experience.

From antiquity action at a distance was exemplified by the phenomena of magnetism and sympathy. But these phenomena remained occult until sympathy was given a manifest explanation, an achievement of the new science of music that emerged at the end of the sixteenth century. Magnetism, however, still remained a subject for investigation, and there were a number of competing explanations of this phenomenon.[24] As we have seen, Hobbes supposed that the principles of magnetism were reducible to those of sympathetic resonance. But one of Hobbes's chief antagonists, Robert Boyle, preferred the Gassendian explanation, for he ascribed magnetical attraction to a subtle effluvia, which, issuing from the lodestone, passed through the pores of nearby bodies. Nevertheless, he admitted that 'Mr. *Hobbes* has another hypothesis [than the emission theory]...; but I know, that divers learned writers have absolutely rejected it, and not one such, that I have heard of, has approved it'.[25]

Like Boyle, More and Glanvill also rejected Hobbes's explanation of sympathy, for they preferred 'the *Platonical Hypothesis* of a *Mundane Soul*', according to which an invisible world soul (function) directs and regulates the mathematical harmony (optimal structure) of the universe. In this hypothesis the world soul has the same relation to the body of the universe as harmony, likewise invisible, has to the body of the lyre. But the interaction between body and soul remains occult. Glanvill, therefore, conceded that for those who preferred a '*Mechanical* account', the phenomenon of sympathy would have to suffice. Hence, as 'in *Musical strings* tuned *Unisons*', so too the imagination of one person (or an angel) may influence that of another person, since 'the motion being convey'd, from the *Brain* of one man to the *Phancy* [certain filaments in the brain] of another; it is there receiv'd from the instrument of conveyance, the *subtil* matter; and the same kind of *strings* being moved, and much what after the same manner as in the first *Imaginant*; the *Soul* is awaken'd to the same apprehensions, as were they that caus'd them'.[26]

It is important to note that Glanvill's explanation of sympathy is not the same as that of Hobbes's resonance theory. Instead, Glanvill followed the mechanical philosophers, for he adopted a translation theory to explain sympathy. According to this incorrect explanation, sympathy takes place, because the instrument of conveyance, the subtle matter, is made up of discrete corpuscles which convey information by pushing in a straight line. Glanvill, therefore, could not provide a solution to the problems raised in his critique of 'Mechanism *upon* Hobbian *conditions*'. Hence, we must look elsewhere to see how these problems were addressed.

2. Localising memory

> ...*if the muse of Plato speaks the truth,*
> *Man but recalls what once he knew and lost.*
> Boethius, *The Consolation of Philosophy* (3.xi)

2.1. As traces

During the first part of the seventeenth century, there were three theories of memory that competed with Hobbes's theory: the trace theory of Descartes, the liquid theory of the Gassendian atomists and the species theory of the Peripatetics. Despite differences in detail, all three theories conceived memory, including remembrance, as localised chiefly in some portion of the brain. Although Hobbes had conceived memory as an infinitesimal vibratory motion in the brain, he regarded remembrance as reverberating throughout the body. Moreover, he treated recollection in the same way, for he supposed that phantasms (the work of memory) are revived after sleep in the same way that phantasms are revived whilst awake, for 'whatsoever strikes the *pia mater*, reviveth some of those phantasms that are still in motion in the brain; and when [after sleep] any internal motion of the heart reacheth that membrane, then the predominant motion in the brain makes the phantasm'.[27] Hence, Hobbes's theory is a partly non-localised theory.

The *pia mater* is the vascular membrane enveloping the surface of the brain and spinal cord and consists of a plexus of blood vessels held in a fine areolar tissue. In Hobbes's day it was supposed that the convolutions of the brain either protected the blood vessels of the *pia mater* or allowed the vessels to penetrate the brain substance more deeply, even though, in antiquity, one anatomist had associated the convolutions with intelligence.[28] In *Body* Hobbes did not mention the convolutions; instead, he conceived the *pia mater* as a membrane, capable of being 'shaken' and, thus, of transmitting motion to the interior of the brain.[29] In circulating round the body, the etherialised (hot) blood 'plays upon' the brain, as well as other organs, thereby making actual their potential to vibrate.[30] But for normal function, there must be an affinity between solids and fluids, which, when 'equally tempered', perform the work of memory by sympathetic resonance.

Descartes adopted a different approach, when he conceived the brain as a soft substance in which animal spirits leave traces, like impressions in wax or creases in paper. These traces are preserved, the animal spirits passing through them again and again, thereby endowing the living creature not only with sensory perception but also with memory. But the work of memory is performed by the pineal gland, the motion of which impels spirits into divers pores of the brain.[31] Once the spirits have passed through a pore, they leave traces of the object and they also make the parts of the brain passed through more easily opened for subsequent passage. When this happens, a special motion occurs in the pineal gland, signifying this is the object we would remember.

That impressions are preserved as memory traces in the substance of the brain seemed highly improbable to Glanvill for several reasons. First, if the brain is such a *'pervious'* substance, the spirits could easily enter or exit almost anywhere. Second, alterations of the ponderous matter of the brain would exert pressure on the pores and close them up. Third, 'the making of one hole in the yielding *mud*, defaces the print of another near it; at least the accession of enlargement, which was derived from such transitions, would be as soon lost, as made'.[32] And finally, 'if *Memory* be made by the *easie motion* of the *Spirits* through the opened *passages*,...how should we recal [sic] the distances of Bodies which lye in a line? Or, is it not likely, that the impell'd Spirits might light upon other Pores accommodated to their purpose, by the *Motion* of other Bodies through them?'[33]

Glanvill's criticisms notwithstanding, Descartes could not provide a mechanism for conservation, because God alone conserves motion in the Cartesian universe. What he did provide was a mechanism for sensation based on the carillon; but he afterwards developed a different theory, based on a different mechanism, which, in 1644, was presented to the English public by Kenelm Digby as follows:

> ...by reason of the continuity of this string or nerve, he [Descartes] conceiveth that the blow which is made upon the outward end of it by the ether, is conveyed by the other end of it to the braine; that end, striking the braine in the same measure as the ether strucke the other end of it: like the jacke of a Virginall, which striketh [i.e., plucks] the sounding cord, according as the musitians hand presseth upon the stop [i.e., key]. The part of the brain which is thus strucken, he supposeth to be the fantasie, where he deemeth the soule doth reside; and thereby taketh notice of the motion and object that are without.[34]

According to Digby, Descartes restricted local change to certain 'strings', which objects 'play upon from the very sense up to the braine: and by their different manners of shaking the braine, he will have it know what kind of thing it is that striketh the outward sense, without removing anything within our body from one place to another'.[35]

If we reduce this account to a diagram (Figure 3.1), we may say that the external world/finger, plays on the external senses/keyboard, thereby activating the 'fantasie'/jack (the slip of wood that constitutes the action at the rear of a key), which plucks the appropriate memory/string located in the brain/virginal. From this reduction three things are clear. First, feeling is due to an alien cause, the striking of the ether upon one of the external senses.

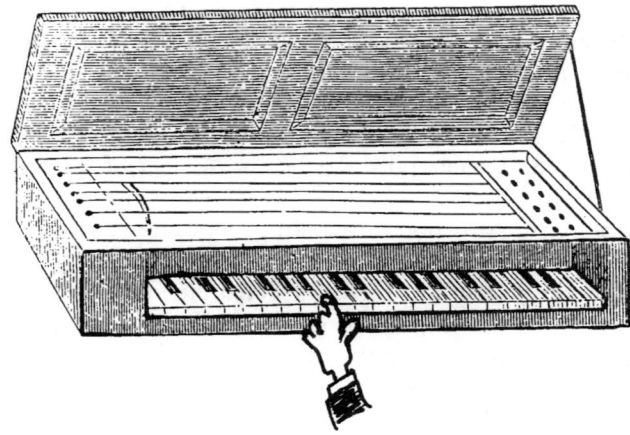

Figure 3.1 Descartes' theory of brain function, after K. Digby, *Two Treatises* (London, 1645)

Second, functions are localised in various parts of the brain. And third, the 'fantasie' replaces the pineal gland as the container of the incorporeal soul. Hence, Descartes' new explanatory analogy is no improvement over the old, because the brain is still a passive instrument: it does not generate functions.[36]

The same point was made in a different way by Digby, who noted that if nothing but motion 'do come into the brain', memory could not conserve anything in it 'and represent bodies to us, when our fantasie calleth for them', for

> How…can we imagine, that such a multitude of pure motions, as the memory must be stored withall for the use and service of man, can be kept on foote on his braine, without confusion; and for so long a time as his memory is able to extend unto? Consider a lesson plaid upon the Lute or Virginalls, and think with your selfe, what power there is, or can be in nature, to conserve this lesson ever continually playing: and reflect, that if the impressions upon the common sense are nothing else but such things, then they must be actually conserved, alwaies actually moving in our head to the end they be immediatly produced,

whensoever it pleaseth our will to call them.[37]

Digby agreed with Descartes that 'all our remembring is performed by means of motion', because he asserted that memory is, for the most part, nothing else but motion: 'For what are words, but motion? And words are the chiefest objects of our remembrance.'[38] But the mere assertion of motion did not explain how information is stored and retrieved.

2.2. As liquid or as species

To address these problems, Digby presented a theory that was Gassendi's not his own, although he claimed to have deduced it 'out of the nature of the objects, the nature of our spirits, the nature and situation of our nerves, and lastly from the property of our braine'.[39] According to Digby, the brain is a 'heape of strings', enclosed by a membrane which 'is very apt and fit to stretch; and after stretching, to returne againe to its owne just length'. Hence, the brain is easily penetrable by spirits, those 'vapours and liquors, whose nature it is, to swell and to extend that which they enter into'.[40] When the brain expands and contracts, the spirits therein are pressed into the hollow nerves (though Digby admitted their 'concavities' could not be discerned). The nerves, which have their own store of spirits, swell like a balloon; and if this swelling takes place in a muscle, that, too, will be swollen and motion will take place.

All these effects, however, are wrought not by the 'intervention of ayery qualities; but by reall and materiall applications of bodies to bodies; which in different manners do make the same results within us'.[41] Thus, when atoms – 'solid material bodies (exceeding little ones)' – are propelled from the objects themselves, they strike the senses and, passing through the nerves, bombard the brain until they find a vacant cell to occupy. From their places of storage, the passions ('natural appetite'), chance or will retrieve the atoms by stirring them up to the same motion with which they first entered the brain. Once stirred up, the atoms slide successively through the communal sense or 'fantasie', in the same manner as they first presented themselves. And when the fantasie no longer requires them, the atoms return to their places of rest 'from whence they were called and summoned by the fantasies messengers, the [animal] spirits'.[42]

If the spirits or 'active *particles*...have no *cement* to unite them',[43] why is it that the atoms drawn from memory are presented to the fantasie with the same motion or circumstances as when they first entered the memory? Digby's answer is twofold. First, if the atoms 'swim' in the same medium, namely, a liquid, vaporous substance, then 'the same body, being in the same medium, must necessarily have the same kind of motion'. Second, in such a medium all the atoms that are of one kind will easily gather together, if nothing disturb them, just as 'when a tuned Lute string is strucken, that string by communicating a determinate species of vibration to the Ayre round about it, shaketh other strings, within the compass of the moved ayre'.[44] Despite the comparison to sympathetic resonance, Digby's theory is not a resonance theory. Rather, memory consists of atoms conserved in the cells of the brain, whereas remembrance is due to the undulating motion of liquid spirits in which they float.[45]

This liquid theory shares a number of features in common with the third and final theory that competed with Hobbes, namely, the species theory of the Peripatetics, according to which impressions are conserved by means of so-called 'intentional species'. Glanvill had dismissed the species theory as a 'superannuated conceit', because species 'have nothing of Matter in their Essential Constitution, but yet have a necessary subjective dependence on it, whence they are called *Material*'.[46] But Glanvill was attacked on his own grounds by Thomas White, a Peripatetic, who observed that sceptics exhibit symptoms of those ills which they objected to in the 'Lovers of Dogmatizing'.[47] In proceeding to detail the species theory, White distinguished between memory, the function of which is to conserve, and remembrance, which is 'a certain Motion whereby that power of using the impressions is reduc'd into Act and Use'.

The work of remembrance is done not by a liquid but by 'atoms' or 'particles', which float in a liquid, subtle 'substance' or 'spirit'. In this way most atoms 'get up' to the brain, though 'tis plain, that many are confounded, [and] many lost; yet, out of the very nature of Multitude,...some are preserved entire, and those enough to serve Nature's turn'.[48] Atoms that reach the brain strike its parts vehemently in order to enter 'empty and hollow places' there. These places are 'all hang'd and furnisht with little threads' to which the atoms stick, thereby conserving the impression. Once stored in the brain, the atoms are called up by the passions – an 'ebullition of Spirits reeking out of the heart'. This motion of ebullition creates a wind or blast which blows past the brain, so that the atoms, 'rouz'd' from their places, 'fly about the cognoscitive part, in a kind of confused tumble', which is neither random, 'nor yet in a certain order', since the motion of different atoms depends on the nature of different passions.

The commonality between Digby's emission theory and White's species theory emerges most clearly in the difficulties both men faced in accounting for auditory memory. Indeed, their explanations of this kind of memory are incommensurate with their explanations of other sorts of memories, as both writers admitted. White pointed out, for example, that the explanation of memory and remembering given for the senses of vision, smelling and taste would not hold for auditory memory, because 'sound is made by a collision of the Air'. Hence, it was evident 'by Anatomy, that it drives the Hammer of the Ear to beat upon the Anvil, by which beat 'tis not to be believ'd but certain particles must fly off and strike the Fancy: the orderly storing up, therefore, of these is apt to constitute the Memory of Sounds'.[49]

Digby, too, admitted that with hearing 'there is a little more difficulty', for, if sound is merely agitation of the air, 'the very striking of the outward ayre against the tympanum would have been sufficient without any other particular and extraordinary organization, to have produced soundes, and to have carried their motions up to the braine: as wee see the head of a drumme bringeth the motions of the earth unto our eare, when we lay it thereunto'.[12] But the central problem remained: how can the motion called 'sound' be conserved in the brain? To solve this problem, Digby proposed an account for auditory memory that is the same as that of White, for he wrote:

> There is a hammer and an anvile: whereof the hammer, striking upon the anvile, must of necessity beate off such little parts of the brainy steames, as flying about, doe light and stick upon the top of the anvile: these by the trembling of the ayre following its course, cannot misse of being carried up to that part of the braine, whereunto the ayre within the eare is driven by the impulse of the sound: and as soon as they have given their knocke, they rebound back againe into the cells of the braine, fitted for harbours to such winged messengers: where they remain lodged with quietnesse, till they be called for againe, to renew the effect which the sound did make at the first....[50]

The hammer governs the motions of the 'anvile' to which it is fastened, so that its blows 'must needs make great difference of bignesses, and cause great variety of smartnesses of motion, in the little bodies which they forge'.

II. MEMORY AS A TIME

> *In my countrie,*
> *if a man will imply that one hath no sense,*
> *he will say, such a one hath no memorie....*
> Montaigne, *Essayes* (I.viii,13)

Introduction
According to legend, Pythagoras discovered musical proportions when he heard sounds produced by a blacksmith's hammers striking an anvil. A conflicting story is told in Genesis (4.21-2), where the proto-musician is Jubal and the proto-blacksmith, his half brother, Tubalcain. During the Middle Ages these two myths were conflated, so that the figure of Pythagoras became a symbol for both proto-musician and proto-blacksmith and, through the latter connection, the human representative of Vulcan, the fire god and inventor of metallurgy (Figure 3.2).[51] Depictions of Pythagoras, however, most commonly show him with a 'canon', a rule or method of demonstrating the musical proportions of ancient *musica speculativa*. Up to and including the sixteenth century, two instruments served this purpose: one was a set of bells, the other, a monochord (Figure 3.3a, b). In the seventeenth century the discipline of mathematics still included the study called 'canonics';

Figure 3.2 Pythagoras as symbol of Vulcan, from M. Agricola, *Musica instrumentalis Deudsch* (Wittenberg, 1528)

Figure 3.3   Pythagoras, from F. Gafori, *Theoria musice* (Milan, 1492)
(a) with the canon as a set of bells
(b) with the canon as a monochord

but, increasingly, this study added other instruments as canons and used them for experiments to demonstrate different aspects of the emerging new science of music that we now call 'acoustics'.[52]

From the point of view of psychologists, the great event of seventeenth-century acoustics was the discovery of the dependence of pitch upon frequency, which varies with the length of the monochord string. If pitch be a frequency, then the way to get a pitch would be to create a frequency. In 1681 Robert Hooke did just this, when he devised a set of toothed brass wheels fixed to clockwork allowing an object to strike the teeth.[53] Rapid rotation produced a musical sound; doubling the speed gave an octave, increasing it one-third gave the fourth and so on.[54] By the time of this experiment, however, Hooke had spent over twenty years investigating the frequency of vibration of the medium of sound, as well as of sound producers, including the frequency of vibration of a fly's wings by the tone or hum they make when flying.[55] Nevertheless, he is known chiefly for the contributions he made to architecture, geology, horology, mechanics, pneumatics, optics, scientific instrumentation and method.[56]

The list of Hooke's achievements is impressive, because the conditions of his life made it very difficult for him to find time for sustained research and writing. Indeed, he was called upon by various employers to provide for their needs, whether it be airpumps and other instruments for Boyle, experiments for Fellows of the Royal Society, lectures for the foundation established by John Cutler and for Gresham College, and surveys and architectural models for Christopher Wren. In 1657 he became a technician (as we now would say) in the laboratory of Boyle, when he also devised many experiments recounted in Boyle's *New Experiments Physico-mechanical, touching the Spring of the Air, and its Effects; made, for the most Part, in a New Pneumatical Engine* (1660).

Boyle argued that the spring or motion of restitution in the air tends outwards, an argument that was answered in two tracts. One appeared under Hobbes's name and is the subject of a study by Stephen Shapin and Simon Schaffer.[57] The other, published under the name of Franciscus Linus, presented an inversion of Boyle's hypothesis, namely, that the spring or motion of restitution in the air tends inwards.[58] But Linus also attributed the immediate cause of Boyle's experimental phenomena to an imaginary line, which he called a 'funiculus'; and it was this that led one writer to conclude that the tract was 'a mere banter of Mr. Hobbs, for he published that notion under the name of Linus as lawyers' Latin for a line, which afterwards he called funiculus or cord, not as his opinion, but to shew what silly things might be imposed upon the world in the way of natural philosophy'.[59]

Boyle was provoked to reply in detail to both tracts for at least two important reasons, one physical, the other metaphysical. First, the two tracts claimed that Boyle's phenomena could be explained equally well by other hypotheses, a claim Boyle had to admit in a number of instances.[60] Second, both tracts addressed issues that Boyle could not ignore if he were to maintain some form of the supernaturalism inherent in the mechanical philosophy with its dualist underpinning.[61] Hence, in 1662 he reissued his *New Experiments* with a long appendix, in which he replied to some of the issues raised in the two tracts. In the course of his reply, Boyle also provided the first complete statement of what now is called 'Boyle's Law': that the pressures and expansions of the 'air' are in reciprocal proportion.[62]

Much has been written about whether Boyle's Law should be called Hooke's Law, and the debate no doubt will continue.[63] This is neither the place to canvass the arguments about the relation of Boyle and Hooke nor to detail how their work intersected, for intersect it did. Nevertheless, there are two reasons for mentioning Boyle's tract and the law that bears his name. First, this law is the second numerical law to illustrate the functional dependence of variable magnitudes (pressure and density), the first being that of the dependence of pitch upon frequency. As we shall see, Hooke later provided a third law, that the displacement and force of a stretched spring are proportional. Second, controversy surrounding Boyle's tract placed Hooke in a difficult situation in relation to Hobbes, a situation that was to continue when in 1662 Hooke became curator of experiments for the Royal Society.

Shortly after this appointment, Hooke met Hobbes for the first time, as we learn from a letter to Boyle, written in 1663, in which Hooke portrayed Hobbes as a dogmatist.[64] Since Boyle regarded Hobbes as a dangerous adversary, one suspects that Hooke provided what his employer would like to hear. This suspicion increases when we consider the evidence provided by Aubrey, one of Hobbes's champions and a constant companion of Hooke, who wrote: 'Mr. Robert Hooke loved him [Hobbes], but was never but once in his company.'[65] Aubrey's statement requires some modification, because Hooke seems to have met Hobbes twice, if we include the 1663 meeting, for on 16 June 1674 Hooke noted in his diary: 'At Hobbes with Mr. Aubery.'[66] Moreover, that the two men were in contact is suggested by Hooke's remark of 7 October 1678, 'book from Mr. Hobbs', and by Hobbes's letter, written in 1679, requesting that Aubrey 'present my service to Mr. Hooke and thank him for the honour of his salutation'.[67]

That Hobbes influenced Hooke's 1665 theory of light has been conclusively shown by Alan E. Shapiro.[68] Much later, in a lecture read in the 1680s, Hooke provided a short critique of Hobbes's concept of endeavour, which he equated with that of Descartes.[69] This equation is hard to understand, given the fact that Hooke's diary, as well as the contents of his library, indicate that he owned many of Hobbes's writings, including both the Latin and English versions of *Body*.[70] Whatever the reason, the evidence is overwhelming that, for Hooke, the 'power' of phenomena such as heat, light, magnetism and weight varies with the frequency of vibrations.[71] And, as we shall see, the same holds true for the 'power' of memory.[72] Indeed, Hooke conceived memory as an internal sense and the source of our notions of time. Accordingly, he developed an insight of Hobbes, who had written: 'rough and smooth, like quantity and figure, are not perceived but by the flux of a point, that is to say, we have no sense of them without time; and we can have no sense of time without memory'.[73]

3. Processing frequencies

> *Memorie is the receptacle,*
> *and the case of knowledge.*
> Montaigne, *Essayes* (II.xvii,334)

3.1. The work of the periphery

Hooke's earliest theory of internal character is preserved in an undated and incomplete manuscript fragment entitled 'Philosophicall Scribbles'.[74] In this fragment there is no evidence of vibratory concepts — hence, my assignment of an early date. Instead, Hooke adopted the Cartesian version of the Platonic trace theory, for he supposed that God sent man into the world, 'almost ready tempered, like a peice of soft wax', to be stamped with incoming impressions from the five external senses. What is stamped is a passive 'common sense' shared by man and animals alike. But humans have something added, which is 'an *active faculty*' that 'collates and compares' the impressions, thereby compounding and composing new impressions and regulating what is defective in others.

In 1665 Hooke published the outline of a different theory, in which he identified the soul with the intellect. The intellect, however, is not a thing but an activity called 'understanding'. In performing this activity, the soul, like the blood, circulates so as

> ...to order *all the inferiour services of the lower Faculties* [sensing, remembering, reasoning]; *but yet it is to do this only as a* lawful Master, *and not as a* Tyrant. *It must not* incroach *upon their Offices, nor take upon it self the employments which belong to...them. It must* watch *the irregularities of the Senses, but it must not go before them, or* prevent *their information. It must* examine, range, *and* dispose *of the bank which is laid*

> up in the Memory: but it must be sure to make distinction between the sober and well collected heap, and the extravagant Idea's, and mistaken Images, which there it may sometimes light upon. So many are the links, upon which the true Philosophy depends, of which, if any one be loose, or weak, the whole chain is in danger of being dissolv'd; it is to begin with the Hands and Eyes, and to proceed on through the Memory to be continued by the Reason; nor is it to stop there, but to come about to the Hands and Eyes again, and so, by a continual passage round from one Faculty to another, it is to be maintained in life and strength, as much as the body of man is by the circulation of the blood through the several parts of the body, the Arms, the Fat, the Lungs, the Heart, and the Head.[75]

According to this passage, which Hooke reiterated on 3 December 1690, 'intellect', the activity of understanding, is the same as analysis and synthesis.[76] But Hooke seems to have had an unusual approach to these terms, since he differed from his contemporaries, most notably Newton, in conceiving 'the analytic method with the "backwards" argument from causes to effects, that is, from the *unknown*, which is guessed at, to the well known'.[77]

After 1665 Hooke's statements about internal character are scattered in different writings. Hence, the interpreter cannot rely on isolated texts but must seek the development of Hooke's ideas from the broad context of his writings generally, some of which still remain unpublished.[78] Although Hooke left no comprehensive treatise, the subject of internal character is of central importance to his philosophy of science, since he believed that '*the True Method of Building a Solid Philosophy*' must begin with 'An Examination of the Constitution and Powers of the Soul, or an Attempt of Disclosing the Soul to its self, being an Endeavour of Discovering the Perfections and Imperfections of Humane Nature, and finding out ways and means for the attaining of the one, and of helping the other'.[79]

Like Hobbes, then, Hooke stressed the importance of self-knowledge and scientific method as a means of regulating beliefs. And, like Hobbes, he also sought to detail the techniques that would assist self-correction.[80] But Hooke, more than Hobbes, explored the physiological limitations that darken our intellect.[81] As part of these explorations, he devised numerous 'artificial' instruments that were intended to increase the power of the external senses, strengthen the memory, enlarge the sphere of the imagination (the source of hypotheses) and rectify the intellect. In addition to experiment, Hooke's instruments included, but were not limited to, hearing aids ('otacousticons') for the ear; spectacles, microscopes and telescopes for the eye; hygroscopes for the nose; and weather glasses for the feeling or temperature sense. Some of these instruments served a dual purpose, for they enlarged the sphere of an individual sense, as well as reduced that sense to a 'standard'.[82] In the case of the temperature sense, for example, 'Heat and Cold are only Relative to our Constitution, as is evident by the Weather Glass, which feels many Degrees of Heat before it is sensible to us'.[83]

Hooke's conception of the workings of the five senses may be inferred from his theory of audition, the most complete statement of which occurs in a lecture, read on 22 June 1676, on the 'theory of sound'.[84] In this lecture Hooke asserted that all musical sounds are produced by a tremulous motion of the 'drum & organ' of the ear, which is excited 'by the like motion of the sonorous medium', which, in turn, receives its motion from the sounding body. As we have seen, not everyone in the seventeenth century accepted that sound is motion; many still preferred to believe with the Peripatetics that sound is a species or with the Epicureans, little hard atoms. To gain assent for the proposition that sound is motion, Hooke provided a short account of 'the structure & fabrick' of the ear.

Although he had read widely in the anatomical literature and had himself performed dissections, Hooke's theory of auditory function seems more indebted to his investigations into hearing aids and experiments on the monochord.[85] Between 1665 and 1668 he produced a number of hearing aids, all of which were 'sharp', that is, pointed at one end. About this time, too, he declared he could produce an 'Artificial Tympanum' if he had the opportunity.[86] These investigations led to the conclusion that the ear, as well as the other senses, served as collectors of information 'to a point'. Thus, for example,

> ...those Rays that proceed from the several Points of any Object that either emits or reflects Light, and fall on the Cornea [horn] of the Eye, shall be all of them collected into so many distinct Points at the bottom of the Eye, and that in the same Order, that the Points were scituated in respect of the Eye, but in a lesser Proportion, according as the Object is farther removed in distance from the Eye, and in a greater Proportion as the Object is nearer....[87]

But how do senses collect information to a point? Hooke answered this question by demonstrating three things about the properties of musical strings. First, if a string is not stretched straight, its movements produce no sensible sound. Second, if it is stretched 'very stiffe', we hear a pleasant, that is, a 'very brisk[,] uniform noyse'. Third, if the string is short and stretched 'very stiffe, it makes soe shrill a noyse that it becomes very offensive'. In each case, Hooke pointed out, there is a 'mechanical and intelligible Cause'.[88]

In the first instance there is insufficient tension of the string. Hence, 'the motion of impulse communicated to ye air, is soe weak & languid that it is not able to move the eare, though left to its greatest flaccidity; even as we find in two strings, if the one be not made of the same tension wth the other, noe symphonick [i.e., sympathetic] motion will ensue'. In the second instance, the

> ...tension has acquir'd a motion brisk enough to communicate its impulse by meanes of ye ambient air to the drum of the Eare, which is by the former contrivance immediately tun'd unison to that sound, & soe is very sensible of it. And it becomes pleasant because it has a middle kind of tension such as is proportionate to it, just as in two strings where the one can be tun'd unison to the other: if either of them be mov'd, they will both be mov'd.

And in the last instance, 'the vibrations of the string are from its exceeding shortness & tension, soe swift that the eare is strained exceedingly, or overstretch't as 'twere, to reach that height of celerity; just as we straine and endanger the breaking of a String, if we endeavour to screw it too high and above its pitch'. Because there is a physiological limit for the kinds of motion that produce musical sounds, all tones 'must be kept between these two [tensions], that they may be neither too low nor too high'.

According to Hooke, the ear functions in a similar way, since it may be 'tun'd as I may soe call it, or stretch't', that is, subjected to stress and strain, because

> ...it has a most curious, neat contrivance of a small film wch is soe expos'd to the air that it is capable of being mov'd by it. Nor is it only like the bare head of a drum, but there is a further excellency in its fabrick, and that is this: that by means of several little bones, nerves & muscles it can be soe tuned, as it were, or stretch't, that it becomes harmonicall or unison to w^{t}soever sound is heard.[89]

By 'harmonicall or unison' Hooke denoted the sympathetic attunement of the ear 'to every particular sound or tremulous motion that affects it'; or, in other words, the ear can 'tune itself' by regulating its tension so that the vibrations of the drum membrane are in phase with incoming vibrations.

In the 1680s Hooke extended this argument to the pupil of the eye, which processes incoming vibrations by expanding and contracting, thereby tuning or modulating the radiations of light so that they are proportionate to the sense.[90] We may assume, therefore, that his theory of the other senses is commensurate to that of the ear and eye, so that, for example, vapours or effluvia may be modulated as they pass through 'cells' or 'pores' of the nostrils, tongue and skin.[91] But if the senses are self-tuning instruments, that is, regulate their own tensions, this regulation will take time. Hooke himself pointed out that in the case of irregular motions or noises, the ear 'hast not time enough to tune itself all the while', whereas in the case of regular motions or musical sounds, it does have 'time enough to tune itself...and thereby to be mov'd more regularly'.[92]

3.2. The work of the interior

From his very first microscopical researches, Hooke became convinced that the sensible motions of creatures are proportioned to their bulk. He returned to this subject in one of his lectures, read at Gresham College in April or May 1682.[93] To convince his audience that velocities may be infinitely swift and that motions may be performed through the smallest of spaces, Hooke argued that

> ...'tis evident first to the Sense of Seeing, that the bigger the Body is, the slower its Vibration, and the smaller, the quicker.... But when...the Eye is unable to assist us any further in distinguishing the swiftness of Vibrations, there the Ear comes in with its assistance, and carries us much further in Bells, where we find by the Tone, that the smaller the Bell, the sharper and more shrill its Sound; and this carries us on to a Sound so sharp, that we only call it screeking, and at length it becomes offensive to the Ear, because beyond that it cannot endure the Sense of a shriller Note or quicker Vibration.[94]

Hence, there must be shriller notes beyond the reach of human ears which creatures of less bulk and finer parts may distinguish. The same would hold true for other senses and even for the organs of speech.

In a subsequent lecture, read on 21 June of the same year, Hooke argued that the brain is the 'Organ' of memory, since it functions as a repository of the motions that constitute sensory data.[95] But Hooke also supposed that the brain itself vibrated, because it was made of material that may receive and retain impressions in the same way that phosphorous, bells, strings and acoustic vases each 'shew their Natures' when the one, phosphorous, is acted upon by the motion of light and the others, bells, strings and acoustic vases, are struck or agitated by the motion of sound. According to Hooke, all these different bodies share a propensity to vibrate, for they have the 'Potentiality of receiving, and being excited by', external impressions.

Hooke then adopted an apparent dualism, for he located the soul as a single point in the brain. To perform its activities, the soul creates, as well as plays upon, the brain instrument, which in turn is played upon by the external world. If the instrument is damaged in whole or in part, the soul's activities will be impaired. But if the instrument is improved, the soul may perfect some of its activities. Hooke allowed for both factors in his account of four soul activities – 'Sensation', 'Cognition' (which he also called 'attention'), 'Remembring' and 'Ratiocination' – all of which are vibratory motions according to which wave fronts are transmitted to and from the central point.

In sensation the soul, by inward vibrations, receives 'impressions' from all the senses, whereas in cognition the soul, by outward vibrations, directs and controls the formation and storage of ideas from the centre of the brain repository. The soul accomplishes this task by linking ideas together in a chain and storing each link in a spiral order (perhaps in this way forming the coils or convolutions of the brain). Accordingly, the soul not only selects but also forms 'some material Part of the Repository into such a Shape, and gives it some such a Motion as is from the Senses conveyed thither; which being so formed and qualified, is inserted into and inclosed in the common Repository, and there for a certain time preserved and retained, and so becomes an Organ, upon which the Soul working, finds the Ideas of past Actions as if the Action were present'. But it is the spiral order of the ideas that constitutes our internal sense of time, for it enables the soul to estimate the flow (period), as well as the intervals (pulse), of time. Indeed, from the spiral store of ideas, the soul may find 'the Ideas of past Actions, as if the Action were present', because past ideas have a power of reaction or 'concurrent repercussion'. Here, then, is what Glanvill had called 'mechanism *upon* Hobbian *conditions*'.

The brain repository has space for millions of ideas (Hooke estimated 7 million) which the soul builds up and stores during life. Moreover, these stored ideas are themselves 'Organical', because experience shows that memory may be improved or impaired. A blow to the head or illness of some sort is known to 'distemper' part of the brain, which then renders that part unfit as an organ for the soul to use. This is so, because the organical parts of memory 'are actually different and separate one from another', 'have their distinct Figures' and 'their distinct Qualifications of Motions and Constitutions'. But even if brains are well-tempered, people differ one from another, some being more active and quick, others being more slow and dull. These differences, according to Hooke, are owing to strength or weakness of memory.

Hooke provided three reasons why memory may be weakened. First, there may be damping – a natural decay in the form and impressed motion of ideas, and this may contribute to the soul's forgetting. Second, as the senses collect and convey impressions to the soul, there may be interference – the interposition of other incoming ideas between the centre and the idea sought in the repository, and this may act as an impediment to remembering. Third, those ideas that are stored at a farther distance from the centre may have fainter vibratory motions than those stored nearer the centre: 'And thence it is, that the Memory of things long since done is for the most part very faint, unless in some cases, where the Impressions made upon those Ideas were at first very powerful, or often recalled, which may be said to be a new forming of them'.

Hooke regarded frequent recall, which strengthens memory, as a creative activity, because the soul, by a 'second Action' called 'habit', newly forms past ideas so that both the 'Form and Qualifications' of the vibratory motion

> ...are renewed and perfected, and for the future it becomes more powerful than the rest of those at the same or lesser Distances, that have not been by such second Radiations so renewed and invigorated; and besides every such Action of the Soul does create and form a new Idea at the Center, which has Impressions that are the Result of those renewed Actions: And this having somewhat the like Figure and Motions or Qualifications, it has a Sympathetick Agreement with the other; and the Impressions from the one do more readily make the Impressions from the other more sensible, in the same manner as a Musical String being moved, does make another String that is unison or harmonious with it, move also, and so together make the Sound the louder, or the Impression the stronger.

The new forming of ideas, in conjunction with past ideas, constitutes thinking, which continues 'almost every moment'. But thinking is most complete as reasoning ('Ratiocination'), which Hooke defined as the soul's activity of

> ...comparing the Re-actions from several Ideas placed here and there in the Repository, and its being sensible of the Harmony or Discord of them one with another, which does produce an Idea wherein all those various Respects are in some means united and impressed upon one and the same Idea. This is an Idea of greater Perfection, and according to the Attention of the Soul in being sensible of more and more variety of former

Ideas, and the Regularity and Order of its proceeding in that Action, and the more steddy and distinct manner in the Course and Progress of it, so is the Idea more compleat, as well as more compouuded [sic]: And this I conceive to be that Action of the Soul which is commonly called Reasoning; and the Conclusion is the new Impression made upon the Idea informing from the comparison of other Ideas which may be contain'd in the *major* and *minor* Propositions.

The perfection of reasoning relies on a large store of ideas, since in this way the soul has a greater 'variety to range and expatiate into, whether these Ideas are only the first and more simple, such as are the Results from the Impressions of the Senses; or the more compounded, such as are made by the Result of comparing several together'. Herein is to be sought the reason why in our younger years we are less skilled in reasoning, for the soul must work with ideas that are 'more simple and less perfect', whereas in our elder years we are more skilled, because the ideas accessible to the soul 'become the more compounded and perfect'.

3.3. The work of the point

According to Hooke's theory, the external senses collect information 'to a point' and transmit this data as vibratory motions to the brain repository. The ear, for example, functions to collect and transmit the millions of sensations we call 'sound' and which, during the life of an individual, are stored as millions of vibratory motions in the brain repository. Most of the sounds we hear are noises, not musical sounds, since the musical scale is limited, the pitches being selected arbitrarily from a much longer series. Frequency, on the other hand, falls into an infinite series, for there is no rate so slow that there might not be a slower, nor so fast that it could not be faster. When frequencies are faster than we can count, we leave the world of sensory imagination and enter the world of infinitesimals – Hooke's 'point'.

In an undated lecture on geometry Hooke defined the word 'point' as '*that which hath no part*'.[96] He then addressed the problem of the '*Minimum Naturae*', by arguing that if there be such a quantity, 'so a Unite may express it in Numbers, Instant in Time, and moment in Velocity'.[97] In the 1680s he asserted: 'there are in every *sensible* Point of Matter a sufficient number of distinct Particles to convey every one of those Motions distinct, without interfering one with another: For as there may be Millions of motions communicated to a *sensible* Point, so there may be as many millions of distinct Particles to receive each of them distinctly.'[98]

Here, then, is Hooke's solution to superposition and interference, the two problems raised by Glanvill. According to Hooke, there is no interference of one motion with another, because every sensible moment of time is composed of 'infinite Instances, or of an indefinite number of other Moments of time of a shorter duration'.[99] Thus, he could explain the modes of vibration of a musical string by the superposition of infinitely small oscillations. Those oscillations are indiscernible because less than a 'human Moment', since if a long but slack musical string is stretched between two pins,

> ...we are able to see and distinguish it, as it moves from one side to the other, and how it returns again, because it makes its Vibrations within the compass of several human moments of time; and if it come within three sensible moments, we seem to see it in three sensible Places. But if it be strain'd yet straighter, so as to make its whole Vibration within one human Moment, we see it as if it were in all parts of its space and in the two *Termini* at once, about which time, and not before, it begins to sound.[100]

In 1687 Hooke once again argued that there are parts of time that 'are abundantly much less than a humane Moment; which, tho' not distinguishable by our Thoughts, yet have their effects, in nature'.[101] He defined infinitely small moments as those which 'a Man cannot distinguish by his Thoughts into a preceding and subsequent moment, or is able to number or distinguish one from another by his Eye or Ear'. To prove this proposition, he appealed to the sense of hearing of skilled musicians, who easily identify pitches by the frequency of isochronous vibrations. But in the case of noises, for those vibrations that are not isochronous,

> ...the Sense runs a step higher and brings us into another Region [than the ear], where we find another prospect of Time, and the Partitions thereof far differing from that of the first and inferior Region, wherein we distinguish the parts of Time by Monades or Unites; for in this [other region] we distinguish

them by Aggregates, Bodies, Bulks, Armies, Thousands, and the like great Numbers, not considering them singly, but together....[102]

Hooke had already mooted that there is something 'higher' than the external senses, for in 1665 he observed that

> ...the Intellect of Man is like his body, destitute of wings, and cannot move from a lower to a higher and more sublime station of knowledg, otherwise then step by step, nay even there where the way is prepar'd and already made passible; as in the *Elements of Geometry*..., where it is fain to climb a whole series of Propositions by degrees, before it attains the knowledge of one *Probleme*. But if the ascent be high, difficult and above its reach, it must have recourse to a *novum organum*, some new engine and contrivance, some new kind of *Algebra*, or *Analytick Art* before it can surmount it.[103]

We now know that Hooke's 'higher region' is the brain or common sensory, the location of the memory store and the source of our notion of time. But why do we require a 'new kind of *Algebra*' as an aid to our knowledge of this region; indeed, what did Hooke mean by a 'new kind of *Algebra*'? If the 'higher region' processes infinitesimals logistically, is it possible that Hooke's 'new engine' processes infinitesimals mechanically? I shall return to this question, as well as to the problem of Hooke's soul/point, at the end of this chapter.

4. Understanding vibratory patterns

> ...*what I feele in my memorie,*
> *I feele in many other parts of mine.*
> Montaigne, *Essayes* (II.xvii,333)

4.1. In musical strings

From the account in the foregoing section, Hooke's theory of brain function ('intellect') may be represented as a combination of circular, radial and spiral lines, the latter of which radiate from the brain centre (Figure 3.4). This representation suggests an orb web, in which the spider – or soul/point – receives data as different modes of vibration. Depending on the data, the spider will or

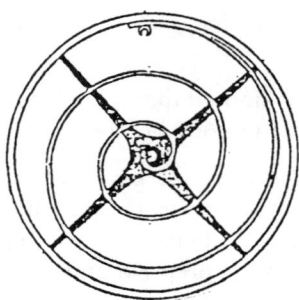

Figure 3.4   Hooke's theory of brain function

will not act. But when action occurs, it is not a simple response to a stimulus, since Hooke's soul/point performs a number of functions, chemical as well as mechanical, just as the spider performs a number of functions, as, for example, killing the prey, wrapping it up for later use, repairing the web and so on.

In antiquity there were two comparisons of the soul to a spider. In one comparison, attributed to Heraclitus, the spider rushes to any part of its web which is damaged; in the other comparison, attributed to the Stoics, the spider sits at the centre of the web, holding the beginnings of the tense threads in order to perceive the incoming messages.[104] In both instances the spider either waits at the hub of the web network, where the radii converge, or hides nearby with a signal strand running to the hub with which it can monitor web vibrations. The radii seem to be the most important communication elements, especially since the spider orients along them in locating a vibrating source. But for activity to take place at all, the spider must maintain the web in a certain degree of tension.

Hooke, however, did not use the spider analogy, for in his theory the soul/point makes the brain by composing, conducting and playing on the memory. According to the semantic field implicit in the theory, therefore, the brain must be a musical instrument, one that combines the different modes of vibration of radial, circular and spiral lines. To discover Hooke's explanatory analogy, it will be necessary to examine some aspects of his musical researches, since Hooke's understanding of vibratory patterns derived from these researches, which, in turn, guided many of his non-musical investigations. Indeed, from his very first publication to the end of his life, Hooke adopted Mersenne's Laws as general principles in nature. He called these principles 'congruity' and 'incongruity', though he sometimes used other terms to mean the same thing.

Hooke's announcement of the principles of congruity and incongruity appeared first in 1661 in a tract on capillary action, in which he explained the rise of liquid in a capillary tube as due to reduced pressure and put forward as a cause of the latter 'that there is a much greater inconformity or incongruity (call it what you please) of Air to Glass, and some other Bodies, than there is of Water to the same'.[105] He did not distinguish between cohesion and adhesion, when he defined congruity as 'a property of a fluid Body, whereby any part of it is readily united or intermingled with any other part, either of it self, or any other Homogeneal or Similar, fluid, or firm and solid body', and incongruity as 'a property of a fluid by which it is kept off and hindred from uniting or mingling with any heterogeneous or dissimilar, fluid or solid Body'.[106]

In 1665 the tract on capillary action was reprinted with important additions in Hooke's most well-known work, *Micrographia*, where he adopted Hobbes's supposition that the world is filled with a fluid ether, the motion of which is due to an innate activity or 'pulse' of heat, that is, a very vehement agitation of the smallest parts in the plenum.[107] Indeed, Hooke attributed the cause of congruity and incongruity to this innate activity, for when a pulse of heat agitates small 'parcels' of matter, 'those that are of a *like bigness*, and *figure*, and *matter*, will *hold*, or *dance* together, and those which are of a *differing* kind will be *thrust* or *shov'd* out from between them', so that

> ...particles that are all *similar*, will, like so many *equal musical strings equally stretcht*, vibrate together in a kind of *Harmony* or *unison*; whereas others that are *dissimilar*, upon what account soever, unless the disproportion be otherwise counter-balanc'd, will, like so many *strings out of tune* to those unisons, though they have the same agitating *pulse*, yet make quite *differing* kinds of *vibrations* and *repercussions*, so that though they may be both

mov'd, yet are their *vibrations* so different, and so *untun'd*, as 'twere to each other, that they *cross* and *jar* against each other, and consequently, *cannot agree* together, but *fly back* from each other to their similar particles.[108]

Hooke also applied Mersenne's Laws to explain how the disproportion of some bodies may be counterbalanced by a contrary disproportion of the same body in another respect, since 'a *unison* may be made either by two *strings* of the same *bigness, length,* and *tension,* or by two strings of the same *bigness,* but of *differing length,* and a *contrary differing tension*; or 3ly. by two strings of *unequal length and bigness,* and of a *differing tension,* or of *equal length,* and *differing bigness* and *tension,* and several other such varieties'. The three properties in musical strings correspond to the three properties in particles constituting bodies, namely, 'their *Matter* or *Substance* [length], their *Figure* or *Shape* [breadth], and their *Body* or *Bulk* [thickness]'. From the varieties of these three properties will arise 'infinite' varieties in fluid bodies, even though these bodies may be agitated, that is, made more or less tense, by the same '*pulse* or *vibrative* motion' that produces temperature changes.[109]

Although congruity and incongruity are always concomitants of fluid bodies, according to Hooke, these same principles are also present in more or less solid bodies. Indeed, he maintained that even the most solid bodies have a propensity to vibrate, because '*all* bodies have some *degree* of *heat* in them', there being no 'such thing in Nature, as a body whose particles are at *rest,* or *lazy* and *unactive*..., it being quite *contrary* to the grand *Oeconomy* of the Universe'.[110] This being the case, congruity and incongruity must be co-efficients in most operations of nature – as those of '*Heat,* and *Light,* and consequently, of *Rarefaction* and *Condensation, Hardness,* and *Fluidity, Perspicuity and Opacousness* [i.e., opaqueness], *Refractions* and *Colours, &c.*'.[111] In his investigations of these and other natural phenomena, therefore, the musical string and its laws remained an important analogue for Hooke.[112]

But the vibrating string could not provide the sole analogue, as Hooke early recognised, because bodies vibrate in different ways. In the case of sound, for example, there is an expansion and contraction of the entire source, whereas in the case of light there is an independent vibration of all the parts of the source.[113]

Moreover, not everything vibrates with the type of vibrations needed to produce light, since there are many bodies that vibrate 'violently', yet do not 'afford' the effect of light, 'and there are other bodies, which to our other senses, seem not mov'd so much, which yet shine'.[114] A solid body, for example, may vibrate, either in consequence of its own inherent elasticity, by which it tends to return to its own proper figure and state when forcibly deranged, or in consequence of an external tension. To the former sort of vibrations belong those of bells and solid masses generally which ring when struck. To the latter belong those of vibrating strings and membranes, such as the parchment of a drum.

4.2. In bells

The modes of vibration of solid masses seemed a particularly acute problem, when Hooke began to study the motions of the earth and to form his theory of universal gravitation.[115] According to the final statement of this theory, which was published posthumously, all parts of the earth execute small, imperceptible and rapid vibrations or spherical pulsations with the centre of the earth as their centre. The ether contained in the terrestrial matter, as well as the ether surrounding the earth, vibrates with amplitudes that decrease with increasing distance from the centre of vibration. As a result of these vibrations, not only parts of the earth itself but also all tangible matter above the surface of the earth are moved toward the centre of the vibrations. According to Max Jammer, this theory was based on an analogy to small bodies that are pushed toward the centre of water waves;[116] but the evidence suggests otherwise, namely, that Hooke's analogue was a bell.[117]

Today we know that the modes of vibration in a bell are influenced by the point of impact of the clapper and by variation in the thickness of the material. In Hooke's day, however, very little was known about the modes of vibration of a bell. Its properties had been extensively investigated by Mersenne,[118] and the bell itself had been used in the early vacuum experiments.[119] Although Hooke contributed to these experiments, it is not known with certainty when he began to investigate the modes of vibration of bells or of bell-shaped instruments. Nevertheless, we may trace some of his investigations from minutes of Royal Society meetings

Figure 3.5   Vibrating segments of square plates

or from memoranda which he jotted down in his diary. Of the greatest importance, however, are a series of experiments which Hooke devised with flour or water in a glass bell.

The first public demonstration of these experiments was performed at a meeting of the Royal Society on 9 March 1670/1, when Hooke mentioned that 'it might contribute to explain the cause of gravity, and suggest an hypothesis for explaining the motion of gravity by'.[120] He repeated this experiment on 23 March of the same year and hinted that upon it depended 'considerable things in philosophy'.[121] Then, on 30 March, he again produced his glass bell with flour in it

> ...to show to the eye, that, according to the several strokes or pulses made upon the glass, the air thence receives as many several impressions; it being manifest by this experiment, that as every different stroke made a different sound, so the making a different impression upon the flour gave it as many several motions. It appeared also, that the powder goes from the place, whence the pulse comes; and that in a perpendicular pulse the powder hath a kind of vibration: as also, that as long as the sound of the bell lasts, the powder seems to be fluid, but, as soon as that ceases, the powder also lies still.[122]

Since the auditors conceived that Hooke's experiment 'might much contribute to the explication of the nature of the internal motion in bodies', he was 'ordered to prosecute it'.[123]

The 1670/1 experiment provides a visible demonstration of surface vibration which is known in textbooks not under Hooke's name but under the name of the German scientist, E.F.F. Chladni.[124] Instead of a glass bell Chladni used rectangular plates on which he spread sand and then damped and excited the plates in different ways. By this means he was able to observe the structure of the resulting vibrations, analyse the sand patterns, and show that the patterns and sounds of a vibrating plate were analogous to the shapes and tones of the modes in the harmonic series of a string. These patterns are now called 'Chladni's Figures', and the lines formed by the piling sand are referred to as 'nodal lines' (Figure 3.5).

It is not clear that Hooke, or any other seventeenth-century researcher, understood nodal lines, which, like nodal points, have no discernible motion. But nodal points had been discovered in the early 1670s and were described in the scientific literature in 1677.[125] Hooke had direct access to this information, because one of the discoverers, Thomas Pigot, not only corresponded with Hooke but also visited him in London several times.[126] If we ignore the problem of nodal lines, we may say that the principles of Chladni's plate and Hooke's glass bell are similar. In the case of the plate, Chladni's experiment shows how the point of excitation decides the position of radial and circular nodal lines, whereas in the case of the glass bell, Hooke's experiment shows how the modes of vibration are influenced by the point of impact.

Despite the Royal Society order that Hooke prosecute this experiment, there is no further mention of a bell until 8 January 1675/6, when Hooke and some others paid a visit to Wren. According to Hooke's account of the visit, 'I told them and explaind the way of the sounding of a bell by the similitude of a wheel moved upon a point like a top and mentiond the severall motions of the moon explainable thereby'.[127] Then, on 8 July 1680 Hooke produced a second glass-bell experiment, in which

> ...the motion of the Glass, fill'd with Water, was observ'd to be vibrative, perpendicular to the Surface of the Glass, and that the Circular Figure chang'd into an Oval one way, and that the Reciprocation presently changed it into an Oval the other way, which he discover'd by the motion of the Undulation or rising of the Water in the Glass, which was observ'd to be in four places of the Surface in a square posture, the same Glass being struck on the edge with a Viol-bow, this square Undulation was very plain, and there was also discover'd another Undulation, by which the Water was observ'd to rise in six places like an Hexagon, and upon farther trials also in eight places like an Octagon; each of these gave their particular and distinct

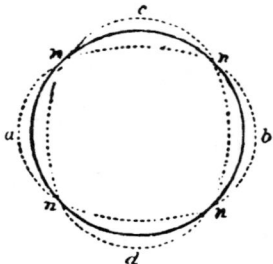

Figure 3.6 Vibrating segments of a bell

Sounds or Notes, the 4 and 8 were Octaves, and the 6 and 4 were Fifths, &c.[128]

In the first part of this experiment, Hooke made the vibration of the glass bell visible, as we may see by reducing his description to a figure (Figure 3.6). In this figure the dark circle represents the circumference of the glass bell in a state of quiescence. When the bell is struck on any one of the segments, *a, c, b, d,* the rim, which is analogous to the sound-bow of a bell, passes periodically through the changes indicated by the dotted lines in the figure: at one moment it is an oval, with *a b* for its diameter; at the next moment it is an oval, with *c d* for its longest diameter. The changes from one oval to the other constitute the vibrations of the bell, the four points *n, n, n, n,* where the two ovals intersect each other, are the nodes. But a bell can divide itself into four, six, eight or any other even (but never odd) number of vibrating segments, as Hooke showed in the second part of the experiment, when he excited the glass with a viol bow to produce the vibrating segments.

Not long afterwards, he speculated that the continued 'Chime of Impulses' from every part of the ether 'do create various sorts of harmonical Motions in concrete Particles, which have their various and admirable Effects in producing the Harmony which is in Nature'.[129] Then, on 14 March 1682/3 Hooke again brought in his glass-bell experiment, this time 'for proving an attraction from the surface of a glass of water to the place struck with a fiddlestick on the side'.[130] And, finally, in an undated fragment, 'Of Gravity',

Hooke listed a number of conclusions drawn from the experiments with bells:

> All Solids have a tremulous Motion, as Bells, &c. ...
> The vibrating Motion of all Globular Bodies is from the Center to the Superficies, and *vice versa*. This shewn by the Bell, Water in a Glass, &c.
> The Motion to and fro at the Center infinitely swift, because condensed conically. ...
> [The] Recess not at once, but similar; whence a circular vibrative Motion, or Pulse of Gravitating Matter. This confirmed by Magnetism, Bell, Water in a glass, &c.[131]

III. FORGING THE MEMORY

> *Bee dum you infant chimes...*
> *Cease all your petty larums, for to-day*
> *Yonge Tom's resurrection is from the clay.*
> Poem on the casting of Oxford Great Tom, 1612
> (Ashmolean MS 36-7: ff.260-1)

Introduction
Although the form of bells may differ, their parts are named as if bells were human bodies (Figure 3.7). At the top there is the crown (1), consisting of loops that rise from the head or relatively flat surface. At the bottom there is the lip (6) or edge round the mouth (7), a large circular opening, formed by the meeting of its inner and outer walls. Other parts include the shoulder (3), waist (4) and hip (5). Sometimes, too, the clapper (8) is called the 'tongue'. In European bells the clapper, an internal and free-swinging part, is the striking agent, consisting of four main sections: (1) a loop by which it hangs from the crown staple, also called the 'interior ear'; (2) a long shaft or shank whose diameter gradually increases as it approaches (3) the ball, or hammer, which contains the greatest mass of metal and strikes the sound-bow when the bell is rung; and (4) an abruptly tapering spur of metal below the ball, sometimes called the 'tail' or, more commonly, the 'flight', since its extra weight is required to make the clapper fly properly.

In Hooke's day bells marked time at regular quarterly intervals, called people to worship, warned of danger and commemorated

1. Crown or cannon, 2. Head or top plate, 3. Shoulder, 4. Waist, 5. Hip, 6. Lip, 7. Mouth, 8. Clapper

Figure 3.7   The bell (*la cloche*), from M. Mersenne, *Harmonie universelle* (Paris, 1636-37)

events. Sometimes, bells would ring through the night, as is clear from the comments Hooke made in his diary for 5 November 1675, 22 October 1677 and for 1688, the year of the Restoration.[132] The prominence of bells is further attested to by Roger North, in whose recollections of seventeenth-century music and musical ideas is the observation that

> ...comon steeple-bells...yeild a most sensible impression, and are signally, not onely regarded, but actually imitated by the comon people, who sound the tones as if a master had taught

them; and being so comon, their melody is almost ingrafted in our natures, and made the musicall scale as if it were borne with us. For it is at least the first musick wee hear, and the nurse's tunefull voice, whose air is comonly the 5 bells, makes an early impression, whereby musicall learning is exceedingly facilitated; which would soon be found true if a meer barbare should be brought to the proof of being taught.[133]

North had been schooled in music by John Jenkins, who wrote several pieces with the name, 'The Bells', one of which included 'cross-peals', and so took account of the intricate systems of change-ringing then developing.[134] Later on, Henry Purcell wrote a 'Bell Anthem' (Rejoice in the Lord alway), the instrumental introduction of which resembles the ringing of church bells.

Hooke, however, advanced knowledge about the 'internal motion' of bells; and he also investigated the strength of bell material. These latter investigations formed part of his work as surveyor and horologist. In the first capacity, he was involved in the restoration of St. Paul's Cathedral and many parish churches which had been damaged or destroyed during the Great Fire of 1666. Indeed, his diary contains specific mention of bells, bell frames or clappers in connection with the restoration of St. Michael, Cornhill, and St. Mary le Bow, Cheapside.[135] In the second capacity, Hooke had regular contact with the clockmakers, William Clement and Thomas Tompion, at one time 'brothers' of the Clockmakers' Company, which means that both men were concerned with the construction of steeple clocks.[136] Moreover, a maker of steeple clocks was on occasion a bell-founder also, the two crafts being associated.[137]

From all the evidence adduced, therefore, we may tentatively conclude that Hooke's model of brain function is a ringing bell, which is a percussion instrument (idiophone). I say tentatively, because we have not solved all the problems, only those concerned with circular and radial lines. As we have seen, those lines are derived from Hooke's experiments with glass bells, for the bell divides into four vibrating segments that are oval, whereas the flour or water within behaves in a different way. The flour, for example, can divide into four or six vibrating parts, thereby producing nodal lines that radiate from the centre, whereas the water will produce ripples. The glass and its contents vibrate together, and everything that interferes with the continuity of the entire mass disturbs the sonorous effect. For example, a crack in the glass passing from the edge downward extinguishes its sounding power, just as a blow to the brain extinguishes its function in whole or in part, as Hooke pointed out.

Descartes also had recourse to a bell, when he conceived sensation by analogy to a carillon and nervous function, by analogy to a bell rope: if a key is pressed, thus tugging the bell rope, a hammer is activated, and a clapper in the brain jiggles, causing us to remember what is stored in that location. Because the pull on the nerve and jiggle in the brain are instantaneous, there is no temporal series and, consequently, no sense of time. Hooke's theory of brain function, therefore, is not Cartesian, as the following five main points of his explanatory analogy indicate. First, sensory nerves transmit pulses as wave fronts which strike the brain, thereby causing a reaction from the brain 'centre'. Second, percussion 'rings the bell', that is, reminds or jogs the memory, a jog that Hooke variously called 'cognition' or 'attention'. Third, reverberation, the amplification of the bell sound, constitutes remembering, because memory travels round and round and maintains itself at the initial strength by drawing energy from a local source, the clapper. Fourth, since reverberation dies down through fatigue or inhibition unless the source of excitation is maintained, so too the circulatory travels of memory will die down and forgetting will take place. And finally, the swings to and fro of the internal clapper constitute ratiocination (comparison).

There are, however, three obscurities in Hooke's theory. First, he assumed that the clapper continues to swing regularly throughout life and that its to and fro motions trace a spiral line. We might ask, therefore, how does the clapper carry out these functions? Second, there is the problem of how the brain processes infinitesimals, those small moments of time indistinguishable by human thought. You will recall that Hooke remarked on the need for a 'new engine' that would help us to understand this aspect of brain function. It remains to discover what this new engine might be. Third and finally, there is the nature of Hooke's soul/point. Let us see how these obscurities might be cleared up.

5. Ringing the bell

> ...*every bell is a wit's Commonwealth*....
> Richard Duckworth and Fabian Stedman, *Tintinnalogia* (1668)

5.1. The mechanics

In a real bell the clapper is fixed at the centre and, when set in motion, swings back and forth like the pendulum of a clock. It is noteworthy that the English word 'clock' originally referred only to the bell on which the hours were struck; later on, the distinction between the bell which sounded the hours and the mechanism that regulated the striking (*horloge*) became blurred. An example of this blurring occurs in the language of bellmen, who speak of bells that are rung or chimed by 'clocking'. Ringing implies that the bell is swung, so that the clapper is made to hit with full force. Chiming consists in swinging the bell just far enough for the clapper to strike the sound bow. Bells also may be clocked by hitching a rope round the tail or flight of the clapper, so as to pull it athwart against the side of the bell.

Bell ringers, however, do not regulate steeple bells. This is accomplished by a number of different mechanisms. In the seventeenth century the most common mechanism consisted of a wheel with a rope round it: the bell ringer tugs the rope which in turn moves the wheel enough for the clapper to hit the bell. When several bells required regulation, the mechanism consisted of a large revolving barrel, similar in principle to that of a music box: the barrel is fitted with little spikes, each of which in its turn lifts a tongue, the extremity of which pulls a wire, which raises a hammer, which, lastly, falls upon one of the bells, thereby striking the tone required of a tune. It is not without interest that on 1 September 1672 Hooke invented 'an easy way for a musick cylinder with pewter tipes [*sic*] between cylindrick rings'.[138] Nevertheless, the music-box mechanism must be discounted, since it regulated more than one bell.

In striking or repeating pendulum clocks, there is a single clapperless bell, which is struck by a hammer (Figure 3.8).[139] In the first part of the seventeenth century, such clocks were regulated by moving weights. But their movement caused many inequalities of motion, which, today, we would call 'non-harmonic'. In 1658

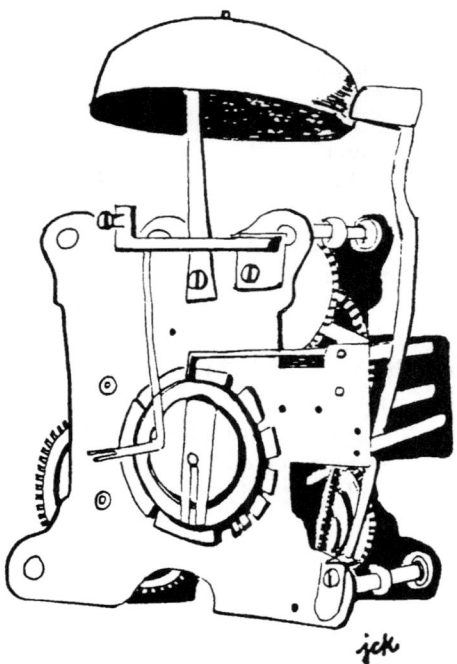

Figure 3.8   Seventeenth-century English striking clock

Hooke sought to improve regulation by attaching a spring to the arbor of the balance wheel, thereby replacing the pendulum with a vibrating wheel that could be moved because it oscillated around its own centre of gravity. Like the older mechanism, this, too, was subject to irregularities. Then, about 1660, he contrived an internal regulator in which the centrifugal force of the swing is used to make the adjustment of a clock automatic (Figure 3.9). According to A.R. Hall, this contrivance resembles a centrifugal governor similar to those used later to provide temperature compensation: 'when the balance is swinging too rapidly, the weights fly outward against the spring or springs, and thus increase its moment of inertia'.[140]

If a centrifugal governor regulates the internal clapper, how do

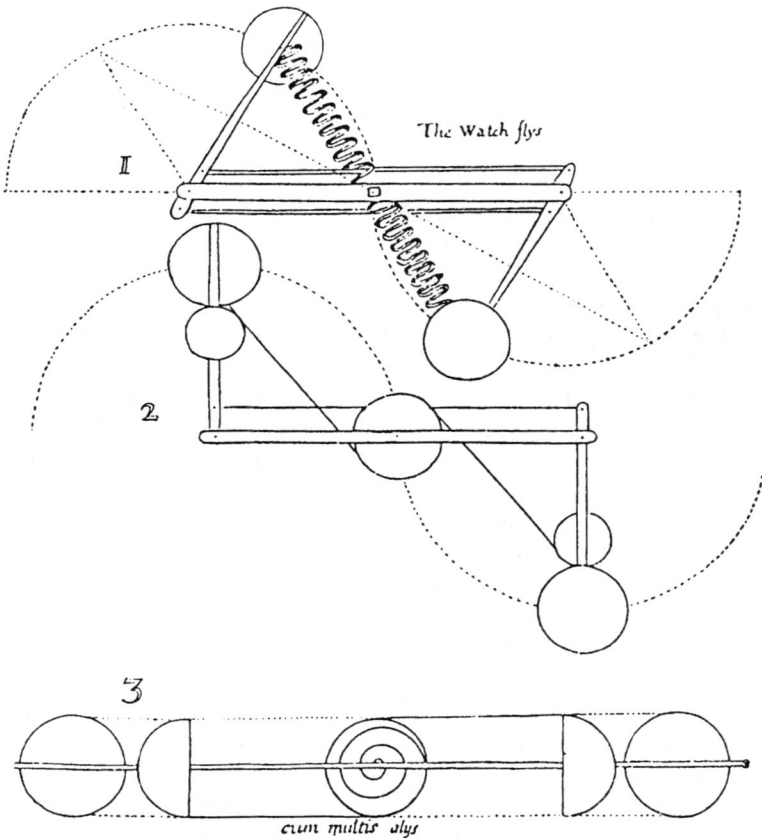

Figure 3.9   Internal regulator, from R. Hooke, *Lampas* (London, 1677)

the to and fro motions of the clapper trace a spiral line? To answer this question, we must turn briefly to Hooke's investigations into the modes of vibration of helical springs. These investigations began as early as 1656/7, when he observed that the *'Method I had made for my self for Mechanick Inventions*, quickly led me to the use of Springs instead of Gravity for the making a Body vibrate in any Posture, whereupon I did first in great, and afterwards in smaller Modules, satisfy my self of the Practicableness of such an

Invention'.[141] As is well known, Hooke's investigations led in 1658 to the law which bears his name and which relates stress and strain to a stretched elastic spring. But he waited until 1676 to announce it in an anagram that transposes into the Latin phrase, *ut tensio sic vis*: as the extension so the force. And in 1678 he finally published details.

According to Hooke's Law, the elastic force called into play by displacement is proportional to the displacement and tends to restore the displaced particle to its equilibrium position.[142] Or, to use Hooke's formulation: 'The Power of any Spring is in the same proportion with the Tension thereof'.[143] To each of the infinite degrees of spring, there corresponds a proportional degree of power. 'And consequently all those powers beginning from nought, and ending at the last degree of tension or bending, added together into one sum, or aggregate, will be in duplicate proportion to the space bended or degree of flexure'. Thus, if the aggregate or sum of powers corresponding to a strain of one degree is one, it will be four when the degree of strain is two.[144] This law applies to all elastic bodies, whether they are pushed in, bent aside or pulled out. Indeed, Hooke himself conceived the vibratory motions of a helical spring as dynamically equivalent to the oscillations of a pendulum and its supposed analogue, a musical string. Moreover, he recognised that what we now call 'simple harmonic motion' is the type of oscillatory motion we obtain when the restoring force is proportional.[145]

To demonstrate his law, Hooke contrived several instruments, one of which was a watch spring coiled in a spiral and mounted on a wheel (Figure 3.10). In 1687 he provided a brief description of a similar contrivance of his own invention − an astronomical instrument to measure infinitesimals, those 'small moments of Time' that human thought cannot distinguish. Used in conjunction with a moving telescope, Hooke's timekeeper assisted in tracing the motions of a star, 'the moments' of which, 'tho exceeding small, will yet be numbred thereby'. The mechanism that facilitated numbering consisted of a pendulum suspended by a round steel wire wheel. When the pendulum was let go, its circulating motion described a spiral line 'which, by equal Angles from the Center, is divided into equal Spaces of

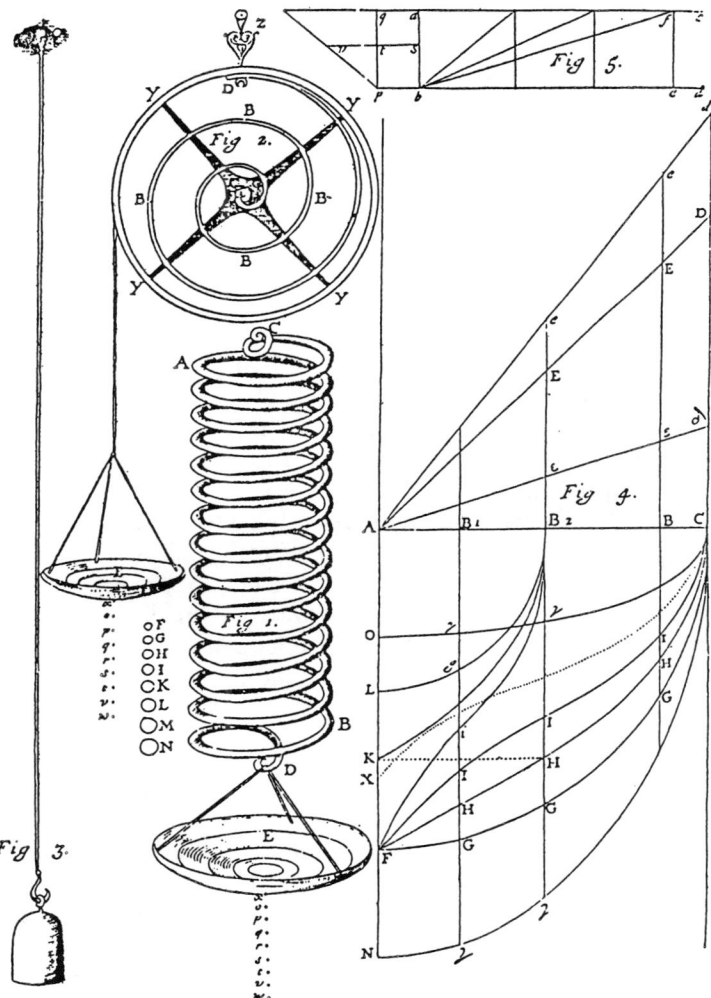

Figure 3.10 Hooke's Law demonstrated, from R. Hooke, *Lectures de potentia restitutiva* (London, 1678)

Time, and thereby the number of the Spaces in that Spiral, past by the Pendulum between the two Transits of the Star, being computed, do give the exact number of third Minutes of Time that have pass[t] between the two Observations'.[146] Here, then, we have Hooke's analogue for the spiral motions of memory's clapper, as well as his 'new engine' for counting infinitesimals.

So far the mechanism of the clapper; but what about Hooke's mysterious soul/point, which is inferred from its activities and from the instruments it makes and uses to accomplish its activities? According to records of the lecture, a number of auditors objected that Hooke conceived the soul as a mechanism. Hooke answered his objectors by asserting that

> ...no such things was hinted, or in the least intended...; it being only designed to show, that the soul forms for its own use certain corporeal ideas, which it stored up in the repository or organ of memory, and that by its power of being immediately sensible of those ideas, whenever it exerts its power for that end, it thereby becomes sensible of those ideas formerly made, as if they were made at that instant, but with this difference, that the farther they were removed from the centre or seat of its more immediate *momentary residence*, the more faint are the reflections or reactions from them; and that this occasions the notion of the distance of time.[147]

If Hooke's theory were mechanical, like that of Descartes, we might call it a 'ding-dong' theory. This label, however, would be incorrect for two principal reasons. First, Hooke's 1680s theory is epigenetic: the soul not only composes, conducts and plays on the memory store during the life of the individual, but also constructs, repairs and maintains the brain instrument. Second, the brain is a vibrating solid. Since Hooke devoted nearly fifty years of his life to that part of physics which is called 'pneumatics' and which is concerned with the properties of fluids (and, later, of gases), it would be a mistake to overlook aspects of those investigations for what they might tell us about his theory of internal character.

5.2. The pneumatics

Today we know that the human body is a heat 'engine' with a built in thermostat. It takes in fuel, 'combusts' it and puts out useful work. But the human 'engine' not only generates the energy for its work but also makes cells, blood and tissues, rebuilds worn-out parts and repairs and maintains itself. In Hooke's theory of brain function, the soul/point does two kinds of work. One kind is mechanical work, which consists in 'ringing' the bell. The other kind is chemical work, which consists in making, rebuilding and repairing the bell. Both kinds of work require a source of energy. Moreover, this source would have to circulate, so that, as Hooke himself hinted, the soul/point would have only 'momentary residence' at the centre of the brain. What is this source of energy? How is it released? And what is the mysterious soul/point?

The first question may be answered by recalling Hooke's indebtedness to Harvey's theory of the circulation of the blood.[148] But Harvey had encountered difficulty in explaining the 'lesser' pulmonary circulation, which is a cycle of warming and cooling similar to that of the blood. As early as 1616 Harvey had recognised the function of the air as 'food', the 'nourishment' of which 'feeds' the *flamma vitalis*: as the flame burns, part of the air is 'consumed', and heat is produced only so long as the loss of air is made good.[149] In 1651 he stated his conclusions in a tentative way only, when he hinted that respiration may have something in common with combustion.[150] It was this suggestion that Hooke developed in 1661 and repeatedly asserted thereafter.[151] The sum of Hooke's argument is that air is a solvent for all sulphurous substances and dissolves them by burning; in the absence of air no such solution can possibly take place however great the heat. Hence, fresh supplies of air are continually necessary for the preservation of animals; moreover, the movement of the lungs, resulting from breathing, is essential for the intake of fresh air supplies. In short, respiration is a kind of burning.

In burning, combustible material catches fire, and the attendant flame is a source of heat, light and, frequently, sound.[152] As we have seen, Hooke treated light and sound as modes of vibratory motion. But he also treated heat in the same way when, in 1665,

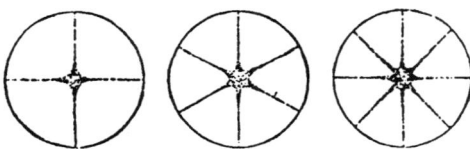

Figure 3.11   Vibrating segments of circular membranes

he compared the agitating pulse of heat to the 'dancing motion' of particles of sand when they are placed on a stiff drumhead that is struck vehemently with a drum stick.[153] This comparison suggests that Hooke's experiments on different modes of vibration pre-date the 1670s, when he publicly demonstrated his glass bell experiment. Indeed, the drum is somewhat like a glass bell, for if the drum membrane is stretched equally in all directions, the sand will pile up as nodal lines in a number of different ways, depending on the point of excitation (Figure 3.11). What is important about this experiment, however, is that Hooke, like Hobbes before him, conceived heat as a mode of vibratory motion; and he reiterated this notion in the undated fragment, 'Of Gravity', when he observed, first, that 'Heat or Excess of motion shakes the Parts of Solids, so as to make them Fluid, which is when a minute Fluid can get between'; second, that solids are 'more easily divisible by Supreme Fluid, which is Fire; and third, that 'Supreme Fluids always recede from the Center radiating; lesser Fluids follow in their place'.[154]

In bell-founding, fire is used not only to fuel the furnaces in which bells are cast, or recast if cracked, but also to penetrate ('get between') and totally mix the metals that are used in making bell metal.[155] The chief goal of bell-founders is to produce bell metal that insures the proper combination of resilience (the capacity to rebound when struck) and resonance. In striving for this goal, bell-founders use alloys – for the clapper, cast iron, and for the bell itself, a hard alloy of copper and tin of low damping capacity. In the case of both bell and clapper, therefore, the substance is composed of two (or more) metals which have been fused. For this to happen, however, 'transmutation' must take place, as Hooke himself pointed out, for

> ...the melting together of Tin and Copper...make[s] a third Body quite distinct in most of its Proprieties from either of those other two; 'tas [*sic*] quite a distinct Colour from either; 'tis of a Consistence abundantly harder than either; 'tis exceeding brittle; whereas the others are both tuff, 'tis much heavier in Specie than either of them, and so for divers other Proprieties, it seems wholly differing from either of the two Ingredients of which it is compounded.[156]

On the analogy of bell-founding, we may suppose that respiration provides the fuel that transforms chemical into mechanical work.[157] But what triggers the release of energy? On Hooke's assumption that respiration is a kind of burning, we may conjecture that the trigger is a spark or fiery particle that is thrown off during the process.

The mass of a spark is as minute as the quantity of its motion is infinitesimal. Could this be Hooke's partly non-localised soul/point? That Hooke may have conceived the soul/point in this way is suggested in an unpublished lecture on geometry, read 4 February 1691/2, when he demonstrated from the 'due proportions of Sound' that 'God by Nature framed our bodies...according to Geometricall Rules'. He then argued that although people may not understand 'the business of proportion or how it comes to passe: they have a body harmoniously constructed and an harmonious Soule to be affected there by', for

> Twas Pythagoras and divers other of the antient philosophers that by search and inquiry found out the reason of it, which I suppose might be one of the reasons why he and Plato asserted the soule to be made of number[,] that is[,] I conceive, they meant noe more but that they were made of almost harmonious and perfect constitution, soe as to be afforded with consonant and harmonious impulses but offended by dissonant and discording influences. And from this speculation it was as I conceive that axiom first sprung...that God doth always act geometrically, that is, by due proportions of number[,] weight and measure. And that faculty of ours of being sensible of it does show us to have...a spark of the Divinity.[158]

Chapter 4
The Daimon Within

I. THE MUSICAL MAN

> ... 'musicalness and unmusicalness'
> are the property of the persistent identity, viz. man.
> Hence...as regards musical man and unmusical man,
> they are a passing-away and a coming-to-be.
> Aristotle, *De generatione et corruptione* (319.b.25-30)

Introduction

In 1648 Hooke's older friend and colleague, John Wilkins, identified two kinds of self-movers or automata: those that receive their motion from something that belongs to the frame itself – as, in clocks, by weights or springs; and those that receive their motion by something extrinsic to their own frame – as, in mills, by water or wind.[1] The former kind of automata have provided the governing metaphor for the so-called 'clockwork universe' of the historians of science, even though other instruments besides clocks may be driven by weights and springs. The latter kind of automata are perhaps the oldest of which we have record. Indeed, when the *Automata* and *Pneumatica* of Hero of Alexandria were first published in the sixteenth century, they transmitted this ancient tradition in which not only water and wind but also heat were the principal sources of movement.[2]

To devise automata operated by variations in the temperature and pressure of the atmosphere, Hero employed the principle of the expansive power of heated air in a glass vessel, or thermoscope. This same principle was applied by the engineer, Cornelis Drebbel, whose hydraulic organ was described by Wilkins thus: 'being set in the sunshine, [it] would of itself render a soft and pleasant harmony; but being removed into the shade, would presently become silent. The reason of it was this: the warmth of the sun working upon some moisture within it, and rarifying the inward air unto so great an extension that it must needs seek for vent or issue, did thereby give several motions unto the instrument.'[3] As we have seen, Hooke's self-mover combines Wilkins' two kinds of automata, for its motive power consists of a clockwork mechanism, as well as a life-giving fluid.

Until the discovery of oxygen in the 1770s, there were many conjectures about the nature of this fluid. Drebbel conceived it as a special 'spirit' in the air essential to respiration in humans and that this ingredient was given off by the heating of nitre (saltpetre).[4] The same notion was adumbrated by Drebbel's near contemporary, Francis Bacon, who stated that 'nitre contains an extraordinary, crude, and windy spirit; which first, by the heat of the fire, suddenly dilates itself; and thus dilated, blows abroad the flame, like an internal bellows'.[5] Bacon classed nitrous spirit under 'pneumaticals', a term he used for spirits that govern nature. These spirits, however, can be regarded as restless airs (gases), for they are relatively permanently rarefied matter, they exude 'breaths' or vapours from various bodies such as fermented liquors, and they are imponderable and intangible.[6] According to Bacon, all material bodies contain pneumaticals that behave like 'subtile or windy spirits'; but living creatures alone possess pure spirit, compounded of air (rarefied water) and flame (rarefied combustible matter). Moreover, like sap in a tree, pure spirit functions as the animating principle, for it is continuous and 'branched' throughout body.[7]

In Bacon's pure spirit we find echoes of the Stoic notion of the soul (*anima*) as a warm breath fed by the exhalation of the blood. But Bacon appears to owe another debt to Stoicism, or at least to the medical version of it, for he believed that sympathy, the motion of consent, results from the affinity (conformity, congruity) between the latent configurations of bodies affected by pneumaticals. Nevertheless, Graham Rees argues that Bacon's 'pneumatic' philosophy is not Stoic; rather, it is 'a chemical system of universal scope couched in the obstinately non-mechanical language of sublimation and rectification, digestion and conversion, sympathy and antipathy'.[8] Hence, Bacon relied on qualitative distinctions to elaborate the nature of tangible and pneumatic substances, at the same time integrating these with a kinematics based on spiral lines, a special kind of harmonic motion employed in the twelfth century for rationalising celestial appearances.[9]

From Aubrey we know that Hobbes once 'assisted' Bacon, though few details seem to be known about the contact between the two men.[10] Still, it might be said that Hobbes improved Bacon's theory in two principal ways. First, even though he retained the belief that pneumaticals govern nature, he rejected Bacon's plethora of pneumaticals, admitting only one, the ether, of which there is a scale of degrees of density. Second, he replaced Bacon's conception of affinity with sympathetic resonance, when he utilised the taut string as a model of the ether. The Stoic doctrine of sympathy had focused on *pneuma* as connecting all parts of a body, thereby offering an interpretation of integrative movement that was independent of physical structure.[11] Hobbes overcame this limitation by recourse to Harvey's circulation physiology: the pulsating (etherealised) blood flows round the body, thereby allowing an interaction between solids and fluids. To these notions Hooke added the pulmonary circulation. Hence, both men contributed to enlarging the imagination of how integrative movement takes place in humans, since, in their theories, function reveals structure.

Nevertheless, hindsight enables us to point to a negative aspect of Hobbes's conception of sympathetic resonance, in which an elastic solid becomes the model for the fluid ether.[12] As we now know, the modes of vibration of solids like strings and bells differ from that of fluids like air in two important particulars. First, the particles of solids are subjected to the condition of never changing their order or arrangement, whereas those of fluids are capable of mutual displacement. Second, each particle of a solid has distinct sides and different relations to space and to the surrounding particles, whereas in fluids each particle is similarly related to those around it in all directions. That Hobbes grasped some of these differences is clear from his treatment of primary impulse, the infinitesimal aggregate motion that, like boiling, 'makes all the parts of the water change their places'.[13]

As we have seen, Hooke made a comparable analogy, for as early as 1665 he described the displacement of fluid particles *inter se*, when he compared the pulse of heat to the 'dancing motion' of particles of sand on a beaten drumhead.[14] Then, in the tract

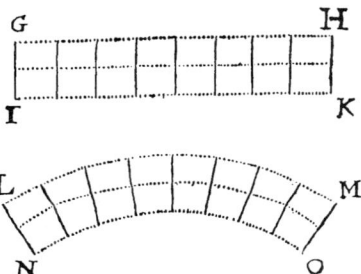

Figure 4.1 Microscopic particles of elastic bodies, from R. Hooke, *Lectures de potentia restitutiva* (London, 1678)

containing his law, he made a clear distinction between two kinds of solids: those which have a simple way and those which have a compound way of springing. In the former category are the hardest solids, like bells (Hooke listed 'Steel, Glass, Wood, &c.'), which have an inherent elasticity, that is, 'have a Spring both inwards and outwards, according as they are either compressed or dilated beyond their natural state'.[15] In the latter category are those solids which spring by flexure, like strings and drum membranes. Despite these insights, Hooke devised a single model to demonstrate elasticity, for he represented all springy bodies, solid as well as fluid, as constituted by a row of eight identically vibrating microscopic particles, each occupying a rectangular spatial domain (Figure 4.1).[16] But he supposed that the microscopic particles do not 'recede and fly from each other', because they are kept together by an external natural force, namely, 'the Heterogeneous compressing motions of the ambient' ether.[17]

According to a number of scholars, Hooke's model is problematic from a modern perspective, in part, because he generalised Boyle's Law to the law of elasticity that bears Hooke's name.[18] But Boyle's Law is a pressure law, in which pressure is defined by the volume of the expansive force, whereas Hooke's Law is an elastic law, in which stress is defined by the proportion of strain. It is Hooke's Law, therefore, that is important for resonating systems. In the foregoing Chapters 2 and 3, we examined two explanatory analogies of internal character based on two different resonating systems, the lute and the bell. But, as noted in Chapter 1, the column of air in a wind instrument also can function as a resonator. When this happens, it vibrates like a helical spring; and in Chapter 3 we learned that Hooke formulated his law by analysis of such a spring.

The helical spring illustrates the principle of elasticity in its most classic and most obvious form, according to E. Williams, for the particular material from which the spring is made is seen as something contingent:

> While it is known that the change in length of a helical spring, such as Hooke used, results mainly from the torsion of the wire, the action of the spring, regarded as a unit, is nevertheless that of either direct tension or direct compression. The torsion is an intermediate element: it is the effect of the direct load and at the same time the cause of the change in length. Viewed in this way, Hooke's observations on the correlation of the primary cause and the ultimate effect hold true.[19]

Hence, although the lute string, the bell and the column of air are different material substances, as elastic bodies they each operate according to Hooke's Law. It will be useful, therefore, to recapitulate some of the points made in Chapter 1, now taking account of that Law.

For the purposes of illustration, let us return to our original example, the musical string, which is a long piece of material of negligible thickness and complete flexibility. But it has the potential to become musical only after it is stretched, that is, pulled apart at its two ends by equal and opposite forces which keep it taut. The magnitude of the elastic force is called 'the tension'. To make the stretched string, or any other acoustic vibrator, alter the pitch of its tone, it is necessary to alter the tension of the vibrator. This is so, because elastic bodies obey Hooke's Law, 'As the deflection, so the force'; therefore, the time of back spring is in each case invariable, and the pitch of the tone produced remains invariable, whatever the amplitude of the vibration must be.

When a taut string is displaced from its equilibrium position by striking, plucking or friction, the force of restitution – that is, the force tending to restore it to its old position – is proportional to the displacement, and the time of vibration is uniform. The same is true of other elastic bodies that are not acoustic, as, for example, a pendulum. When the bob of the pendulum is displaced, or deflected, or pulled aside a little, the amount of the deflection is always very nearly proportional to the force which was used to produce the deflection. If the swings of the pendulum are not too big, the motion may be considered harmonic motion, in which the accelerating force increases with the distance of the body from some fixed point. Under such conditions, the swings about this point will be made in equal times whether they are large or small ones. Although Galileo discovered these properties of the pendulum, it was Hooke who made the first attempt to understand simple harmonic motion in an elastic context.[20]

But Hooke's Law also opened the way to new investigations into the problem of how air 'fits' into musical pipes. Although Bacon and Hobbes, briefly, and Mersenne, extensively, had devoted attention to the production of sound in different kinds of aerophones, none of them had understood this problem.[21] The first step toward a solution was taken by Roger North, who argued that air in a pipe fits like a long helical spring: 'all the propertys that may be affirmed of any spring (forme and condition considered) will be true of air included in tubes; but it is wholly by lengths, for latterally it is confined and cannot spread'.[22] Indeed, North provided an illustration to show that whatever is done by the monochord, or musical string, vibrating laterally, will be done by a column of air in a pipe or tube trumpet vibrating longitudinally (Figure 4.2); 'and the consequences as to sound will be alike in both'.[23]

If we view the history of the seventeenth century through the lens of the history of acoustics, the story told so far suggests that there were three successive advances in understanding modes of vibration, beginning with solids that spring by flexure (vibrating strings), continuing with solids that have an inherent elasticity (bells) and concluding with the motion of fluids in enclosed spaces (air in wind musical instruments). With these advances the ground was laid for a theory of internal character as a 'consort' of different musical instruments, in which a fluid medium is given a central role. It is North's achievement to have constructed such a theory, which has only recently come to light with the editing

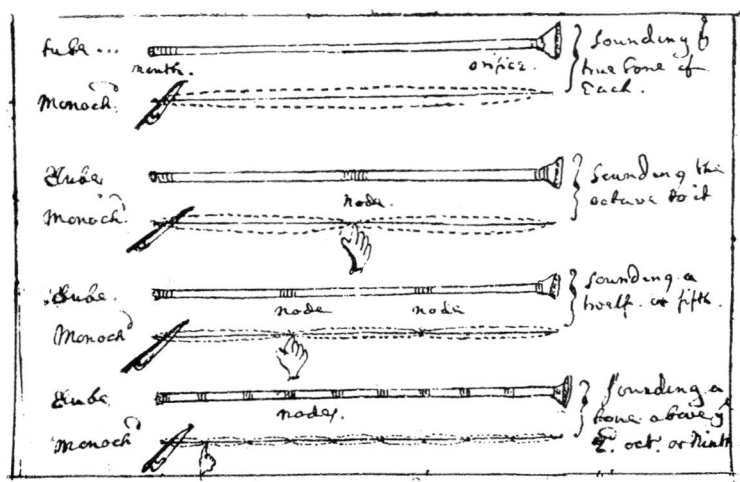

Figure 4.2 Tube trumpet, showing longitudinal vibrations, from R. North, *Theory of Sounds...1728* (BL Add MS 32535: f.138)

and organising of his music manuscripts. Prior to this, North's reputation rested chiefly on his work as a life writer and, more recently, as the first theorist of biography.[24] But his theory of biography, taken by itself is incomplete, since North sought to teach, by both good and bad examples, the art of living.[25] Hence, it was necessary for him to understand the 'springs' of human thought and action.

At first, North's understanding was Cartesian, for, in an early text, he wrote: 'There are some who fancy a resilition or springyness in all bodys, which I cannot assent to, finding it inconsistent with the nature of body, which is infinite or perfect hardness, and every spring supposeth a yeilding and a force to result.'[26] Later on, when he began working on *Notes of Me* and lives of three of his brothers, he rejected Cartesian impenetrability, as well as mind/body dualism. The latter tenet left the visible face of human nature as a tantalising illusion, as Roy Porter points out, for 'if the ego was hidden, if mind was but a ghost in the machine, how could inspecting the outside of the machine tell you about the ghost?'.[27] To solve this problem, North turned to Hobbes, who, in *Leviathan*, had written: 'He that is to govern a whole

Nation, must read in himself, not this, or that particular man; but Man-kind: which though it be hard to do, harder than to learn any Language, or Science; yet, when I shall have set down my own reading orderly, and perspicuously, the pains left another, will be onely to consider, if he also find not the same in himself.'[28]

In this passage Hobbes used a literary metaphor, conceiving mankind as a text to be read. But in *Body* and its companion volumes, where he set down his 'orderly' reading of the 'book' of mankind, he offered a different metaphor, conceiving people as extended in three dimensions with resistance, thus bringing together the Stoic tenets of tension (physiology) and goodness (ethics). North also adopted these tenets. But in his reinterpretation, the 'book' of nature is a musical score, written in acoustical signals, and nature itself is a large-scale model of musical activity. Body is a 'consort' of musical instruments that has the potential to play together harmoniously. Mind is the conductor of the consort, for it has the potential to interpret the musical score so as to direct which instrument, or group of instruments, is to play at appropriate times. The potential of body and mind is made actual by spirit, which is the composer as well as the musical score that the unity of body and mind expresses.

In the first part of this chapter, I shall show how North solved the mind/body problem by examining separately the three aspects of his musical metaphor: body, mind and spirit. By the term 'body', North denoted the knowing subject, that is, the whole personality consisting of thoughts as well as actions. By the term 'mind', he signified the knowing process. And by the term 'spirit', sometimes used in the plural, he meant life or animating principle. This principle is not occult; rather, it is a tenuous pneumatic substance contained in the air. During respiration, which North likened to combustion, this tenuous substance functions as a source of excitation, thereby actuating the potential energy of bodily instruments to function as a combination of acoustic vibrators and resonators. To explain living creatures, therefore, North adopted a functional approach to body, whereby the instruments or nerves and muscles, the conductor or central processing unit, and the creator and regulator or spirit must all cooperate else there is no knowledge and, indeed, no life. Hence, North's conception of nature proceeds from the assumption of the immanence of life and function in organised matter. Neither of these can exist independently of each other, since, as he himself stated: spirit makes the difference between a living and a dead corpse.[29]

As a biographer North was concerned with life lived. But he believed that his depiction of a life 'cannot be good, if the peculiar features, whereby the subject is distinguished from all others, are left out. Nay, scars and blemishes, as well as beauties, ought to be expressed; otherwise, it is but an outline filled up with lilies and roses'.[30] Once body is thought of as a life, indeed, as this or that particular life, the biographer will be confronted with the problem of the dynamics of living experience. To solve this problem, North needed to find a controlling metaphor that would enable him to depict a wide range of living experience, including the experience of illness, for disease processes threaten one's ability to be oneself and, even after recovery, one may be changed in important ways. Since North used musical activity as a model of normal function, the range that constitutes health, it might be asked: what was his model for abnormal function? In the second part of this chapter, I shall consider this question.

1. Organised body

> *The several kinds of Instruments*
> *are commonly used severally by themselves:*
> *as a Set of Viols, a Set of Waits, or the like:*
> *but sometimes, upon some special occasion,*
> *many of both Sorts are most sweetly joined in Consort.*
> Butler, *The Principles of Musik* (94)

1.1. As the consort

In his treatment of body as knowing subject, North posited one substance: matter. He then argued that all 'our capacity lys, 1. in the use of our sences, 2. in the movement of our members; and from these two are to be deduced the understanding of all humane things'.[31] To treat these capacities, North assumed the two Stoic tenets of tension and goodness: that every body is a tensional field made up of inward and outward action; that through this two-way motion the utility and existence of body is preserved. Thus, he wrote: 'the body is a mobile engin like a compage of springs, that on the least percussion, will fall to shaking

The Daimon Within

and vibrating a long time, which is from an interne principle, and not [from] the force that occasions it'.[32] A principal feature of body, therefore, is its unity, for it has functions and states or conditions.

Since body's states and conditions are modes of vibratory motion, North had recourse to the isochrony of 'springs' and other systems having equilibrium configurations along axes. But it would be a mistake to conclude that North conceived people as exemplifications of the pendulum condition, because he made a distinction between pendulums and 'springs'. Pendulums are

> ...actuated by gravitation, which is an exterior principle, and continually works, and both augments the reducing force, and resists the imprest force.... But it is not so with the elasticks, for those are actuated by an interior principle, which at every returne ceaseth to work, till the imprest force hath invigorated it againe, and when free from exterior impulse, the springs when not unduely strained will goe, and returne isocronically to the last.[33]

According to North, no physical pendulum is truly isochronous unless it is regulated by some clockwork mechanism, whereas 'elasticks' are isochronous, as is proved by musical strings, 'which have all the propertys of springs'.[34] By the term 'elasticks', therefore, North denoted acoustic vibrators, since a pendulum is an elastic body but is non-acoustic.

During a period of more than forty years, North sought to understand the functions not only of acoustic vibrators but also resonators, as may be discovered in his essays and treatises relating to sound and sound producers.[35] The chief catalyst for these writings was his brother's theory of sound, which was based on two suppositions: first, that sound results from the percussion of matter against air particles, or air particles against other air particles; and, second, that sound is transmitted as a series of 'cracks' caused as the air rushes in to fill an evacuated space.[36] North was to replace these suppositions with two others: first, that sound results from the vibration, as a vibrating spring, of either the material of the generator or of an enclosed quantity of air; and, second, that sound is transmitted as the result of the simple harmonic motion of air particles acting on other particles according to the laws of kinematics.

Although there is considerable evidence that North's thinking about sound underwent developments between c.1698 and c.1730, the theory which he developed after c.1720 resembles that of Christiaan Huygens, whose kinematic theory had been published in 1690 as *Traité de la lumière*.[37] In that work Huygens made numerous comparisons between sound and light; but he recognised both positive and negative aspects of the analogy, for he noted that although both light and sound are propagated by waves, they differ in three principal ways: their generation, their medium of propagation and their mode of propagation. First, sound is produced by the motion of the entire source, whereas light is produced by the motion of every point of the source. Second, sound is propagated in the air, but light is propagated in the ether which freely penetrates all matter. Finally, sound is propagated through the air, the particles of which are not in contact except during collision, while light is propagated through the ether, which consists of particles in contact.[38]

In following Huygens, North argued that for people and musical instruments to sound, such bodies, or parts of them, must first become agitated so as to shake all the contiguous air.[39] When the agitation is equal-timed, the pulses occasion the simple harmonic motion of air particles, the particles then acting on each other according to the laws of impact. By means of the air, an invisible and impalpable body, sound spreads around the spot where it has been produced by a vibratory motion which is passed on successively from one part of the air to another. The spreading of this motion, taking place equally rapidly on all sides, forms spherical surfaces or waves. These waves, ever enlarging, strike our ears. Sound, therefore, is transmitted by a composition of pulses.

For immediate knowing to take place, however, sensible presence, by itself, is insufficient, for there also must be attention. Hence, pulses must be notable, that is, they must engage the attention and lead to sustained reflection and thought. Since our perception is 'a notice of pulses, or remarkable alterations of body',

> ...these things cannot be all observed at once, but successively one after another, which gives the idea of time. And as all are not of equall circumstance, but some more eclattant then others, so wee are attentive to some, and let others pass, with litle or no notice. And often the pulses from memory, shall have force to prevail and be attended to rather then others without us, which is called not minding. And there is no sleep or moment of life without attention to (that is perception of) one thing or other.[40]

The pulses that are notable, however, are so swift that they consist of indiscernible moments of time.

Previously, both Hobbes and Hooke had remarked on the indiscernible nature of pulses, but it was Hooke's tooth-wheeled experiment that lent conviction to this notion. Although that experiment was shown publicly to the Royal Society in 1681, it had been devised earlier as an aural demonstration of Francis North's 'ocular scheme' for representing musical pitches as a temporal flow of equable pulses (Figure 4.3). According to Roger North,

> The ingenious Mr. Hook put this scheme of music into clockwork, and made wheels, with small lingulæ in the manner of cogs which moving, each upon its pin, as the wheel turned, struck upon an edge, one after another, equably; the wheel turning slow, *the pulses were distinguishable, and had no other virtue*; but then, turning swifter, *the distinction ceased*, and a plain musical tone emerged. This for one. Then, another wheel was contrived to strike three to two (for instance) and *as the distinction began to fail, and continuation to take place*, we might hear a consort 5th coming on, and settling in the manifest accord so named.[41]

North's notable pulses, then, are those that Hobbes had called 'insensible' and Hooke, 'less than a human moment'; that is, they are real but infinitesimally small vibratory motions. When pulses meet this condition, they excite the tympanum of the ear,[42] the chain of events taking place internally being the same as that which happened externally. The vibrating tympanum transmits the pulses to the nervous system, which, in turn, vibrates and transmits the pulses to the brain, which coordinates the various pulses and elevates them into consciousness as images, so that the mind, by

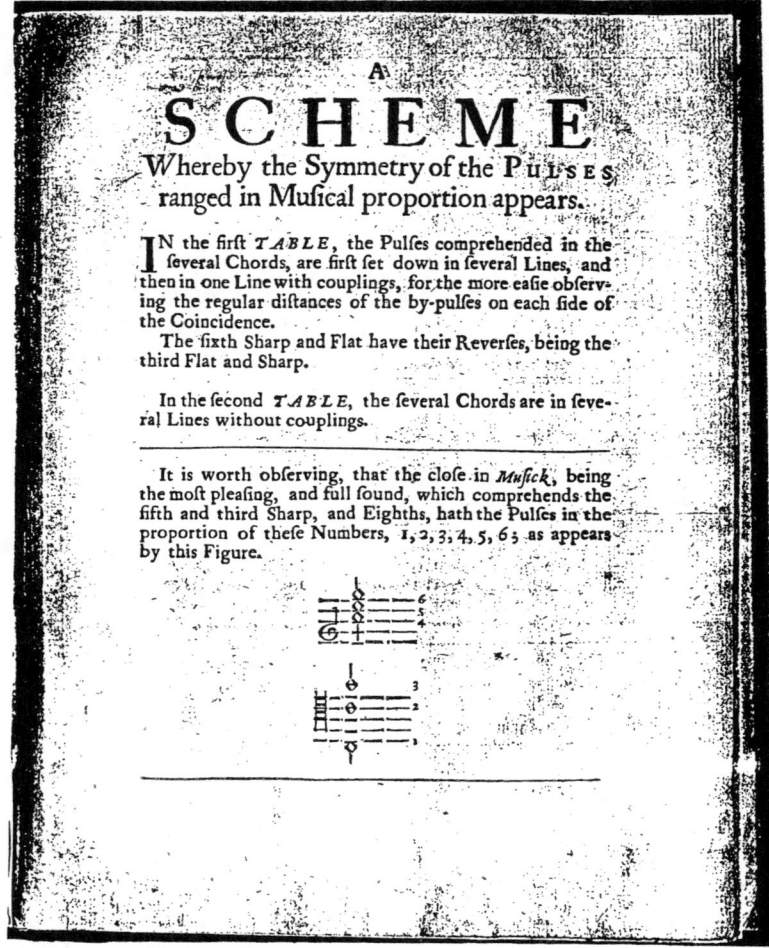

Figure 4.3 Method of representing musical pitches as a temporal flow of coincident pulses, from F. North, *A Philosophical Essay of Musick* (London, 1677)

Tab: I.

16
8
4
2
1
Octaues.
3
2
Fifths.
4
3
Fourths.
5
4
Third sharp.
6
5
Third flat.
6 } 3 ᵈ flat.
5
3
Sixth sharp.
8
5 } 3 ᵈ sharp.
4
Sixth flat.

Tab: ii.

Octaues.
Fifts.
Fourths.
Third sharp.
Third flat.
Sixth sharp.
Sixth flat.

its presence to the brain, then 'reads' the images in the act of perception.

In the 1644 *Tractatus opticus* Hobbes had posited an internal phantasm or mental representation, although he left the nature of this representation implied rather than stated. North, however, was explicit, for he conceived the images represented to, and seen by, the mind as rules of vibrations; and, in a development of Francis North's scheme, he exemplified these rules in a series of 'punctations' (L. *punctum*, pl. *puncta*), one of which is illustrated in Figure 4.4. In this punctation the parallel vertical lines represent the flow of time, and the points represent the pulses. The lowest row represents the pulses that correspond to the fundamental tone ('key'); the pulses above correspond to the intervals of the octave, 12th, 15th, 17th, 19th and 22d. These intervals form what North called the 'full accord' (he never used the terms 'harmonic' or 'overtone series'), which, with some octave transposition, is represented in current common musical notation above the punctation.

From this punctation alone, it is clear that sounds co-exist and do not obliterate each other, because they are dynamic processes in the air, of which each of them is a certain modification. Such modifications can undergo superposition without losing their identity, whereas a superposition of static states does away with them. We may conclude, therefore, that the brain is not a wax tablet on which images are impressed or a piece of paper on which creases are made. North himself suggested that the brain or 'residence of thought' is like the reflecting telescope invented by Newton. According to this comparison, the concave mirror or speculum is the cerebellum ('sensorium'); the eyepiece or combination of lenses for magnifying an image is the cerebrum ('brain'); and the eye, moving to and fro, is the mind.[43] But North insisted: 'I doe not argue extention, or locality of the mind otherwise then it hath power over this particular matter, to which in every humane body it is affix't.' Mind, therefore, differs from the instruments of body only in its function as a conductor 'to determine among the capacitys of the body, which shall be imployed, and which not'.[44]

1.2. As the conductor

To fulfill its function as a conductor, the mind scans the images transmitted to the brain, 'and so passing and repassing seems to

The Daimon Within

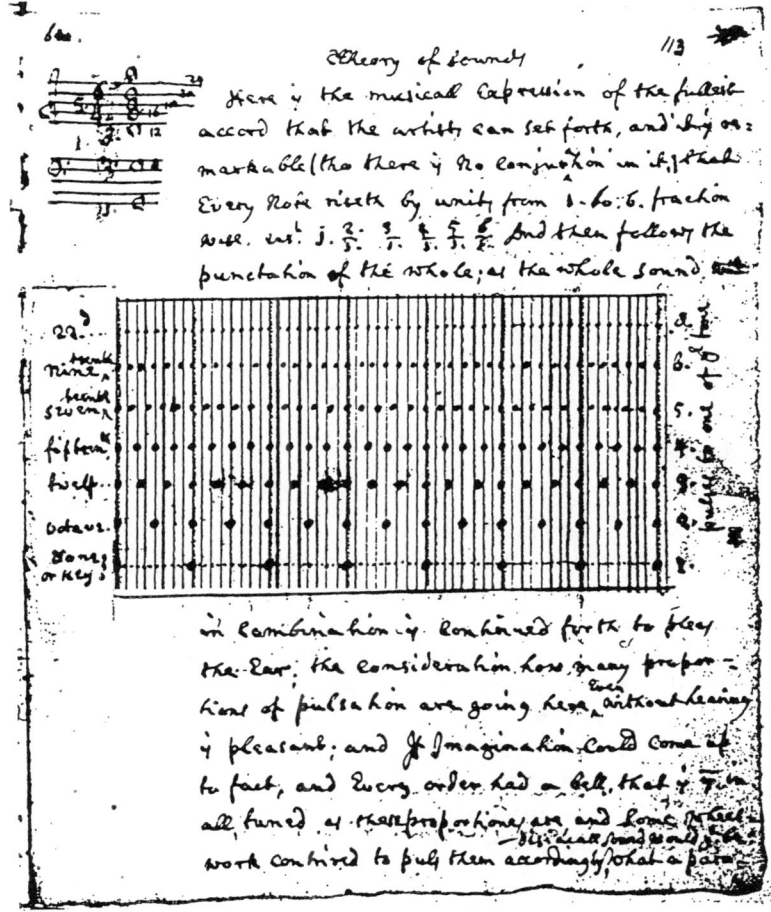

Figure 4.4 Mental representation as rules of vibration, illustrated by a 'punctation' of the full accord, from R. North, *Theory of Sounds...1728* (BL Add MS 32535: f.113)

```
            1
           1 2
          1 2 3
         1 2 3 4
        1 2 3 4 5
       1 2 3 4 5 6
```

Monochord Divided	Intervals Produced	Ratios of Frequencies	Order of Perfection
1	Unison	1:1	(Most perfect)
2	Octave	2:1	
3	Fifth	3:2	
4	Fourth	4:3	
5	Third ♯	5:4	
6	Third ♭	6:5	(Least perfect)

Figure 4.5 Key to Figure 4.4

dilate the observation'.[45] Yet, despite the rapidity with which it performs this action, the mind can attend to only one image at a time, because in the act of perception the mind must perform various computations on the data represented to it. In performing these computations, the mind employs three powers: the external senses, the memory and the imagination. These powers are not separate faculties; rather, they are different functions of mind. North, therefore, followed both Hobbes and Hooke, who explicitly connected mental activity with computations. But North went further in his treatment of the chronological sequence of mental function as different kinds of computations. Let us begin with his explanation of the power of hearing.

Since data are transmitted as a composition of infinitesimal pulses, peripheral processing occurs subconsciously and involves counting. The method may be illustrated in the key to Figure 4.4 (Figure 4.5), showing North's punctation in numbers, followed by the mechanical derivation on the monochord. The bass or fundamental tone (1 in the computational model) is the normative sound in determining the character of harmonic sonorities, all the upper parts being more or less perfect as they have more or fewer pulses that coincide with pulses of the bass. But the ratios of simple consonances stop at 6:5, because we know only the numbers 1 to 6 by forming ideas of so many bodies. Beyond this, we know only hypothetically and 'by names where of the signification is granted'.[46] Hence, the mind's power of distinguishing pulses is limited; and the measure is given from our ability to move some part of our body and which is done 'actually or mentally, when ever wee mark or number things passing by us'.[47]

But when pulses strike us faster than we can count, the mind is unable to separate them in conscious thought into preceding and succeeding moments of time. To process such pulses, the mind employs a second power, memory, which gathers them into larger units.[48] These units, which North regarded as appearances or mental fictions, consist of discernible pulses, the computation of which occurs consciously and involves comparison. Pitches, for example, do not merely exist at the moment they are heard, they also endure in the memory and relate to what came before and what follows after. The memory accepts or rejects a pitch as harmonically functional by a process of comparison, and in this way the musical scale is formed.[49]

The names by which we designate appearances are conventional and not intrinsic to bodies, for North acknowledged that 'wee have litle else, but names, to be concerned with in this theory...[and] it must be no surprise if some termes occurr, without a sufficient vocabulary, but I shall take care, whatever names are assumed, the things shall be clear enough'.[50] Accordingly, names such as 'noise' and 'tone', 'accord' and 'discord', 'high' and 'low', 'harsh' and 'smooth' are common terms for various combinations of vibrations that are impressed on our organ of hearing and transmitted to the mind to read. Nevertheless, there is a correspondence between reality and appearances, for 'altho the mind hath no distinction of the elements of continued sounds, yet there is a resentment of the reall propertys that attend them, but yet in different ideas, whereby every alteration or variety amongst them is vertually perceived and one composition is distinguish't from another'.[52]

Once the mind is stocked with data from sensation and memory, it forms new ideas by means of its third computational power, imagination, which combines the data in order to yield new ideas.[8] North explained this computational process by recourse to a logical calculus of ideas conceived as a combination of simple

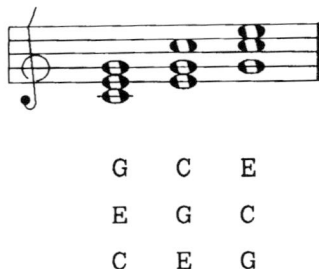

G	C	E
E	G	C
C	E	G

Figure 4.6 Chord inversion

into complex concepts. In his version ideas are like pitches: we all employ the same musical lexicon, and musical thinking is merely the concatenation of pitches according to a rudimentary probabilistic mechanics – the art of combinations and permutations. Simple ideas consist of single pitches, as well as pitches in relation, since it is the scale 'out of which all variety of harmony and melody is derived'.[53] Complex ideas consist of larger levels of structure, starting with the formation of chords, whereby the notes may 'counterchange' their situations by means of the combinatorial procedure we now call 'chord inversion' (Figure 4.6).

In the knowing processes just described, the imagination plays a major role, for it serves to represent the images received from the external senses, to bring the images back into consciousness from memory in the absence of the sensed object, and to combine the images in order to yield new ideas. In each of these roles the imagination provides images for the mind to read. Nature, therefore, is a visible language, for it can be seen by the mind. But to exist as a sign, nature must be interpreted. In North's account, reading involves interpreting, for although sense data are necessary for knowledge in that they form the raw material in which the knowing power exercises itself, North's emphasis is on the way the sense material is handled and articulated, for he detailed how the mind follows certain patterns in action. Forms are automatically imposed on sense input by the person receiving, thus enabling the knowing subject to order reality.

The forms imposed are judgments, for they concern relations between things. Indeed, counting, comparing and combining all involve different kinds of relation. The tendency to perform judgments is active from the first moment of contact between people and their environment. But the criteria of such judgments derive from our ability to feel pleasure and pain, because nature constituted all creatures with an instinctive attraction toward those things which promote their own well-being and a complementary aversion toward their opposites.[54] North's theory of pleasure, therefore, is a conscious-quality theory, for 'tho life is a burthen from bodily defects, yet moderate sensations, simply considered are pleasure; becaus they give a consciousness of our being, which is better then not to be'.[55] But his theory also is motivational, for pleasure is analysed in terms of realisation of the good – the object of striving.

Because people have a universal tendency, which is the mind's aspiring to omnipotency, that which we most seek is relief from ignorance. Hence, 'every item of knowledg gained, is so much ground in the way of the soul's impetuous tendency, and therefore cannot but be pleasing'.[56] By knowledge, North signified 'whatever is plainely exposed to the soul to be understood'; by ignorance, whatever induces 'doubdt, upon doubdt'.[57] The former is pleasant; the latter, painful. The opposite of knowledge occasions a desire in us to clear the doubts, uncertainties or confusions. If this desire is ungratified, we are in pain. But even pain can lead to pleasure, for 'it must be granted, as eas is often purchast with labour, which by contrariety setts it off, so by doubdt ther[e] is a way of knowledg, which makes study, that of it self is painefull, a most aggreable pastime to such as are used thereout to gaine knowledge'.[58]

On this view, the affections and passions of the mind can be defined in terms of endeavour. Experience alone brings on endeavour,[59] because the foetus brings 'onely the instruments of motion, a little determined by instinct'.[60] Before people can compose and govern their own 'economy', therefore, they must acquire self-knowledge, the first beginnings of which are in infancy, when we become acquainted with our own members through a process of 'experiments'. But North did not suggest by this term 'a process so firme, as our experiments of things are, who have strength of attention, reflexion, and designe; but weak in the same degree as children are, whose ideas are weak, and [whose] will [is] scarce awake...[so that] the more children are tost[,] danc't and playd with, the faster they come on, and have more knowledg and spirits. For all that to them is a sort of travell over their owne microcosm.'[61]

In this way the child develops strength, which is the learner's ability to exercise tension against resistance and, thus, to discriminate between different degrees of resistance. We now call this discrimination 'kinaesthesis', which is an intrinsic endowment that consists of various states of tension or contraction of the muscles. By this endowment the learner acquires knowledge of the consistence of bodies – their degrees of hardness and softness – and, hence, of the world 'out there'. But this kind of learning is not restricted to children, for it is the basis of all learning, even adult learning, for 'men growne up...have no other principle whereby to distinguish one member or part of their bodys from another, but onely the memory of the various sensations peculiar to them'.[62] Hence, because 'wee have not power to move any member or part to the porposes of life or arts, but by slow degrees and tryalls...all that wee doe in life, is acquired, as musick is'.[63]

If knowledge is entirely empirical, the truth of what people apprehend depends upon external impressions of a sufficiently clear and distinct kind. But people are prone to err, and there are two principal sources of error. One source is from the mind itself as subjective delusions occasioned by disorders in the body.[64] The other source is from excited inference, since our 'sences, or imagination doth not deceiv us, but our hasty and immature unweighed conclusions from them are so fallacious that we have scar[c]e a just opinion of any thing without us'.[65] Hence, judgments made in response to our environment provide us with an understanding of what is only apparently good and apparently evil. What, then, are the criteria for judging what is really good and really evil? According to North, the basis of moral choice is a causal understanding of events and the consequences which follow from them.

By causal understanding, North signified analysis ('resolution'), according to which simple motions or forces are imagined which, when logically compounded, provide a causal explanation of complex phenomena. What, for example, makes a person tick? One cannot find the answers as a watch repairer can do, by taking the watch apart. But one can take a person apart in imagination, that is, hypothetically. In so doing, the power of human understanding 'is magnifyed, and proved by algebra', which is like the watch repairer's art — a taking apart in order to show the pieces, for it is 'a method of working a proposition, without ideas of the subject matter', wherein 'the demonstration and the method of working it, is rather, as the word imports, a shewing things in peices, like explaining a watch, then proving'.[66] Analysis, therefore, is an exercise of the imagination, which should lead to a precise set of mathematical rules.[67]

2. Animating principle

> Music...being natural unto Mankind,
> Not to be animal Musicum,
> is not to be animal rationale.
> Butler, *The Principles of Musik* (120)

2.1. As the composer

In North's interpretation of body in motion, there are two kinds of cause: primary and secondary. When, for example, he wrote of 'mechanicall causes of all agencys that usually affect us by means of hearing',[68] North denoted secondary causes ('occasions'), for he observed: 'As to the operations of the mind, I look upon the action of things sensible to be occasions onely, and not causes of those ideas that are framed in the imagination'.[69] Since an account of nature based on secondary causality leaves us in the realm of what is only apparently good and apparently evil, recourse must be had to primary causality to understand what is really good and really evil. North's conception of primary causality is a cosmic one, for he adopted a thoroughgoing monism, in which the basis of nature is a subtle ether, which North also called 'the spirit of the world'.[70]

When considering people, North's spirit is not to be confused with the animal spirits of the physiologists, for he stated that the physician, Thomas Willis, 'and others that use the terme, animal spirits, seem to intend the same as I doe, but yet I subtileize more'.[71] Nor is his spirit to be confused with the vital ('natural') spirits of the body, the fluids that flow through vessels ('veins, arteries, vessells of milk, limpha &c.'). Blood, for example, a 'hott spiritous and fermenting juice', is one of the natural spirits that functions, like other natural spirits, as 'agents' which activate the solids to spring or to function in a 'peristaltick way'.[72] To perform their work, however, natural spirits must become 'airy', that is, lively; and the source of life and, hence, of motion is the penetrating cosmic spirit.

Like the ether of Hobbes and Hooke, North's cosmic spirit is a very tenuous, invisible, elastic medium extended throughout the universe, for

> Body is extended, and of that nature no one is more perfect then another, but the least have the same pretensions as the greatest; but if we would consider the perfection of that nature [body], it consists in extension or space in infinitum, as philosofers now hold: and the other nature[,] spirit[,] which consists in power, may be all alike as to essence [i.e., extended in space], yet [the]...advances are in power and the perfection is in the Almighty.[73]

The assumption of spirit's extreme tenuity is in strict accordance with North's hypothesis that spirit is omnipresent not only within body but also within the apparent emptiness of the space between bodies. As the active principle of matter, spirit functions 'like a spark firing the powder in a mine: it is not the spark that heaves the bastion, but some other mechanicall power derived from the latent energie of matter at large in the world. And if the globe of earth were of like composition as gunpowder is, it were the same thing.'[74]

To release the latent energy of body, spirit works 'just at the incoation of the power of body, and then in the way of explosion is disperst over the whole, by the machination of the organs and parts of it.'[75] In this way energy is released as a compressional wave, and it is this that 'heaves the bastion'. Indeed, North himself adopted the name 'comprest' wave, which, like sound waves, can be transmitted through fluids (liquids and gases). Moreover, like the energy we call 'sound', so too 'in almost all naturall energyes, every scruple of change, (substantiall or circumstantiall,) in the cause, by a due attention will be found corresponde[nt] in the effect'.[76] This is Hooke's Law: as the extension, so the force.

In humans, firing takes place in the cerebellum, from whence energy is released, since

> In the fabrick of humane body there is certeinly a comune sensorium, or a concentration of all the organized mechanicall powers of it, or where every movement of every part hath corrispondent action, tho in minutenes[s] actually infinite: this sensorium hath bin guessed but never found; it is not the heart, brain, nor glandula pinealis; but most probably somewhere about the brain, because all the radiations of sensible power are found to derive from that part; nor can it ever be discovered, becaus it is so small, or rather a mathematical point.[77]

But body is not merely a passive recipient: it actively and vitally collaborates with spirit in that it undergoes certain dispositions. Indeed, like the bodies we call 'nitre', 'sulphur' and 'charcoal', so, too human bodies, from 'very insensible touches', are made 'to move an immense weight, whereof the opperations are manifestly mechanick in all respects but the occasion, which is lodged like a spark of steel till it exerts itself, and produceth a spacious effect'.[78] Body's potential, then, is made actual by spirit.

In addition to creating life and motion, spirit regulates the world by pneumatic action, for its component particles endeavour to press inward from the surfaces of ordinary bodies or to press outward from the interspaces of those bodies. By means of these two opposing tendencies, spirit maintains ordinary bodies in a dynamic state of equilibrium or 'posture of rest'.[79] But equilibrium conceals an internal dynamic tension of competing forces or 'ballance of impulses', so that apparent rest is thoroughly kinetic. Thus, when ordinary bodies are displaced from their positions of equilibrium by some additional force, the particles of spirit behave like the restoring forces acting on a bent spring, musical string or oscillating pendulum.

By these same pneumatic actions, spirit mediates between the properties of external objects and the consciousness of the perceiving mind. In North's account of the knowing process, every stimulus from the outside is conducted from the specific sense organ excited by it to a central processing unit which coordinates the various impressions, elevates them into consciousness and then releases the impulse reacting to the sensation. The mind 'gives the inception that occasions the whole to work with its proper forces; and the externall incidents of the body, or sense, administers objects to affect the soul, and so returnes are reciprocally made'.[80] The vital function of the central processing unit, unifying all the activities of body and maintaining and regulating its contact with the external world, clearly defines a dual direction of communication. But it is only through the incessant movement of spirit that this two-way communication is established.

2.2. As the musical score

To prove the universal law of causality, it is necessary to look for observational sources of evidence. North relied on inferences based on signs and events in his physical surroundings. Since, in his philosophy, modifications of spirit take place in body as modifications of tension or 'tone', nerves and muscles may be either tense or relaxed, just as the mind may be 'nerved up' or 'enervated'.[81] The effects of tonicity and flaccidity, therefore, are visible not only in objects such as pendulums, springs and musical strings but also in the external movements of the human body, including expressions on the face. Hence, internal movements result in an 'air' or external sign, for example, of a particular passion or affection of the mind. Although the word 'air' here means external manner, appearance or mien, it is the result of an internal character: a tense or relaxed spirit.

North's theory of air as a unity of internal and external character derived from and informed his theory of musical ayre. In the several writings expounding this theory, the term 'ayre' is an omnibus word. It may mean melody, song or tune; but this usage is rare. More often, it may mean the tonality ('complexion'), the mode ('character'), major or minor, or the various tempi ('manners'), slow to fast, of a piece of music. The term 'ayre' also may signify 'common measure', the harmonic rhythm that maintains the interaction (sympathy) between the different parts (melody and harmony) of a composition. In this usage ayre is analogous to the pneumatic action of spirit, because harmonic rhythm 'runs thro the whole work and, like the soul, animates the mass, which would be dead without it'.[82]

North, however, wrote three theories of music, in the first of which he did not make a consistent distinction between these various uses.[83] In the second theory he developed his conception within the confines of a separate treatise, in which he explicitly stated that 'time' represents actions and melody, thoughts and affections, the two aspects together symbolising the whole personality – the actions of the body as well as the passions and affections of the mind.[84] But he also used the term 'ayre' to refer to a composer's spirit – his 'wit' or 'anima', which becomes manifest as musical style or excellence of expression.[85] In the third and final theory North presented his most fully developed conception of musical ayre in conjunction with a history of music, in which he argued that music is the invention of humans and a representation of their changing history and habits.[86] Through music, therefore, we may read the score called 'human nature'.

II. THE UNMUSICAL MAN

Every foolish man is mad.
Cicero, *Paradoxa Stoicorum* (4.27)

Introduction
In the tradition of musical ethos, the cultivated man is the musical man, one who is harmonious – consistent or coherent – not only within himself but also with the rest of nature. The obverse, the uncultivated man, is unmusical, because disharmonious. In the seventeenth century writers identified two kinds of unmusical men – those who are so because of defects of constitution, and those who are so because of defects of character. The first type is the demented man or man without reason, a state which may occur at birth or develop later through habit, illness or injury. The second type is the overly passionate man, who, although he has the power of reason, fails to use it to regulate his conduct. In the context of the exercise of tension, we may say that a man with a defect of constitution is distempered, whereas a man with a defect in character is untempered.

According to Hobbes, an understanding of each of these requires consideration of the strength of materials and the motions he called 'passions', for by these we may discover the differences between one individual and another at any given time.[87] For example, he pointed out that 'we observe our own body, and find that by the indisposition of the eyes, the brain, the nerves, and the heart, that is, by obstructions, stupidity, and debility, we are deprived of light [i.e., intelligence], so that a fitting disposition of the organs to receive impressions from without is likewise a necessary part of the cause of light'.[88] But he supposed that defects of constitution, as well as of character, arose chiefly from passions that are contrary to nature and, thus, to reason.

Hobbes identified three types of passions that are contrary to nature – weak, indifferent and excessive passions, for 'to have weak Passions, is Dulnesse; and to have Passions indifferently for every thing, GIDDINESSE, and *Distraction*; and to have stronger, and more vehement Passions for any thing, than is ordinarily seen in others, is that which men call MADNESSE'.[89] If we recur to his taut-string model, we may understand weak and excessive passions as too little or too much tone. In the case of too little tone, or hypotonicity, the self will be slack and motion, sluggish. That this is Hobbes's meaning is clear from his definition of 'DULNESSE, *Stupidity*' and the like, the names of which 'signifie slownesse of motion, or difficulty to be moved'.[90] Hence, in the case of too much tone, or hypertonicity, the self will be so highly strung and motion, so agitated, as to produce madmen.[91] But what about indifferent passions? How are these to be understood? Since Hobbes defined indifferent passions as distraction – a divided mind, we may conjecture that his model was a false string (Figure 4.7).[92]

In 1694 William Holder provided a brief description of false strings in his summary account of the work on musical sounds from the time of Galileo and Mersenne up to and including Hooke and Francis North. According to Holder, a false string is thicker in one part of its length than in another. When set vibrating, the thicker part vibrates more slowly and, hence, sounds lower, whereas the more slender part vibrates more swiftly and, hence, sounds more acute. Thus,

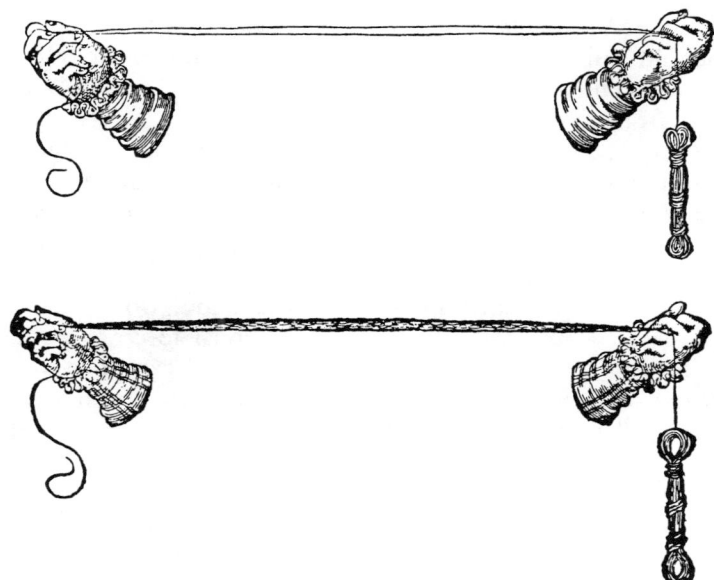

Figure 4.7 True and false strings, from M. Mersenne, *Harmonie universelle* (Paris, 1636-37)

> ...whilst two Sounds so near one another, are at once made upon the same String, they make a rough discording Jarr, being a hoarse Tune mixed of both, more or less, as the String is more or less unequal: And if the thicker Part be next the Frets [on a viol or lute], then the Fret...will render the Tune of the Note too sharp; and the contrary, if the slender Part of the String be next the Frets; because in the former, the thicker Part is stopped, and the thinner sounds more of the acuter Part of this unhappy Mixture: As in the later, the thicker Part is left to sound the graver Tune, and thus the Fret will give a wrong Tune, though the Fault be not in the Fret, but in the String....[93]

But Holder went farther, for he speculated that since nerves were made of small fibres, like lute strings, they too might be false. In such a case, nerves would not be fitted to correspond with commensurate impressions and motions. The same might be true of harder parts of the body, since a glass bell, when regularly framed, will tremble and 'echo' its own tone when struck, but when irregularly framed, the tone will be uncertain. Holder, however, raised these matters merely 'by the by; and only for a Hint of Enquiry'.[94]

Holder's conception of the nerves as fibres that vibrate was uncommon in the seventeenth century, when the prevailing consensus, deriving from antiquity, was that nerves as well as muscles were hollow.[95] Both Descartes and Gassendi had explained neuro-muscular function as a dilation of nerve and muscle caused by the flow of animal spirits from the brain. Both men also supposed that the muscle required additional force to perform its function. To account for this, Descartes had explained muscle inflation by recourse to quantity: the muscles, which contain spirits, inflate because of the in-flow of additional spirits. But afterwards he adopted Gassendi's explanation of muscle inflation by recourse to quality: when the animal spirits flow into the already full muscle, there is a chemical reaction or 'shooting out' which provides the added force, allowing the muscle to contract.[96]

3. Disorganised body

> ...*all pipes or wind-instruments have a blast, as well as a sound.*
> Bacon, Sylva sylvarum (9: 72)

3.1. As flatus

In the second half of the seventeenth century, the mechanical philosopher and physician, Thomas Willis, became one of the most important exponents of the inflation theory.[97] Like the two earlier philosophers, Willis adopted a dualist metaphysic, for he imagined that sentient beings had two souls, a rational soul, which is incorporeal, and a sensitive soul, which is corporeal. But he added that the sensitive soul is itself twofold, consisting of vital (flamy) spirits, enkindled in the blood, and animal (airy) spirits, distilled from the blood in the cerebral and cerebellar cortex. He then localised all function, voluntary and involuntary, in different parts of the brain, the voluntary in the cerebrum and the involuntary in the cerebellum.[98] But the instrument of these instruments is the animal spirits, because they are the 'immediate organ' of neuro-muscular function.

Although indiscernible, Willis regarded spirits as real, impenetrable particles of matter, a 'sufficient stock' of which, flowing from the brain into the nerves and muscles, 'actuates all these passages, and blows them up into a certain Tensity'.[99] Muscular motion depends further upon a constant influx not only of animal spirits but also of blood, for the former alone, without being associated with the latter, cannot perform muscular motion. This performance takes place in the following manner. In contraction the animal spirits 'shoot out' of the tendons into the fleshy parts of the muscle, whereas in relaxation they 'shoot back' from the fleshy parts into the tendons. The initial shooting, which inflates the muscle, is caused by a 'conflict', or chemical reaction, between the saline-spiritous particles of the animal spirits and the nitro-sulfurous particles enkindled in the arterial blood. But the shooting back of the spirits from the fleshy fibres to the tendons is not a chemical but a mechanical reaction (recoil).[100]

As long as the animal spirits are alone and their passage is unhindered, the sensitive soul will remain quiescent in its 'Natural State or Condition'. But when the spirits enter into a chemical process, the sensitive soul, moving from its 'wonted' state, exhibits two 'Chief and Primary Gestures': 'to wit, either she stretches forth her self into a greater Compass, by profuse Pleasure, as if it affected to be dilated beyond the bounds of the Body: or being overthrown by Sorrow or Grief, she is contracted more narrowly, and runs herself within the wonted Sphear of her Emanations: from this twofold Affection of the Sensitive Soul, all the other Passions take their Origine'.[101] Because all internal structures are 'tubulated',[102] dilation and contraction results from the quantity and quality of the inflowing spirits. For example, when the nervous system supplies spirits of too heterogeneous a nature, muscle contraction (a tightening) will be too powerful and uncontrolled, resulting in an extension of the sensitive soul 'beyond its measure'. But when too few spirits are supplied by the nerves, the result will be weak contractions (a loosening) and, hence, a depression of the sensitive soul.[103]

Willis's dualism committed him to a description that separates container ('mediate' instrument) from contained ('immediate' instrument). There are a number of containers; and these include, from inside out, the fluids in which the vital and animal spirits float, the tubulated membranes through which the fluids flow and the external covering housing these. But Willis's medical philosophy is reducible to the spirits and, particularly, the animal spirits, for these ultimate elements constitute the '*Hypostasis*' or essence of the sensitive soul.[104] In treating the sensitive soul in health, Willis sometimes wrote of the animal spirits, as of other bodily instruments, in military terms. This metaphor enabled him to combine mechanical and chemical readings of internal character, as well as to retain a separation between structure and function. For example, he wrote that 'certain Machines or Braces, like to a Drum of War, are appointed for the Drum of the Ear'; but for the drum to function, the muscles ('Braces') that control the drum stick ('Hammer') must be 'actuated', that is, inflated. When that happens, the tendons shorten, causing the drum stick to rise, thereby making tense the drum membrane. In this way the drum fulfils its function, for it transmits 'Sonorific Particles' to the brain.[105]

According to Willis's military metaphor, the brain is like a command centre, the organs of the body are like 'regiments' and the animal spirits, like 'soldiers'.[106] When contiguous one with another, the soldiers are 'like an Army in Array; for they after a Military fashion, whilst they move not from their station, and keep Order, perform their Offices; and whether they be set in Battel Array, or on the Watch, they perform the Commands carried outward from the Brain, themselves being almost immoveable, and effect Motion, and deliver presently to the Brain the news of any sensible thing Impressed, whereby Sensation is made'.[107] For Willis, the temper we call 'health' arises from the structure of the regiments (e.g., a cracked or a normal 'globular' brain), from the quantity and quality of the soldiers and from the sympathy (consent) between the two. If one or more of these aspects is hindered, the soldiers cannot fight, and the war machine collapses.

Although Willis adumbrated a doctrine of sympathy, he did

not interpret collapse as destruction of a structure when it is required to store excessive energy. You will recall that this happens when the rhythm of a vibrator coincides with the resonator's natural frequency of vibration, so that the resonator's movements become too much for its strength and it collapses. Willis, however, could not resort to resonance as a means of explaining collapse, because his doctrine of sympathy is a mixture theory, according to which each individual has a peculiar 'natural Instinct', that is, 'Idiocrasie' or temperament.[108] Sympathy, therefore, is defined as an *'agreement in qualities'*,[109] and it is this that determines the gestures of the sensitive soul. For example, if the mixture of spirits in the muscle is congruous, the reaction will produce loosening and tightening within the measure that constitutes health; but if the mixture is incongruous, the result is disease.

To account for incongruous mixtures, Willis would have to posit additional chemical processes. And this is just what he did when he described diseases of the brain and nervous 'stock', including various 'sleepy' diseases, palsy, apoplexy, delirium, phrensy, melancholy, madness, stupidity (dullness), foolishness, gout and colic.[110] These different diseases are abnormal manifestations of the two passions of the sensitive soul, elation and depression. In both cases, however, the 'formal reason' or 'conjunct cause' resides in the quality of the animal spirits, since 'morbific matter', like 'mines' and 'incentives', may act as catalysts, thereby accelerating or retarding the chemical reactions in the body.[111] Hence, instead of a shooting there will be a 'blasting' or a lack of blast, because the spirits' '*Copula*'s have divers sorts of adjuncts, some of which induce an *Elastick* and very *explosive* virtue, as in the Convulsive Distempers, and others a Stupor, numness [sic], or immobility, as in the sleepy diseases, and also in the *Apoplexy* and *Palsie*'.[112]

Various commentators have supposed that the chemical reaction between the arterial blood and animal spirits produces an expansive force like the explosion of gunpowder.[113] These commentators notwithstanding, by the term, 'explosive', Willis denoted flatulence, for when the blood contributes its activating ingredient, the spirits become 'highly flatuous and apt to be rarified', so that the chemical process in the muscle is a 'letting off' like breaking wind.[114] But when the letting off is beyond the normal 'Instincts of wind', the spirits 'break forth into Meteors, *viz.* Winds, Hurricanes, and horrid Thunder'.[115] Because the muscle inflates beyond measure, the spirits, which recoil from the fleshy fibres to the tendons, strike each other beyond measure. But it is the force of these instantaneous impacts, and not the wind, that triggers the changes in the layers of containers, as, for example, boiling or whirling motions of the fluids, corrugations or wrinklings of the tubes and convulsive motions of the arms and legs.[116]

3.2. As ructus

In Willis's theory of inflation the model is a mechanical machine, in which chemical energy is transferred directly into work. Against this model, Hobbes, Hooke and North used a thermodynamic machine, in which chemical energy passes through an intermediate stage of heat. We may conclude, therefore, that the mechanical philosophers focused on the generation of energy to run the machine rather than to integrate the activities of the organism.[117] Willis continued this focus, for he conceived the war machine as a collection of little machines so constructed as to provide a constant and perpetual wind. The source of this energy is a chemical process; but the 'Energie or the Act of the [sensitive] Soul it self, from which every Function of the animated Body primarily and chiefly arises', is wind.[118] This approach, of course, did not cease with Willis. Indeed, when Roger North came to write *Notes of Me*, he recurred to Willis's theory to describe, ironically, one of his own illnesses.[119]

The diagnosis of the attending physician, John Masters, was acute fever, but North believed his greatest difficulty was a pain in the stomach. Consequently, he had 'a disposition perpetually to eruct': 'This I strove so much in when I was alone, thinking if I could raise the wind (*as it seemed to be*) I should be well. And by a perpetual striving to eruct, I have fixed on myself an eructation, which is but a convulsion of the aesophagus, which I shall never quite wear off, and was plainly at first derived from this error of conduct; but it grows less, and I hope will become inconsiderable or nothing.'[120] You will have noticed North's aside — that the wind 'seemed to be'. He afterwards elaborated on this, when he pointed out:

> It is with many as I found it to be with me, that a disorder or convulsive motion of the fibres of the stomach, or mouth of it, is believed to be wind, and medicines go accordingly, as ginger and warm drugs; whereas *it is not so*, but plain convulsion. In my sickness, when the fever began to wear off, in sleeping *I had an image of thought*, as if a small point or seed within me grew and swelled as if it would have blown me up. This came two or three times, and was great pain, and caused the doctor to be sent for, who with a cordial kept down the evil.

In this description North highlights his own folly, which is contrary to reason and which, in this instance, derives from a (temporarily) darkened imagination, for whilst he was ill, he conceived that his 'general convulsion of the stomach' could be explained in Willisian terms by ferments (seeds), intumification and 'want of spirits or good order of them'. But regaining health, he once again recognised that 'these sick images are strange things, and few that are sick observe them, but think the reality is according to their sense'.[121] To appreciate North's irony, however, we need to know three things. First, the attending physician, Masters, was a pupil and associate of Willis.[122] Second, Willis had been physician to North's sister-in-law before her marriage and continued in this role afterwards, so that he and North were acquainted.[123] Third and finally, North had constructed a theory of inflation different to that of Willis. Since he supposed that the larynx and some other parts in humans function like wind instruments, let us return to his example of the tube trumpet mentioned at the outset of this chapter.[124]

The tube trumpet has no finger holes, so that changes in pitch are determined by variations in the tension of the player's lips. The trumpeter's lips are the source of energy, but the variations in their tension determine the degree of 'blast' — the power or rate of energy expenditure. When a blast from the trumpeter's lips excites vibrations of the column of air in the tube, at any instant the air will possess both kinetic energy of motion and potential energy of displacement or deformation. But for the air's vibrations to continue, there must be a continual source of excitation, because the 'spring' of air in the tube, being more rapid than that of wire springs, stops sooner. Hence, North was careful to consider 'the action, as it must be derived from the lipps, and continued to the vent at the orifice, from whence the sound seems to proceed'.[125]

According to North's account, sound is first created by 'eruptions' of the air from the lips:

> ...the air in the tube cannot give way to the eruption from the lipps all at once, therefore there must be a compression, the wave of which passeth along, and vents at the orifice, and the air within the tube being distended returns back to the mouth peice, and there compressing[,] stopps the eruption succeding and as the nature of spring is, dilates againe towards the orifice, and at that instan[t] a distension next the lipps, lets goes another eruption; and so alternatim by equall times; the air of the tube at the lipps, distending and compressing governes the eruptions, which a compressure stopps, and the distention letts goe; and so pulses continue by equall times, as the quantity of air in the tube qualifyes its spring.[126]

When there is a 'conformity' between the action of the lips and the air in the tube, the waves follow each other 'with perpetuall addition of force from the lipps...as a great bell raised with (comparatively) a little force'.[127]

By 'conformity' North denoted the reinforcement or prolongation of sound by synchronous vibrations. We now call this reinforcement by the name 'resonance'. Since the inflation theory of the mechanical philosophers ignored vibratory resonance, it is not surprising that North put their theory, in both its Cartesian and Gassendian versions, to the test of criticism. According to him, 'the vanity of the present anatomick philosophy concerning muscular motion' consists in two things: (1) 'of their making an expedition of animall spirits from the braine to the energitick muscle, and back again upon every movement of a member'; and (2) 'of the explosion and consequently swelling of the muscular spirits or humours, whereby the tendons are drawne'.[128] Such a theory was 'improbable', because it assumed two things: that the nerves were hollow pipes and, therefore, as turgid as muscles; and that the muscles enlarged in quantity when working. Both assumptions were demonstrably false ('never found'); for nerves are not hollow pipes, and muscles exhibit 'onely an action of shrinking which rather contracts then enlargeth the space'.

The Gassendian version of the inflation theory exhibited additional problems, according to North, for it failed to clarify whether shooting took place in the muscle only or was 'devided from the brain'. If the former, 'what principle is it that walks about the body to give fire on all occasions?'. If the latter, either the nervous system must ascend to the muscle or 'emissarys' must pass. In North's theory firing takes place only in the cerebellum. There, a spark functions like the trumpeter's lips as a source of excitation, raising compressional waves that enable the body to perform its work. North, however, did not dwell on this point; rather, he singled out a principal weakness in the inflation theory of the mechanical philosophers, when he asserted that even if its principal tenet was granted, muscle inflation would require such a strong 'blast' that 'work' would have more advantage than 'power', 'which is not to be imagined', since 'there is need to throw all the advantage on the side of the power opposite to the weight'.

Here is North's most telling criticism, for power (muscular strength) is the ability to exercise tension against resistance (weight). In the performance of this exercise, 'the whole body is at work, head, hands, shoulders, etc. all in alternate action assistant to the main course'.[129] This is so, because 'the positive force of a muscle, is like that of a spring allwais bent which is opposed by some other like in opposition to it, and if any one yeilds the other draws, and è contra'.[130] From North's premiss two things follow: first, 'that the movement of the parts are not by inspiring the muscle that seems to work, but by enervating the antagonistick'; and second, 'that upon generall motions of the body, the muscles draw, and remitt alternately, and the whole body, and not onely the members im[m]ediately concerned, move to maintain the alternative of force generally thro out the whole'.[131]

4. Elastic limit

> *The motion upon pressure and its reciprocal viz. motion upon tension, we call motion of liberty....*
> Bacon, Sylva sylvarum (8: 279)

4.1. The scale

In his pathology Willis provided a general character of the madman as a person who possesses abnormal strength.[132] But he did not supply case studies of the mad, as he did in treating other passions that were contrary to nature. Instead, he suggested that the reader 'go to the *Hospitals* of mad people, where they may behold, not without a wonderful spectacle, as it were a new and monstrous nation of men, contrary to rational people, and as it were our *Antipodes*; all which, if they were gathered together in one place, and that all, Madmen and Fools[,] were joyned to them; I know not whether this world would not be equally divided between them and the sober and prudent'.[133] At issue here is the question of persistent identity: what sort of animal is man, as a species? The traditional answer, transmitted through textbooks on logic, was that reason is an essential attribute of man.[134] The mechanical philosophers continued this tradition of essentialism. But Hobbes, Hooke and North took a different position, for they held that reason is only an accidental attribute, which man may acquire through education and study but which man is always capable of losing.[135]

There are many ways of losing temporarily or permanently this accidental attribute called 'reason'. One way is through illness, which North believed could darken the intellect by presenting distorted images to the mind, as he showed us in the case of his own folly. The implication is that health is a condition for the development of reason – a life lived in harmony with nature. Since North conceived life as a springy force field, the condition for strength of mind and vigour of body is a moment-to-moment exercise of tension against resistance, in which the springy force field neither contracts too much nor expands too much. But since

The Daimon Within

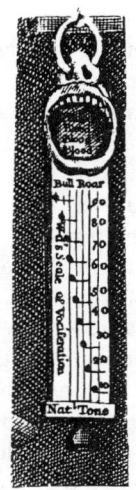

Figure 4.8 Scale of degrees of tension, detail from W. Hogarth, *Credulity, Superstition and Fanaticism* (London, 1762)

it cannot contract without drawing equally at both ends or expand without pushing equally at both ends, there is a danger, as Hobbes had intimated, when he wrote: 'equal powers opposed destroy one another'.[136] Hence, there will be a limited scale of tensions in health, just as there is a limited scale of tones in music.

In both cases, health and music, the scale will consist of different frequencies of periodic vibrations, and the limits of the scale will be determined by the nature of the instruments, or particular combinations of acoustic vibrators and resonators, some of which will be more, others less resilient. When the scale is exceeded on the minus side, there will be too little tension, or dullness.[137] As the degrees of tension rise, so too does power, considered as rates of energy expenditure. As the scale continues beyond measure, our complex internal tensions will consist of a mixture of a very large number of frequences. When this happens, a person may become a fast-moving projectile, as, for example, by shooting out the arm in anger or by flinging about the entire body in an epileptic fit. Sometimes, too, these movements may be accompanied by sudden, sharp noises – crepitations, roars, screeches, and the like (Figure 4.8).

From his very first treatise on music, North recognised that unmusical sounds were different in degree, rather than in kind, from musical sounds. But he paid particular attention to two very 'egregious' noises. These noises were explosions triggered when glass drops are broken or when gunpowder is fired.[138] Although glass drops were first introduced to the Royal Society on 4 March 1660/1,[139] this phenomenon had already occupied a number of European researchers, who had shown that the head of a glass drop withstands hammering on an anvil without fracture, whereas if the tail is broken with the mere pressure of a finger, the whole explodes with a loud crack into a powder. How was this phenomenon to be explained?

In 1662 Hobbes provided a probable explanation by analogy to a crossbow.[140] The sum of his argument may be stated as follows. Until the bow is strung, the string lies slack. As the bow is bent, its 'spring' or elastic force is felt. When the string is fitted to the bow, it then bears the elastic force and acquires tension. If the bow remains in a bent state for a long time, it loses its spring or 'endeavour of restitution to its former posture'. But if we take a new bow, one that has not yet lost its endeavour of restitution, and if we fit a string to this bow and then set it at liberty by cutting or by suddenly breaking the string, there will be a very visible motion – indeed, the bow may break into 'shivers'. Glass drops are similar, according to Hobbes, for when the tail of a glass drop is unbent, all its many threads will be 'shivered in pieces' like so many little crossbows. For Hobbes, therefore, the terms 'spring' and 'endeavour of restitution' are synonymous and denote 'a principle or beginning of motion in a contrary way' to that of the force which bent the glass drop or the crossbow.[141]

In 1665 Hobbes's 'solution of continuity' was improved upon by Hooke, who identified the source of stress as thermal contraction on cooling, for he grasped the principle that molten glass in cooling changes in a narrow temperature range from a viscous fluid to a hard elastic solid.[142] The outer layers of the drop harden first, forming a rigid enclosure of relatively unchanging volume within which the still hot interior glass endeavours to contract as it cools, thereby bringing the outer layers into a state of compression, balanced against high tensile stresses in the interior. If the tail is broken, thus exposing the tensile core, a disintegration front propagates in both directions from that point with a speed similar to that of transverse sound waves in glass, leaving behind it a pattern of multiple fractures that divide the material into needle-like splinters.

This coupled wave of stress change and fracture bears an analogy to a detonation wave in an explosive, in which a stress wave triggers (in that case chiefly by its thermal effect) the release of chemical energy that reinforces and sustains it. If explosive behaviour is compared to exterior ballistics, then we need to know something about interior ballistics and, particularly, gunpowder, which, in *Body*, Hobbes had described as a compound of nitre, brimstone and coals, beaten small.[143] To fire this latent energy, a flint is struck, the spark falling on the powder. Because the coals take fire, the powder's explosive power is released, and this in turn activates the motions of heat ('nourishment') and light ('flame') from the brimstone and, subsequently, of sound ('vehemence') from the nitre.

But Hobbes also pointed out that if, before beating it, the nitre is laid upon a burning coal, a sequence of events takes place: it melts and, like water, quenches the part of the coal it touches; then, 'vapour or air' flies out where the coal and nitre join. But the crucial part of the sequence occurs when the vapour

> ...bloweth the coal with great swiftness and vehemence on all sides. And from thence it comes to pass, that by two contrary motions, the one, of the particles which go out of the burning coal, the other, of those of the ethereal and watery substance of the nitre, is generated that vehement motion and inflammation. And lastly, when there is no more action from the nitre, that is to say, when the volatile parts of the nitre are flown out, there is found about the sides a certain white substance, which being thrown again into the fire, will grow red-hot again, but will not be dissipated, at least unless the fire be augmented.

In this passage we have a short description of the chemical transformation that takes place during burning: the combustible material catches fire, and the attendant flame is a source of heat, light and sound. When the fire is extinguished, the burned material is utterly changed in appearance – most notably, it no longer is combustible. Not long after Hobbes published this description, Hooke formed his notion that a nitrous component in the air was an essential agent in combustion and respiration; his subsequent investigations into gunpowder and explosions helped to reinforce this notion, as a number of commentators point out.[144]

For North, however, the two kinds of explosions reinforced a different notion, namely, that when an elastic body becomes too tense or too compressed, an abrupt change will take place, and springiness will give way to permanent deformation – to the empty negativity of non-elasticity. We now call the point at which the abrupt change takes place 'the elastic limit'. This concept did not develop until the nineteenth century, according to E. Williams, who conjectures that 'the main hindrance to fixing a limit of elasticity lay in the very real difficulty in conceiving the idea of a hard and fast line of demarcation in qualitative change', so that 'it may well have been that the change-over was thought of as a gradual one, allowing of no possibility for fixing a sharp, let alone constant, line of demarcation'.[145]

North, however, did recognise that a limit to springiness existed, because he understood elasticity as a process working toward qualitative change. When this process is internalised as the *daimon* within, it becomes a controlling metaphor for the life of an individual person. To illustrate how this is possible, I shall draw upon North's treatment of the distempers and death of three of his brothers, one of whom is the doctor, another, the knight, and a third, his lordship. These epithets refer, respectively, to Dr. John North, a clergyman, who was master of Trinity College, Cambridge (1677); Sir Dudley North, a merchant, who was sheriff of London (1682); and Francis North, first Baron Guilford, a lawyer, who was Keeper of the Great Seal (1682). In what follows, however, I have been guided by North's assessment of each brother's 'natural temper and propensities, such as of one kind or other all men living have, and which came into the world with them, and are in their power to alter no more than complexion or stature'.[146]

4.2. In expansions

In the life of Dr. John, we discover a 'vigorous and active spirit' quartered in a 'slight and feeble machine of flesh'.[147] His weak constitution gave rise to 'natural timidity', which led to a 'propense disposition to fear'; and this, in turn, had the worst effect 'upon his spirits when applied to the consequences of his life', for it 'not only sullied his character by making him seem avaricious, but even shortened his days'. From the very beginning, therefore, the ground is laid for a portrait of a man who is unmusical because of a defect of constitution. A little further on we learn that the doctor is actually unmusical, for he '*Attempted music upon the organ, but failed*'.[148] Unfortunately, the doctor made no advance in finding any 'favourite diversion or manual exercise to rest his mind a little, which he held bent with continual thinking'. Since, on North's theory, there can be no thinking without vibration, the doctor will be stressed over and over again, so that fatigue or weakness will ensue; and this could become serious enough to lead to ultimate fracture if the intensity of vibration is sufficiently great. To retain his sanity, therefore, the doctor had a struggle 'to curb excesses growing upon him'.[149]

One way to curb such excesses and, thus, to prevent fracture, is by a vibration damper, a device that either reduces the amplitude of the vibration or reduces the communication of vibration energy from the vibrator to its surrounds. That the doctor had a vibration damper is clear from his peculiar method of self-government ('*autarchia*'), in which he would use 'his friends as spies upon himself to discover his own failings, and for that end used to be very sharp upon the company, and if anyone that he might be free with had a sore place, he was sure to give it some rubs, and harder and harder till they must needs feel, and then they fell to retaliating, which was his desire'. The retaliatory friction of the doctor's friends, by which North usually means the brothers, is a damping device, for it reduces the vibratory energy that produces 'heats' which 'kindle and exasperate'.[150] But when the friends were not around to serve their purpose, the doctor's 'humour was to hold all within himself'.[151] Consequently, his 'mind was full and wanted a discharge, and that drew a weight upon his spirits'.[152]

Since deformation is an energy-storing process, the doctor's pent-up spirit is waiting to break out in an explosion, as Peter Millard rightly points out,[153] for this is precisely what happens, as North takes us through a sequence of the doctor's illnesses leading to his final collapse. The 'distemper came upon him by these steps': 'first a cold, then an unusual quantity of rheum discharged at his throat, and the tonsil glandules tumefied, and at length his uvula. And as the course of these colds is, a deal of spitting and venting of rheum at his mouth followed'.[154] This was nothing remarkable by itself, but it was made so by the physicians' remedies (as North remarks in an aside, 'I fear that in my report of this case I may offend the medical faculty').

Instead of sending the doctor home to his mother to be nursed, the physicians

> ...fell in pell-mell with their prescriptions to divert this flow of rheum from discharging at his throat and mouth, and to send it another way. But first the cause, as they said, must be removed, which was to be done by rectifying his digestions, that rheums might not breed so copiously, and then they might safely stop the vent. And in order to this, a circulatory course (as they called it) of physic was prescribed, enough to have purged a strong man from off his legs.

Inspite of the purging at one end, the rheums were never vented at the other, so that they once again began to flow, till at last, 'his body growing weaker, and his disease stronger, the humour, having no vent at his mouth as it naturally tended (for all those pores were closed), broke out in his brain, and threw him down all at once in a desperate apoplexy'.[155] Once again, the physicians were called for; and once again their regimen proved fruitless, for they assumed that if he fell asleep he would never wake again. Hence, they prescribed 'perpetual noise and clangour of one sort or other to keep him awake'. The doctor's mother, coming to Cambridge, put a stop to this nonsense, dismissing the 'musicians' and staying on to nurse him through this second 'crisis'.

The stroke that led to apoplexy, like the explosion of gunpowder fired, resulted in a transformation of the doctor, for 'the mine was fired, and all the fracas it could make upon a poor mortal bulwark of animated earth [was] determined, and what remained was only ruin and confusion as the blast had left it, never to be recovered into its former order and strength again'.[156] There were three external signs of the doctor's transformation. First, he was left with a 'numb-palsy': his 'mouth and face was drawn up on the lame side, and his left arm and leg altogether enervous'. Then, the 'seat' of his memory was 'ruffled by the disease falling upon his brain and nerves, which had made such havoc that he had no firm notion of himself or of anything'.[157] Damage to the doctor's 'thinking and memorial capacities' led to the third alteration, namely, a propensity for low, even smutty tales that made him laugh; and this 'unseemly laughing' affected his speech, which had been 'touched, and never perfectly recovered'.[158]

The blast made the difference between manhood and puerility: 'the former hath a large stock of useful memories, and also strength habituated to action, which the latter wanting, runs after levities and anything for variety, without choice, unless appetite or inclination (and even that flows from experience) draws it'. Eventually, however, the doctor regained 'his faculties of mind and powers of his body in some measure', but he continued to have many 'apoplexies and palsies' and, finally, a series of epileptic fits. As they 'accelerated', the doctor became increasingly weak, so that his 'chief ease was his couch, where he usually lay expecting fits and wishing for death, the only means to free a limpid soul, as his certainly was, from that dungeon of flesh in which he lay stuck fast as in a mire'.[159] But the 'weakness of body continually increased';

and, at length, the doctor lost all resilience, for 'in one of his fits as was supposed...he went out rather than died'.

If the doctor was a thin, melancholic man, who continually worried about his health, then Sir Dudley was the opposite: a corpulent, cheerful man, who never worried about his health. This lack of worry is remarkable, because the knight's constitution, like that of the doctor's, was weak: he was given to colds, and these were so bad that they left him 'phthisical; and that sat upon his lungs so that he could not, at any time after that, bear a swift or violent motion'.[160] Although he 'never looked upon himself as long-lived', he maintained 'tolerable health', occasionally interrupted by injuries that discomposed his body or illnesses that depressed his spirit.

In one illness, a distemper of the bowels, the knight perceived that 'a girdle...circled him round', though it did not appear outwardly at all. As a means of remedy, he took brandies and 'clysters and was hacked about the streets, and all means were applied that could be thought on to ease his griping and renew the peristaltic motion which seemed to cease within him, and not without danger of inverting'. At last, he agreed to try the regimen of his biographer, which was to swallow 'a great deal of water-gruel'.[161] The knight drank tankard after tankard 'till his bowels were so full, that his lady feared some rupture'. When the rupture comes, a disintegration front propagates in both directions from the tensile core, like the breaking of a glass drop, for the knight was surprised

> with a discharge up and down, all at the same instant, not as a work of nature, by vomit or stool, but as the effect of a compression even against the force of nature resisting it. Such an explosion of all that was within him, happening in that manner, was a crisis, the doctors said, they had never known before. But it cured him all at once; and he never had any like complaint as long as he lived after.[162]

The knight had spent many years as a merchant in the Levant, but after his return to England, he and North discovered an easy friendship based on many common interests.[163] In 1690 the knight moved to his biographer's house in Covent Garden, during which period his 'time of change' arrived. The first manifestation of the change was a return of colds. These, in turn, affected the knight's lungs. But as 'it was his resolved way to carry his evils about with him which he could not shake off', he continued to suppose that his usual 'immane coughing and striving' would lead to eventual well-being. But health did not return, and the knight's countenance began to manifest 'an unusual deadness', for his breathing was noticeably affected. Although his physician, John Ratcliffe, prescribed a pectoral, the knight resolved 'not to be a subject of the artist's experimentations', for his nature was to accept his fate.[164] Thus, 'in all good sense, conscience and understanding, perfect tranquillity of mind and entire resignation, he endured the pain of hard breathing till he breathed no more'.[165]

4.3. In contractions

Unlike the doctor and the knight, Francis North, first baron Guilford, possessed a sound body, full of spirit and flame. His lordship's natural temper, therefore, was airy and his propensity, expansive. Consequently, he had to overcome 'many natural infirmities', including 'his innate modesty [i.e., bashfulness], and how apt he was to passion, and, upon any offence, to inflame; and more than ordinarily inclined to be amorous: not forgetting that, coming into the world with little in present, and nothing expected from his family, he was very solicitous of keeping within compass, and then to improve his fortunes'. But his lordship 'broke through his temper, and acquired a commendable assurance, and kept under his passions to such a degree as made him be thought mild and dispassionate'.[166]

In forming this second nature, his lordship employed a method of self-examination, for

> ...withal, 1. That when he fell under any deliberation of great concern to him, and the point was nice, and stood almost in *aequilibrio*, he took his pen, and wrote down the reasons either way, as they fell in his mind, in any words, or manner of expression; and had that paper, for the most part, lying in his way; which gave him frequent opportunities to weigh the cogency of them. 2. When he observed himself, in his mind, unsteady, or disturbed, he set down the truths that ought to confirm him; and so upon occasion of diverse emergencies of his life.[167]

The resulting 'speculums' were intended to reflect the 'inner-man, his excellencies and imperfections', somewhat like mirrors reflect the outer-man. North provides numerous examples of his lordship's speculums, in some of which, especially those 'reflections upon his person and state', we discover a man striving to achieve Stoic apathy, as in this speculum: 'Let me not disquiet myself afresh with lamentable and melancholy apprehensions of what may happen; or renew those excessive and continued groans, attended with fear on every side, which break my rest, and even deprive me of my senses'.[168]

Stoic apathy is frequently misunderstood to mean absence of passion; but in the context of the exercise of tension, it denotes (the ever elusive) tranquility of spirit. Although his lordship sometimes achieved this state, it was precarious, because in the course of improving his fortunes, various responsibilities, private and public, began to weigh heavily; and the load increased by an order of magnitude after his lordship's appointment as Keeper of the Great Seal, the second most powerful post after the King. With this appointment began the decline and final collapse of the most notable of the three brothers, because the demands of the office, coupled with the slanders, factions and other discords of political life, laid an insupportable weight upon his spirit. North suggests that it was ill usage that 'lay burning' in his lordship's 'most sensible breast', and this in turn led to 'a state of judicious despair; and then no wonder that a distemper, otherwise of an ordinary crisis, got the better of him'.[169]

The distemper began with a a bad cold 'that obstructed all the passages on one side of his head, and he had very great pains there, and, withal, a fever'.[170] But even after the physicians performed a phlebotomy and prescribed a diet, his lordship continued to lay restless 'under a burning acute fever, without any notable remissions, and no intermissions'. The physicians then prescribed cortex and, afterwards, opiates ('quieting potions'), but his lordship continued to have his headache and want of sleep.[171] Indeed, he 'ranted' and renounced the physicians as his 'greatest tormenters', because all the while 'he had axes and hammers, and fireworks in his head, which he could not bear'.

The 'rage' of the disease, 'which was the effort of nature to throw off the venom that caused it', was subdued by cortex,

...but the venom, then afloat, was let sink into his [lordship's] constitution: and it is now found that, without there be an intermission of the fever, the cortex doth but engraft the venom to shoot out again more perniciously. And so, in his lordship's case, he had a seed of a malignant fever in him, which turned to a malignant chachexy [sic], kindling and burning in the centre of his very vitals, making little shew but in his pulse, and a general pain, and continual uneasiness, languor, and want of sleep.[172]

A cachexy is a depraved condition of the body in which nutrition is defective.[173] On North's account, this condition arose from a 'seed' or chemical ferment in the blood. This ferment is not benign, for it poisons the blood, thereby affecting the brain, which is deprived of its nutrition.

As a result, all 'that was peculiarly good in his humour' left him.[174] Indeed, the man who once had been benefactor to his family and friends now turned niggardly: 'He concerned himself strangely about his economy, and the abuses of it, and every thing should be new-modelled, and his family reduced; and he, that was never so well as when his house and table were full, began to look upon us as inmates, and would needs go out, and take an account of his stables'. Thus began his lordship's 'time of change', for even after the fever left, his countenance remained 'sunk' and 'spiritless'. Although the physicians continued to ply him with new doses 'under the name of cordial powders',[175] it was 'his strength of mind', not the physicians' cordials, that continued to 'carry him through all'.[176] Eventually, however, he took to his bed, where he began 'to agonise, and be convulsed, and, by virtue of the doctor's cordials, lived longer, than was for his good'.[177] During this period of decline, he would strive to get up, then to lie down again. At length, having striven to rise, he said, '*It would not do*; and then, with patience and resignation, lay down for good and all, and expired'.

Chapter 5
Sounding the Depths

I. BODY MUSIC

> ...how great...are those powers...
> [through which] we can grasp and understand the world around us.
> Cicero, *Nature of the Gods* (2.147-149)

Introduction

I have now come to the end of my story, insofar as this kind of subject matter can be said to have a beginning, middle and end. My broad purpose was to show some of the ways in which the technology and semantic field of music have been used to understand internal character. To do this, I narrowed my focus to the seventeenth and early part of the eighteenth centuries, since it was this period that laid the groundwork for research programmes and special subjects that have been pursued in increasing detail ever since. All stories, of course, have 'heroes'; and mine have been Hobbes, Hooke and North, who, because of their neo-Stoic orientation, presented a more 'rounded' conception of the self than did the mechanical philosophers. But these three men also suited my purpose, for their controlling metaphors enabled me to illustrate how a stringed, percussion and wind instrument could model aspects of internal character.

No doubt, there were many motives that led each of these men to write about internal character, yet it is tempting to believe that at least one of the reasons stemmed from the personal experience of illness. Hobbes, for example, became seriously ill in France during 1647, and the result was 'the shaking Palsy'. According to Aubrey, the shaking manifested itself in Hobbes's hands before 1650,

> ...and haz growne upon him by degrees, ever since, so that he

haz not been able to write very legibly since 1665 or 1666, as I find by some letters he hath honoured me withall. Mr. Hobbs wase for severall yeares before he died so Paralyticall that he wase scarce able to write his name, and that in the abscence of his Amanuensis not being able to write anything, he made Scrawls on a piece of paper to remind him of the conceptions of his Mind he design'd to have committed to writing.[1]

Yet, Aubrey noted that 'the decay of his [Hobbes's] Vital Heat in the extremity of old age, accompanied with the Palsy to that violence,' did not chill 'the briske Fervour and Vigour of his mind, which did wonderfully continue to him to his last'. Even so, as the shaking progressed, Hobbes's ability to act in the world declined. It is not so remarkable, therefore, that he chose a bundle of taut strings as a symbol of internal character.

If we apply Hobbes's conception of the 'work' of memory to that of muscles, three points emerge. First, rest is only an appearance, since body is maintained in a state of equilibrium by a real but infinitesimal vibratory motion. This is like muscular tonus, the sustained partial contraction of muscles which is a condition of health. Second, when a body is set vibrating by an impact, a blow or friction, the reaction is equal to the action, and this is like muscular force. Third, the two kinds of impulse, taken together as endeavour (*conatus*, effort), are like the kinaesthetic sense: the perception of movement, weight, resistance and position. Indeed, the shaking palsy would have made Hobbes acutely aware that he was losing muscular *tonus*, a natural endowment, and with it, the ability to exert muscular force – will power.

Hooke, too, was chronically ill, for he had the 'pissing disease', diabetes. Because nothing was then known about the nature of the disease, Hooke's problems were compounded by treatments that were empirical in the true sense of that word. Sometimes the treatments 'wrought well', but mostly the result was giddiness, clouded vision, loss of smell and taste, nose bleeds, headaches, swollen ankles and leg cramps, digestive problems, fevers and sweats, heart palpitations, hand tremors, insomnia, incubus and melancholy. For a period of time, too, Hooke had recurring *tinnitus* or ringing noises in his ears.[2] Once, he attempted to solve this problem by singing, 'which made me not hear the noyse in my head'.[3] On another occasion, a friend recommended putting warm honey into the ear, then moving the honey about with a wool applicator inserted with the finger.[4] Even when Hooke ceased to record details of his condition, he continued to punctuate his diary with exclamations to the deity, some of misery, when he felt particularly ill, others of gratitude, when his condition improved.[5]

In the case of North, there was a childhood illness, probably meningitis, an act of 'great violence of nature', because it 'weakened the faculties of the body as well as of the mind'. This illness impaired North's thinking, or so he believed, 'for the mind cannot work without the actions of the body, which are its immediate instruments'.[6] Hence, he often felt insecure, and this feeling, in turn, led to recurrent bouts of melancholy and to periods of 'crisis'.[7] The most severe crisis occurred with the death of three of his brothers, who also had been North's closest friends; during this period, too, North lost his public offices.[8] When the crisis passed, North was left with this 'advantage': 'I have ease and repose in my mind so as if ever I am overwhelmed in irremediable calamity and pain, I may, if I find I cannot bear them, put a period to free myself, and in this thought I have great comfort, and have had and shall continue to have all my life long'.[9]

Regardless of motivation, all three writers shared a common approach to self-knowledge and self-restraint, according to which the criteria of conscience are internal and relative. But these criteria become reasonable through an intellectual process that includes methods of developing and testing hypotheses. As I have tried to show, Hobbes and North were particularly concerned with the inwardness of morality and with the notion of virtue as a disposition, not a habit. This, too, had been the concern of the ancient Stoics, who acknowledged that virtue may be taught but that the most potent teacher is the life of the individual. North put this belief into practice, through life writing; but Hobbes acknowledged it, when he wrote:

There is...no such Inconsistence of Humane Nature, with Civill Duties, as some think. [For] I have known cleernesse of Judgment, and largenesse of Fancy; strength of Reason, and gracefull Elocution; a Courage for the Warre, and a Fear for the Laws, and all eminently in one man; and that was my most noble and honored friend Mr. *Sidney Godolphin*; who hating no man, nor hated of any, was unfortunately slain in the beginning of the late Civill warre, in the Publique quarrell, by an undiscerned, and an undiscerning hand.[10]

For Hobbes and Hooke, self-knowledge served an additional purpose, for by knowing ourselves we come to know our limits as observers and, accordingly, become more aware of the need for measuring instruments. By means of such instruments we are able to move from observation language to explanatory language, one that may be translated into symbols and in this form enter a theory which, as an intelligible whole, will give meaning to its terms.

When internal character is symbolised by means of the technology and semantic field of music, the resultant theories may be said to explain inner music, the world-in-there. But there also is a world-out-there; and this world may become musical, because it 'sounds', and so becomes a 'language' which 'speaks' of physical structures and interactions behind them. In 1605 Bacon provided a striking image of both inner and outer worlds, when he wrote: 'this variable composition of man's body hath made it an instrument easy to distemper; and therefore the Poets did well conjoin Music and Medicine in Apollo; because the Office of Medicine is but to tune this curious Harp of man's body and reduce it to a Harmony'.[11]

From one point of view, that of the patient, body, the world-in-there, is like the strings of a harp. If these strings each retain their appropriate tensions, body has the potential to produce harmonious sounds. This is its normal function, so that health is a harmony. Following from this, disease becomes loss of tension in one or more of the strings. When this happens, function – or at least its range – is impaired, because the strings go out of tune and discord follows. From another point of view, that of the physician, body is the world-out-there, for the physician's role is to temper the strings, thereby reinstating their tensions and, thus, their harmonious relation one to another so that the instrument will once again have the potential to produce musical sounds.

If we retain the physician's point of view, we might well ask: are sounds signs of health and disease? and if so, what music does the body play? To answer the first question, I shall sketch briefly the discovery of methods and instruments for amplifying internal body sounds. To answer the second question, I shall focus on that aspect which the Stoics called 'incorporeals'. These are not mind, as the mechanical philosophers believed; rather, it is what words assert that constitutes non-body. For the Stoics, as A.A. Long points out, acts of thought are private, physical modifications of internal character (the *hegemonikon*), 'but the sense of the words in which they are expressed is immaterial, objective and something which others can grasp'.[12]

Hobbes repeated this Stoic theory of incorporeals, when he made a distinction between imagination as possessing an idea and conceiving as inferring by reasoning that a thing exists: 'We infer by reasoning that there is something within the human body that gives it animal motion – something by means of which the body feels and moves; we call this, whatever it is, the soul, without having an idea of it'.[13] The implication is that substance is not conceived but only inferred by reasoning. Thus, although words are the 'body' of our reasoning, statements made and inferences drawn are non-body, because they are the work of reason – the patterns which the mind imposes upon reality. The discovery of internal body sounds as signs of health and disease provides an apt illustration of this point of view.

1. Playing and listening
1.1. Techniques

> *In our sense of hearing...we find*
> *a marvellous power of discrimination in the perception of...*
> *pitch and tone, and also of many different qualities...,*
> *sonorous or dull, smooth or rough, low or shrill, firm or flexible.*
> Cicero, *Nature of the Gods* (2.144-146)

Internal body sounds had been noticed from the time of Hippocrates, but their utility as signs was not widely appreciated until the sounds themselves had been identified in all their variety.

The first steps toward identification were taken by Hooke, who proposed that 'it may be possible to discover the Motions of the Internal Parts of Bodies...by the sound they make, that one may discover the Works perform'd in the several Offices and Shops of a Man's Body, and thereby discover what Instrument or Engine is out of order, what Works are going on at several Times, and lies still at others, and the like'. Although he feared his contemporaries would regard this proposal as 'mad, foolish and phantastick', experience had encouraged him of its possibility, since he had been able to hear very plainly 'the beating of a Man's Heart, and 'tis common to hear the Motion of Wind to and fro in the Guts, and other small Vessels, the stopping of the Lungs is easily discover'd by the Wheesing, the Stopping of the Head, by the humming and whistling Noises, the sliping to and fro of the Joynts in many cases, by crackling, and the like.'[14]

But Hooke went farther, for he asserted that two things were requisite if internal body sounds were to become more audible: either the motions producing the sounds must be increased, for example, by striking the body; or the organ of hearing must be made more powerful, for example, by an 'otacousticon'. Thus, he enunciated clearly three important things: first, that sounds are signs of internal body motions in health and disease; second, that although these sounds may be heard by the naked ear, they may be made more resonant, either by striking the body or by employing a hearing aid; and third, that internal body sounds are various, because they consist not merely of simple sounds, or sounds in isolation, but also of compound sounds, or sounds in relation. Nevertheless, only a small number of physicians after Hooke described particular body sounds;[15] and a more general approach was not taken until 1761, when Leopold Auenbrugger announced a 'new' method for identifying body sounds.[16]

According to this method, which Auenbrugger called 'percussion', the physician was to 'play' on the body like the musician plays on a drum. To elicit the variety of sounds by percussion, therefore, the parietes of the cavities of the body were to be struck in such a manner as to enable the examiner to judge the degrees of resonance of the parts beneath. In so doing, the physician could hear two classes of sound: natural and morbid. Auenbrugger described natural sound as resembling 'the stifled

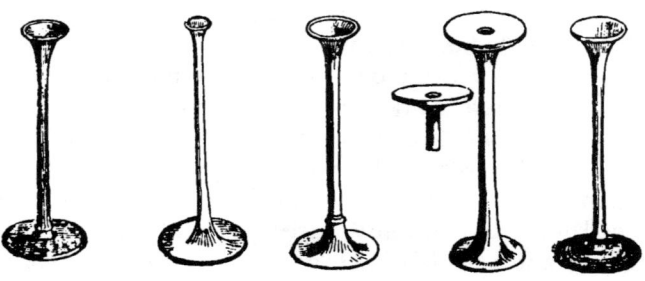

Figure 5.1   Firm stethoscopes (wood, ivory, metal), from S.S. Alison, *The Physical Examination of the Chest* (London, 1861)

sound of a drum covered with a thick woollen cloth or other envelope'.[17] When the volume of air in the chest is diminished, natural sound becomes dull or even absent, thereby signifying morbidity. The chief characteristic of significant sound, therefore, was loudness and its modifications, clearness and dullness. These modifications, in turn, depended on the volume of air (augmented or diminished) in the chest. But Auenbrugger also recognised that silence (absence of sound) could have significance.

In the tract announcing his discovery, Auenbrugger failed to provide adequate descriptions of the method itself or of the specific differences of percussive sounds. Like Hooke's proposal, therefore, Auenbrugger's tract excited little attention. This situation changed after 1819, when René Laennec brought Auenbrugger's invention into prominence by providing detailed descriptions of the attributes and relations of the sounds heard in percussion, as well as in a 'new' method. According to the new method, which Laennec called 'mediate auscultation', the physician listens with instrumental aids to sounds arising from the exercise of functions such as respiration and circulation and compares those emanating from diseased organs with those ascertained by previous experience to exist in a healthy condition.

Laennec's instrumental aids were the stethoscope, which he devised to listen to lung sounds, and a wooden rod or cylinder, which he used to listen to heart sounds. His stethoscope was like

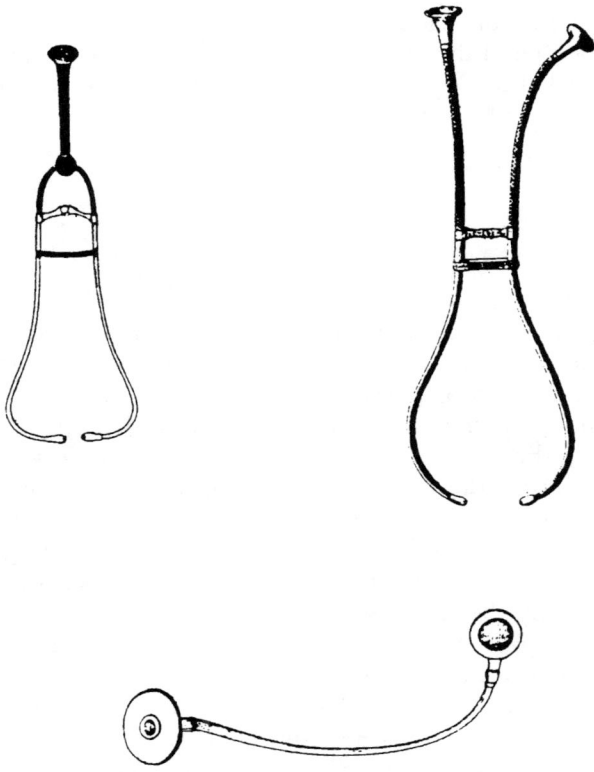

Figure 5.2 Flexible monaural and binaural stethoscopes, from S.S. Alison, *The Physical Examination of the Chest* (London, 1861)

a trumpet, that is, it was firm in form (Figure 5.1); afterwards, a number of physicians proposed alterations which, eventually, led to the flexible form we know today (Figure 5.2). In whatever form, Laennec was convinced that hearing instruments would enable physicians to study the internal motions of the body more exactly than one may do by opening and inspecting living animals. Indeed, he asserted that 'the ear appreciates much more exactly the smallest intervals of sounds, and their shortest duration, than the eye can judge of similar differences in motion'. As proof of this proposition, he pointed out that 'the least practised musician will detect the omission of a note in the midst of several double crotchets, should they be in harmony, and will easily distinguish a point added to the value or duration of one of them, although it be prolonged by but the 12th of a second'.[18]

1.2. Instruments

Above all nature has given us the hand,
so apt a tool...for the playing of string- and wind-instruments.
Cicero, *Nature of the Gods* (2.147-149)

Initially, the methods of percussion and auscultation were applied to explore the region of the chest. As their use became more widespread, so, too, physicians began to explore other regions of the body, at the same time proposing various modifications to one or the other method.[19] In percussion, for example, the physician struck the patient with his fingers or with a percussion hammer (Figure 5.3a, b). But in phonometry, a modification of the percussion method, the physician placed a vibrating tuning fork on the surface of the patient's chest, abdomen or head to determine, by the loudness or softness of the tone, whether the subjacent organs do or do not vibrate simultaneously, that is, whether they are permeable or impermeable to air.[20] If a tuning fork was unavailable, a pitch pipe or *flûte d'accord* could serve similar purposes.[21] In autophonia, a modification of mediate auscultation, the physician observed the effect of his own voice on the chest of the patient. With the ear placed in apposition to the chest, but not pressed too firmly against it, more or less resonance is perceived, when words are pronounced with a loud voice, and in a manner to secure reverberation through the nasal passages.[22]

Immediate methods could not be pursued too often, especially with female patients, for whom nineteenth-century sensibilities demanded that some instrument be interposed between physician and patient.[23] Following from the notion of mediate auscultation, therefore, where a stethoscope is interposed between the patient and the ear of the physician for the purpose of increasing or modifying the sound, some physicians proposed mediate percussion, in which solid material is interposed between

(a)

(b)

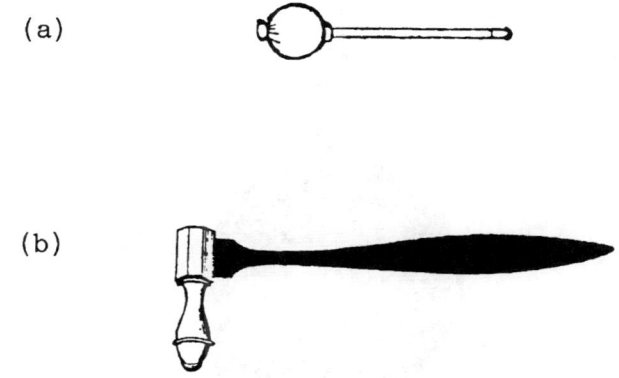

Figure 5.3   Percussion hammers
(a) from H.I. Bowditch, *The Young Stethoscopist* (New York and Boston, 1846)
(b) from S.S. Alison, *The Physical Examination of the Chest* (London, 1861)

the parietes and the striking finger, hammer or tuning fork. A number of instruments, called 'pleximeters', were devised for this purpose, including thin discs of wood, ivory, cork and India-rubber, with and without different kinds of tongues or lips to be used as handles. Sometimes, pleximeters were joined to the percussion hammer itself. One physician went so far as to advocate the use of a water-filled balloon, which he interposed between the stethoscope and the patient, since he believed that water is a better conductor of sound than air (Figure 5.4).

The proliferation of hearing, striking and related instruments illustrates the creative activities of physicians, rather than the ready acceptance of the new diagnostic methods. Indeed, some patients, as well as some physicians resisted their introduction. For the patients, the sight of the stethoscope or other instrument, as well as the idea that an examination was about to be made, caused fear, distress and agitation. Hence, the physician was to attune himself to the patient's psychological state,

Figure 5.4 Hydrophone, from S.S. Alison, *The Physical Examination of the Chest* (London, 1861)

thereby establishing sympathetic conditions necessary for a successful examination.[24] For the physicians, the methods required learning new skills; these skills, involving both aural and manual dexterity, took time to learn; and, in the case of teaching hospitals, the new skills had to be imparted to younger physicians.[25]

Nevertheless, with the recognition that sounds were important signs for detecting health and disease, the methods of percussion, or examination by striking, and auscultation, or examination by the ear, did become accepted practice in one form or another. Although these methods have been amply treated in the historical literature, the actual process of discovery and identification of the sounds has had little attention.[26] Yet, sounds must be named to become useful in diagnosis or prognosis; and for science to develop, two further steps are required: there must be a vocabulary of abstraction; and there must be an account of how the sounds originate in the body. Let us see how biomedical scientists solved these problems.

2. Creating theories
2.1. Naming

> ...*the voice is projected*
> *in accordance with the orders of the mind.*
> Cicero, *Nature of the Gods* (2.147-149)

Laennec must be credited with creating and defining most of the names employed in physical diagnosis of chest diseases. Nevertheless, his nomenclature was not accepted uncritically, and additions and emendations were made for three principal reasons. First, Laennec had been convinced that a well-formed language should derive from classical sources, but some physicians argued against an excessive reliance on classically-derived terms.[27] Second, as Laennec's work became more widely known, his vocabulary was altered in translation.[28] Third, and most important, not all physicians had the same powers of aural discrimination, and this was a source of disagreement about terms. For example, one physician thought that metallic sounds in the thorax of a patient were comparable to the tones of a musical snuff-box, whereas, on examining the same patient, another physician supposed that the vibrations of a tuning key would convey the best idea of the sound.[29]

Since names for sounds were based on the subjective judgment of individuals, a number of physicians sought tests that could help to bring about intersubjective agreement. These tests included reproducing sounds on a pitchpipe or other musical instrument for the purpose of comparison, as well as representing sounds graphically for the purpose of analysis. Indeed, Laennec himself had recourse to musical instruments (he played the flute); and

Figure 5.5 Graphic representation of humming murmur, from R. Laennec, *A Treatise on Mediate Auscultation* (London, 1846)

Figure 5.6 Graphic representation of the pulse, from F.N. Marquet, *Nouvelle méthode facile et curieuse, pour connoitre le pouls*, 2d edn. (Amsterdam and Paris, 1749)
(a) the norm

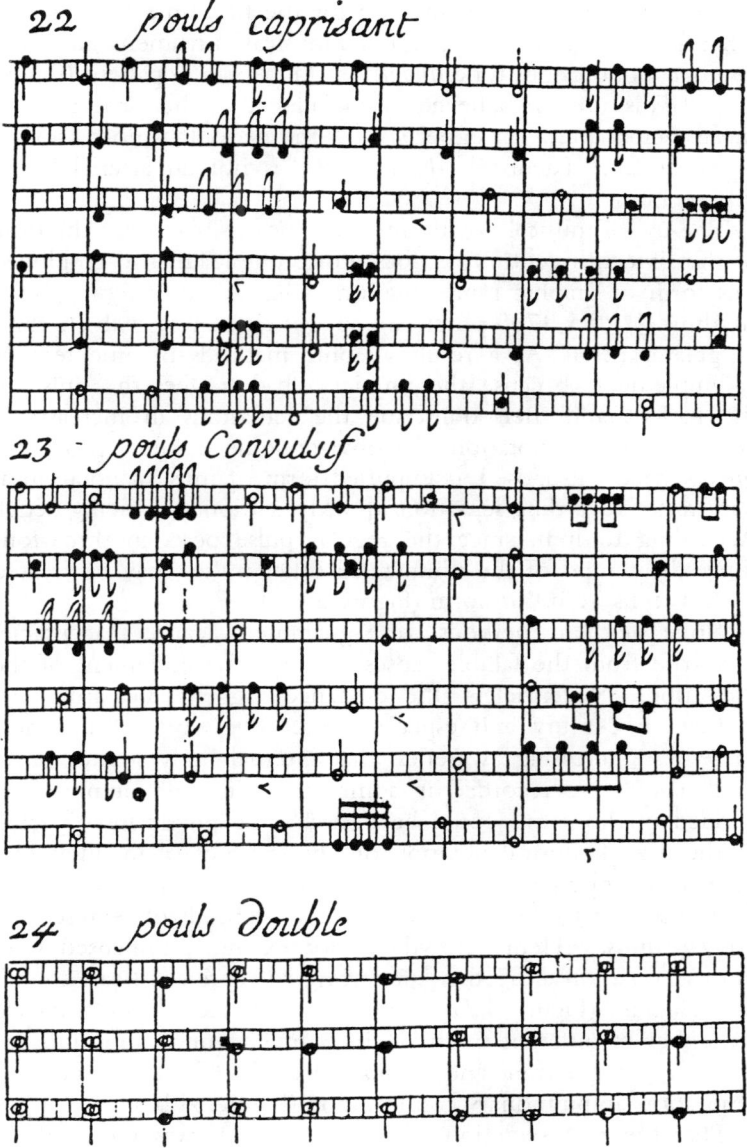

Figure 5.6
(b) deviations from the norm

in 1826 he used musical notation for the first time to represent what he described as 'the sound of a musical instrument executing a rather monotonous tune (*chant*)' in the neck of a patient (Figure 5.5).[30] This tune, he believed, was produced by the carotid artery, the principal artery on either side of the neck. It is now known, however, that Laennec's *chant d'artère* is not an arterial but a venous hum.

The use of musical notation was not new, since, from the time of the sixteenth century, if not before, physicians had employed this form of graphic representation as an aid to analysing pulse rhythms.[31] After 1700 physicians sought to analyse such rhythms in greater detail. As a result, graphic methods became tedious to implement, because the physician had to feel the pulse of the patient and then transcribe the sensations in increasingly complex musical notation. To obviate some of these problems, one physician proposed a simplified form of musical notation as a means of recording sensations quickly without sacrificing detail. According to him, since the regular pulse beats in three-four time, the tempo of the minuet, all other pulses may be treated as deviations from this norm (Figure 5.6a, b).[32]

None of these methods were guarantees against inaccuracies that arise from the fallible senses or subjective judgment of the transcriber. Nevertheless, the evidence suggests that from the eighteenth century and especially after the work of Laennec, there was increasing awareness that internal body sounds of all kinds should be recorded in some way, although opinion was divided on how this could be done. Some physicians objected to the use of musical notation on the grounds of intelligibility, since many physicians lacked the appropriate training in music. Others sought to devise more universal methods of representing body sounds.[33] Henry Bowditch, for example, dispensed with musical notation altogether, preferring to represent heart sounds in a diagram (Figure 5.7a), whereas Somerville Alison proposed a number of different methods, including an undulating line for the 'wavy respiration' and 'acoustical circles' for the 'oscillating respiration' in pulmonary consumption (Figure 5.7b, c).

That the representation of internal sounds was intended, in part, to facilitate naming is clear from the debate about the nature of heart sounds. Those who examined the acting heart

(a)

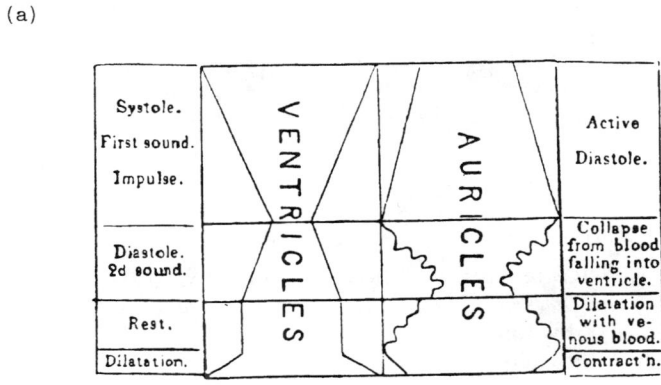

(b)

(c)

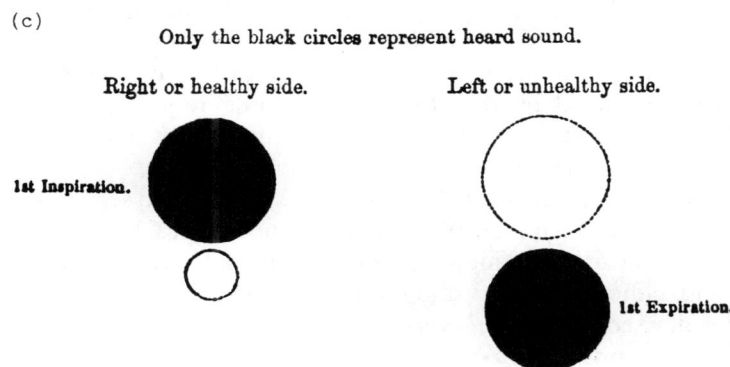

Figure 5.7   Other methods of representing body sounds
(a) Heart motions, from H.I. Bowditch, *The Young Stethoscopist* (New York and Boston, 1846)
(b) 'Wavy respiration', from S.S. Alison, *The Physical Examination of the Chest* (London, 1861)
(c) 'Oscillating respiration' in pulmonary consumption, from S.S. Alison, *The Physical Examination of the Chest* (London, 1861)

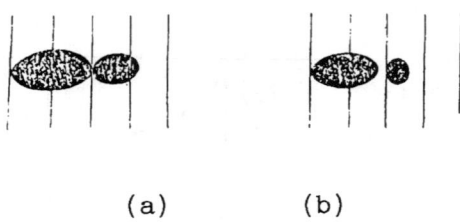

(a) (b)

Figure 5.8 Representation of heart sounds, from C.J.B. Williams, *The Pathology and Diagnosis of Diseases of the Chest*, 4th edn. (London, 1840)
(a) Laennec's rhythm
(b) Williams' rhythm

by auscultation heard at each pulse two sounds following each other in quick but regular succession, after which there was an interval of silence until the next pulsation. To ascertain the rhythm of heart sounds more precisely, Laennec supposed that the period of a pulse (that is, the time from the commencement of one double sound to the commencement of another) could be divided into four equal parts and that two of these parts were occupied by the first sound, a little more than one part by the second sound, and the remaining part by the interval of silence.[34]

According to Laennec's supposition, the first and second sounds are long, and the interval of silence is short. But Charles Williams disputed Laennec's findings, for he supposed that the first sound is a long, rather dull sound, and the second, a short abrupt flap. Hence, he devised a modified version of musical notation to represent heart sounds, in which he compared Laennec's findings (Figure 5.8a) with his own conclusions about the average rhythm of heart sounds in a healthy male adult (Figure 5.8b). For Williams, the male was the standard, from which females and children deviated by having the first sound 'rather shorter and less dull, more like the second'.[35]

In identifying internal body sounds, first Laennec, then other physicians, assigned names on the basis of the impressions the sounds conveyed to the sense of hearing. Accordingly, the names tended to imitate, more or less, the sounds produced in the body. The most explicitly mimetic name was the Greek term for the rumbling sound in the intestines, *borborygmos*. This term had been coined long before Laennec, although after him the term '*borborygmi*' was used generally for stomach rumbles, whereas various species of rumbles were designated differently according to language group (e.g., in German, *gurren, kollern, poltern*).[36] Terms for heart sounds were also explicitly mimetic and included, for normal sounds, tic-tac, too-to, blob-blob, lubb-dup, lumb-dup, lung-dup and, for abnormal sounds or murmurs, bullub-dup, lubb-dupup, lubb-durrup, to-to-too.[37] But the majority of terms were derived from names corresponding to the sounds themselves: babbling, bleating, blowing, bubbling, buzzing, cantering, chinking, chirping, chopping, clapping, clicking, clinking, cooing and so on.

All these terms exhibit a belief in the connection between the phonic or orthographic form of words and the thing they designate.[38] Indeed, Laennec himself recognised this in the case of what he called 'simple sensations', which, he argued, 'can only be conveyed by comparisons'.[39] Some English writers, however, were sceptical about mimeology. Samuel Gee, for example, agreed that terms must correspond to 'clear and distinct ideas', but he cautioned that 'when we read about "la rudesse de l'inspiration, qui devient râpeuse, granuleuse, au lieu d'être légère, moelleuse, et caressant à l'oreille," we seem to have passed beyond common sense into mere fancy and fine writing'.[40]

Gee's criticisms were not particularly acute, since mimetic language presents very specific problems for physicians. In the first place, such a language is as indefinite as it is diverse. For example, Laennec's *râle crépitant humide* was known under such different terms as moist crepitous rhonchus, crepitation, crepitating *râle*, crepitant rhonchus, crepitant *râle*, minute crepitations, crackling of pneumonia, small crepitations, vesicular *râle* and *râle sous-crépitant du catarrhe pulmonaire aigu capillaire*.[41] In the second place, mimetic language creates confusion, because the idea conveyed to the mind of the reader is frequently different from that intended by the writer. Finally, mimetic language raises difficulties in interpreting words according to a writer's meaning, because there is no standard by which to measure their true signification.

2.2. Classifying

> ...*the evidence of our senses*
> *leads to the inventions of the mind....*
> Cicero, *Nature of the Gods* (2.151-154)

Science cannot develop from mimetic language, for it requires a vocabulary of abstraction. But how was such a vocabulary to be achieved? According to prevailing opinion, the physician should accustom his ears to the many varieties of sounds in the chest, so that by experience he could know and name (distinguish) them. But it was conceded that the art of the physician did not consist merely in 'reading off' the sounds separately or in combination. 'Reading' required interpretation; and for a correct interpretation of the physical expression of disease, the physician had to acquire knowledge of the laws through which sounds occur. Accordingly, the object became to investigate the varieties of sounds by describing them consistently with acoustical laws and the observed characters of the phenomena. In this way, it was supposed, the terminology would become more definite.

In pursuit of this goal, some physicians utilised the principle of sound conduction, thereby identifying as many types of sounds as there were organs in the body. Although Laennec himself had adopted this principle, it became popular after Pierre Piorry drew attention to the increased sense of resistance which invariably accompanies the dull percussion sound. Since the various organs of the body (liver, spleen, heart, for instance) differ considerably in consistence and size, thereby offering very different degrees of resistance to percussion, the tactile phenomena were then regarded as strictly analogous to the acoustic properties of the percussion sound. In this way a nomenclature sprang up, in which sounds peculiar to the heart, liver, spleen, etc. were spoken of.[42]

Other physicians relied on the principle of sound production, thereby identifying sounds produced by striking, by breathing, by speaking and by beating.[43] But to ascertain the different varieties of sound within each type, additional principles of demarcation need to be employed. For example, Auenbrugger and Laennec had divided thoracic percussion sounds into two opposing types: clear and dull. This demarcation was challenged by Josef Skoda, who in 1839 subjected the work of both Auenbrugger and Laennec to searching criticism, because he supposed that thoracic percussion sounds should be divided into four types: full/empty; clear/dull; tympanitic/non-tympanitic; high/low.[44]

Skoda intended the terms 'full' and 'empty' to bear reference to the size of a vibrating body, as in the different sounds given by bells of different sizes. According to him, the faintest sound from a large bell, or the loudest ringing of a small one, conveys to us at once the idea of the size of the bell in vibration – the former sounds full, the latter scanty. Later in the nineteenth century, however, it was recognised that the difference was due not to the size (volume) of the resonant chamber but to the material of which its walls were composed.[45] Skoda's division, therefore, ceased to be tenable, as Walter Walshe pointed out, when he proposed a new division based on the four attributes of musical sound: loudness ('amount of intensity of resonance'), pitch, timbre ('quality') and duration.[46]

Other physicians had already used these attributes to characterise sounds heard not only in percussion but also in auscultation. Sometimes, however, they weighted the attributes differently, as in the case of Austin Flint and Charles Williams. The former physician emphasised the value of pitch as a 'feature highly distinctive, easily appreciated, and...of considerable importance'. Indeed, he claimed to be the first to draw attention to this attribute.[47] But the latter physician assigned greater value to duration because of his interest in rhythmically recurring sounds. For example, since Williams believed that the function of the heart is characterised by its action, he supposed that functional disorders, arrythmias, could be classed into (1) increased action (palpitation), (2) irregular action and (3) defective action. But respiration also is rhythmical; and Williams claimed to be the first to describe a new variation in respiratory sounds, namely, that which affects their duration.[48]

Although acoustics did help to introduce a language of abstraction, as well as a more uniform terminology, it did not bring about a more uniform classification. There were two reasons for this. First, acoustics emerged as a new science during the seventeenth century, so that by the nineteenth century the distinction between noise and musical sound was well understood. Of the four attributes of a musical sound, only two – pitch and loudness – had been adequately explained. In 1830, for example, John Herschel speculated that timbre ('quality') probably was due to 'the law which regulates the excursions of the molecules of air originally set in motion'. But of the qualities of musical sound 'and the molecular agitations on which they depend, we know too little to subject them to any distinct theoretical discussion'.[49]

Second, to describe internal body sounds consistently with acoustical principles, physicians relied chiefly on typologies, in which taxonomic categories are steps in logical division.[50] Typologies have two advantages. First, users do not require prior knowledge of the principles of acoustics, only an ability to carry out the procedure of division. Second, typologies provide convenient identification keys, whereby the investigated physical sign is placed into one of the classes of an already existing classification. But these advantages are outweighed by one single disadvantage, for typologies can provide an unlimited number of taxonomies. This is so because of the importance of the demarcating principles, the choice of which establishes the differentiating characteristics of sound. Hence, the replacement of one demarcating principle (e.g., sound conduction) by a different one (e.g., sound production) can result in an entirely new taxonomy.[51]

Nevertheless, typologies may be useful, as John Hughlings Jackson pointed out at the end of the nineteenth century, when he asserted: 'we must have types, not definitions, and consider cases presented as they approach this or that type', since 'there is, really, no such thing as "genuine" or "real" epilepsy' or other diseases, 'except in this arbitrary sense'.[52] By this assertion he did not mean 'to underrate the scientific study of disease in advocating the separate clinical study of it for practical purposes', for he allowed there was a need for 'scientific or theoretical classification' as well as for practical typologies. What, then, is the difference between these two taxonomic procedures? As Kurt A. Hoeline points out, classifications are tools for answering well-formulated, precise and limited questions, whereas typologies are heuristic tools. With classifications we are more or less in control of the ordering process, but with typologies this control is not always possible.

Even if the variables are well identifiable and measurable, there is still no guarantee that these...give a true understanding of the meaning that the typological centre represents. E.g. a musical chord consists of a number of tones well defined by their frequencies. Yet the resulting new entity, the chord, is more than the superimposition of these frequencies. The mathematical workup does not necessarily lead to an understanding of that new entity.[53]

Hoeline's remarks relate to mathematical and statistical typologies, whereas our physicians utilised logical methods. Nevertheless, his main point is applicable to our case: since there can be as many typologies as there are physicians practising percussion and auscultation, this taxonomic procedure cannot provide a scientific basis for understanding disease.

2.3. Explaining

> *By synthesis and analysis*
> *we can then devise...arts of life....*
> Cicero, *Nature of the Gods* (2.147-149)

Laennec had understood disease by its effects, since he believed that causes were unknowable. His work with the stethoscope, therefore, had been an exercise in relating auscultatory sounds with 'lesions', for he believed that a disease was always associated with some lesion, even if that lesion was not organic or detectable by the science of pathological anatomy.[54] Afterwards, increasing efforts were made to understand disease based on knowledge of the disorders that trouble the laws and functions of bodily organisation. To gain this understanding, physicians were to learn how sounds may be produced, transmitted and modified; and how the contents of the body may produce sounds or change them. The method of procedure was to compare the two 'mechanisms' in question. By thus learning the acoustic relations of the body not merely as isolated facts but as parts of an applied science, some physicians sought to move from empirical diagnosis toward rational pathology.

Such was the aim of Charles Williams, who applied the comparative method by considering the contents of the body as so many different musical instruments. Since muscles, such as the heart, produced sounds in health by contractions and expansions, he supposed that the tonicity or flaccidity of a muscle would alter sound in the same way as a tense or relaxed string alters the sound of a stringed musical instrument. But since morbid sounds, such as heart murmurs, were produced by the passage of liquids through solid tubes or apertures, he supposed that this passage would alter sound in the same manner as the passage of air alters sound in wind musical instruments, producing thereby either noises or musical sounds. But the murmurs of 'water instruments' and the music of wind instruments also have these differences: 'that liquids, being more sluggish than air, are less susceptible of the sudden motions which constitute sonorous vibration; and not differing so much in density from the solids in which they move, liquids will have little of those reflected or echoed vibrations which increase and modify the sounds produced in air-filled tubes'.

With these qualifications in mind, Williams believed it would be possible to explain the murmurs heard in the heart and arteries by referring to parallel instances of the tones of wind instruments; and this explanation, he claimed, could be extended to the rhonchi, respiratory and vocal sounds of the windpipe and its branches, which he described as the most complete and diversified wind instrument. Thus for example, the type of murmurs classed as sonorous rales (rhonchus in Williams' vocabulary) – grating, sawing, droning – have their parallels in reed instruments, whereas those classed as sibilant rales – blowing, hissing, whistling and cooing – have their parallel in flutes. In the former, the vibrating resistance of the solid is chiefly concerned, and its vibrations are transmitted to the adjoining parts as well as to the current, so as to produce a 'thrill'. In the latter, however, there are no perceptible vibrations in the solids, and the sounds are propagated in the direction of the current.[55]

Williams did not base his conclusions on speculative grounds, for he had conducted a series of laboratory experiments to prove that the production of sounds by liquids closely resembles those which regulate the same phenomena produced by air in tubes. To this end, he attempted to simulate those exercises of physiological function involving motion of fluids through a tube. His apparatus consisted of an India rubber ('caoutchouc') tube, 18 inches long and three-quarters of an inch in diameter. This tube was attached to the stopcock of a reservoir in which there was water to the depth of from 8 to 10 inches. For some experiments, the apparatus was modified, whereas for other experiments, the fluid was made more glutinous. But the chief purpose of all the experiments was to find the 'essential physical cause' of murmurs by bringing about changes to the current of liquid when pressure was exerted in different ways.[56]

CONCLUSION

> *One may say that we seek...to create a second nature in the natural world.*
> Cicero, *Nature of the Gods* (2.151-154)

There are two points to notice about the foregoing account, one linguistic, the other musical. In the domain of linguistics, the activities of naming, classifying and explaining internal body sounds follow a sequence of three stages which may be characterised as mimetic, analogical and symbolical, although, on the historical evidence, these stages overlap and cannot be compartmentalised. According to Ernst Cassirer, language always passes through these three stages in maturing to its specific form. Moreover, these stages, he asserts, represent 'a functional law of linguistic growth, which has its specific and characteristic counterpart in other fields such as art and cognition'.[57] We might also make a further distinction between marks and signs, following Hobbes, who wrote: 'words...connected, signify the cogitations and motions of our mind. The difference, therefore, betwixt marks and signs is this, that we make those for our own use, but these for the use of others'.[58]

In the domain of music, the three traditional assumptions, encoded in Bacon's metaphor, continued to guide the theory and practice of auscultation and percussion long after the seventeenth century. These assumptions were that health is a harmony; that the patient's body is like a musical instrument or group of musical instruments; and that physicians required skills similar to those of musicians to play on the body instrument. But the physicians' skills were to be acquired by long practice and would vary with the method used or the task to be accomplished. The most general skills included a cultivated ear to distinguish the different internal body sounds, as well as the ability to 'read' sounds as physical signs and interpret their significance. In the case of percussion, there was the additional skill of manual dexterity, although as one writer noted, those 'who are accustomed to play on musical instruments, especially the piano, already possess the necessary command over the wrist'.[59] As the diagnostic aids gained acceptance, other requisite skills included the ability to record sounds in musical notation and to reproduce them by imitation on musical instruments or in laboratory experiments.

If the patient's body is like a musical instrument, or group of musical instruments, what music does the body play? From the foregoing account, the answer must be mostly noisy and sometimes tuneful music. My main concern in this book, however, has been to tell how some writers of the seventeenth and early eighteenth centuries conceived internal character as a silent musical activity by recourse to mechanical models (musical instruments) and sometimes also to mathematical abstractions, both of which yield purely symbolic representations of nature. Hence, it does not follow that one is more 'realistic' than the other.[60] Indeed, historical evidence shows that both kinds of symbolic representations produce science – an account of the relations among symbols or signs, which should not be confounded with the real cause of phenomena. Like the composers, therefore, the scientists create entities by means of arbitrary conventions: they lay down symbols and at the same time prescribe the rules according to which they must be combined. Creativity, therefore, is the work of imagination *and* reason, as Hobbes insisted, when he wrote:

> Stones and inanimate things seem to be unable to err simply because they have no power of reasoning or imagination. So it is natural to infer that in order to err one needs the power of reasoning, or at least of imagination; both these powers are positive, and they are given always, and only, to those who err.[61]

Notes

CHAPTER 1: CONCEIVING THE INCONCEIVABLE
1. For models, see Hesse (1963), whose argument and examples form a useful complement to the story told in this book.
2. E.g., Fodor (1975).
3. E.g., Hale (1971), Pagel (1958), Rabelais (1530-34: 295-301), Randall (1983: 158), Robinson (1972: 11-59), Rose (1973: 1-35), Virchow (1958).
4. See Kassler (1984a, 1984b).
5. E.g., in the system devised by Erich M. von Hornbostel and Curt Sachs, for which see Kassler (1984c) and sources cited there.
6. I.e., aided by concepts from musical instrument technology.
7. For the reception, see Mintz (1962); for one explanation of this reception, see Shapin and Schaffer (1985), who argue that the hostility between Hobbes and the mechanical philosopher, Boyle, was due to different conceptions of scientific method.
8. Hesse (1962: 101).
9. E.g., Brandt (1928).
10. E.g., Dijksterhuis (1969).
11. Diogenes Laertius, *Lives of the Philosophers* (7.158); see also Sambursky (1959).
12. P. Fletcher, *The Purple Island* (Canto 5.47-8); see also Cohen (1984: 77, 93, 122, 177, 201, 235 *et passim*).
13. I.e., the theorem published in 1822 by Fourier, according to which any periodic vibration, however complex, may be considered as built up of a series of simple harmonic motions whose frequencies are in the ratios 1 : 2 : 3 : 4 etc., the frequency of the complex vibration itself being the first member of the series. This series is called the harmonic series. Boring (1942: 325-6) points out that the theorem is synthetic, as well as analytic, for it shows that any periodic motion at all can be reduced to the sum of a series of simple harmonic vibrations.
14. For Hobbes's criticisms, see Shapin and Schaffer (1985).
15. Hunt (1978: 112-21, p.121).
16. *Ibid.* 35-7 does not mention Joshua, although he provides a number of ancient accounts of tunnel location techniques as instances of the

234 *Inner Music*

practical application of acoustical principles for military purposes.
17 See, e.g., Tobias (1970-72).
18 Helmholtz (1877: Ch.6). Boring (1942: 400-2, 404-19, 431-4) cites Haller as the only 'precursor'.
19 Some commentators, e.g., Boring (1942) and Tobias (1970-72), describe Helmholtz's theory as a place theory, since there is a separate 'string' for each frequency of the sound wave. Later, investigators came to see the problem as one of the total hydrodynamics of a tube with elastic walls and not as a series of nearly independent resonators. Hence, it was supposed that the cochlea, a spiral-shaped tube, acts like the spiral-shaped musical instrument we call 'French horn'. The fluid within the tube is traversed by long and short waves, and the waves close into arcs and strike different places on the basilar membrane, much as a pianist's fingers work the keys.
20 By Sorge in 1744, Romieu in 1751 and Tartini in 1754.
21 Leibniz (1714: 532): 'Music charms us, although its beauty only consists in the harmonies of numbers and in the reckoning of the beats or vibrations of sounding bodies, which meet at certain intervals, reckonings of which we are not conscious and which the soul nevertheless does make.'
22 Schrödinger (1956: 169-71).
23 Kostelijk (1950); Littler (1965); Tobias (1970-2). Although the basilar membrane is an elastic membrane, it appears to have no tension in any direction. If tension really is zero, two things follow. First, Helmholtz's supposition that the 'strings' are under transverse tension would be false. Second, displacement of the membrane would not grow in linear relation to the applied signal, so that the law formulated by Hooke (*infra*) would not hold in this case. Some scientists conjecture that the membrane may have a small but definite degree of tension, even though a determination of this may not be easy to make experimentally.
24 See Kassler (1979, 1: 249-53, 2: 864-71) for the music theories of D'Alembert and Rameau.
25 Diderot (1966: especially 155-63).
26 This odd sentence may be glossed by reference to a well-known experiment. If one takes a goblet and places the base in a large vessel of water filled nearly to the top edge of the goblet, it is possible to observe ripples spreading with regularity as the glass edge is sounded by the friction of the finger. At first, the waves will be uniformly spaced, but if the tone of the glass 'leaps' an octave higher, at that moment the aforesaid waves will divide into two, a phenomenon that shows that the ratio involved in the octave is two (2:1).

27 I have re-instated Diderot's *clavecin* (Eng.: harpsichord), which the translator has rendered as clavichord (Fr.: *clavicorde*), since the two instruments are different in shape, construction and action.
28 See Cassirer (1957) and Hewes (1977). Variants of the resonance theory, e.g., the ding-dong theory, the echoic theory, share a common belief that language has always been vocal-auditory and, hence, developed from calls and cries.
29 Diderot (1966: especially 97-108).
30 Kassler (1984a).
31 The term 'paideia' was not limited to education in the formal sense, according to Anderson (1966: 2).
32 Edmonds (1957, 1: 15-9, p. 15).
33 Anderson (1966: 57).
34 See Plato, *Phaedo* (85e *seq*., 88d), and the criticism in Aristotle, *De anima* (407b30 *seq*.). Gottschalk (1971) concludes that the association with Pythagoreanism was made later and that the harmony doctrine probably was 'improvised' by Plato 'as a model of what was entailed in real terms by the analogy with which Simmias had begun'.
35 Scaltsas (1990) shows that Plato's criticism of the second theory is unfair to the heuristic value of the model. Like Gottschalk (1971), however, he assumes that mixture, not tension and relaxation, is the only approach to the attunement model, even though one of its promoters, Aristoxenus, *Elementa harmonica* (1.10-12), made sound a function of tension and relaxation.
36 Freeman (1952: 73-77); Kirk, Raven and Schofield (1983: 214-38, 322-50).
37 Kassler (1982, 1986).
38 Kirk, Raven and Schofield (1983: 181-213); see also Lloyd (1970: 37).
39 A comparison between a crossbow and a lyre-type instrument, the *phorminx* (see Anderson 1966: 3-11), occurs in Homer, *Odyssey* (21.404-11) thus: 'subtle Odysseus had been weighing the great bow in his hands and looking at it all over. Then, just as a man who understands the *phorminx* and song easily stretches a string round a new *kollops*, tying the well-twisted sheep-gut at both ends, so Odysseus strung the great bow without difficulty. Then, taking it in his right hand, he tested the string, and it sang out beautifully like the voice of a swallow.'
40 Kirk, Raven and Schofield (1983: 280-321); see also Solmsen (1950).
41 Mathieson (1975).
42 Spiegel (1973: 214-19); Hall (1969, 1: 137-63).

43 Galen (1951: 13, 17).
44 Dijksterhuis (1969: 22); Tracy (1969: 164).
45 Aristotle, *Physica* (Book A 5.188b; 7.190a-190b, 7.191a).
46 Bogard (1979); Bolzan (1976); Joachim (1903).
47 Tracy (1969).
48 Galen (1951: 12).
49 Spiegel (1970); Wilson (1959).
50 Nussbaum (1978: 143-64).
51 Rist (1985: 38); see also Hahm (1977).
52 Solmsen (1961: 183) suggests that Tertullian continued the tradition of the soul as a *pneuma*, or exhaled breath, because he made an analogy to '*flatus in calamo*' (air in a flute): as the *flatus* emerges at the openings of the flute, so does soul at the sense organs.
53 Rabelais (1530-34: 295-301, p. 301) converted Galen's chemical model into an economical one: as the pneumaticised blood circulates, organs become lenders and debtors.
54 Wilson (1959: 311-4).
55 See, e.g., Hutchison (1983, 1984).
56 Harvey (c.1616-18: 37, also 7).
57 *Ibid.* 123, 227, 229.
58 Harvey (1627: 111).
59 *Ibid.* 143, 147.
60 *Ibid.* 111.
61 *Ibid.* 151.
62 Ammann (1967); Godwin (1979).
63 Fludd grasped that a string does not produce a pitch effectively until it is drawn so taut as to be virtually unstretchable, but he did not realise that any increase of string tension strains the soundboard proportionately. But Hobbes (Ch.4.II.4.1. *infra*) grasped the principle – the greater the draw, the greater the bend – by recourse to the archer's 'monochord', a crossbow. Subsequently, Hooke (Ch.3.III.5.1. *infra*) gave the principle a quantitative determination.
64 See, e.g., Chamberlain (1971: 125): the preacher is cantor; his exegesis of the whole Bible, cantus; all virtues, tones or specific consonances; the virtue of virtues (charity), canticum canticorum; vice, canticum diaboli; the cithara, mortification of sins; the psalterium, inner devotion to God; the tuba, preaching or tribulation in charity; the tympana, control of lust.
65 See, e.g., Michael and Michael (1989).
66 For the publication history, see Descartes (1632: xliii-xlv).
67 E.g., Descartes (1637: 114).

68 Descartes (1632: 71-2).
69 *Ibid.* 33-5; see also Descartes (1637: 89).
70 Descartes (1632: 46).
71 *Ibid.* 47.
72 Descartes (1637: 89).
73 *Ibid.* 90, who did not distinguish clearly between sensory and motor nerves.
74 Oatley (1978: 57).

CHAPTER 2:   THE PARADOXES OF POWER
1 Hobbes (1651: 81).
2 Sacksteder (1982c) lists the secondary literature. Smart (c.1756-63: 78) exemplifies the confusion, because, initially, he followed received opinion, which held that Hobbes was an atheist (i.e., one who identifies the creating principles of the universe with God, not one who denies God's existence), and later changed his mind: 'Let Crispus rejoice with Leviathan – God be gracious to the soul of HOBBES, who was no atheist, but a servant of Christ, and died in the Lord – I wronged him God forgive me.'
3 Hobbes (1650a, 4: 4; 1640: 3-4).
4 Hobbes (1650a, 4: 9, 11; 1651: 88; 1656a, 1: 377ff.).
5 Sambursky (1959).
6 Hahm (1977: 153-6, 243-8).
7 Rist (1985: 45).
8 Lloyd (1970: 99-124).
9 Anderson (1965: 133).
10 Kassler (1979: xxv-lxii; 1982).
11 Plato, *Philebus* (55e1-56a3) developed the purely speculative (Pythagorean) aspects: once any art is deprived of numbering, measuring and weighing, what is left will be mere guessing and empirical concern with the senses. Thus began the long tradition in which 'intelligible' was treated as distinct from, and ranked superior to, 'sensible'.
12 According to Dostrovsky (1974-75: 183 n.4), the word 'frequency' was used only occasionally during the seventeenth century, when it was more common to refer to the pitch of the sound or to the number of vibrations.
13 Cohen (1984); Drake (1970). This theory has been superceded, since it mistakenly assumes dependence on phase relationships.
14 Cohen (1984: 92). Brandt (1928: 78ff., 150, 157, 393) states that in 1634 Hobbes visited Mersenne daily, and in 1635-6 he met Galileo at Florence.

15 Dear (1988: 5-6).
16 Dostrovsky (1974-5: 185-8) represents them algebraically.
17 Galilei (1638: 95-108); cf. Hobbes (1650a, 4: 34-7, 1656a, 1: 485-505). See Drake (1970) and Palisca (1992) for the musical experiments of Galileo and his father, Vincenzo.
18 Hobbes (1656a, 1650a, 1650b); but see Hobbes (1662: 9-10): why pendulums of equal lengths perform their vibrations in equal times, but not if they start from unequal angles.
19 Ariotti (1971-2).
20 Galilei (1638: 84, 95-6, 107, 188-94, 239-40).
21 Hobbes (1656a, 1: 316). A geometrical construction using only straightedge and compass is called 'Euclidean'. It is not possible to square the circle in this way; but it was difficult to prove that this was so, and the impossibility was finally proved only in the closing decades of the nineteenth century. In his attempts at quadrature, Hobbes (*infra*) also used Archimedean constructions.
22 E.g., Brandt (1928: 322).
23 According to Ariotti (1971-2: 380), Descartes rejected Galileo's insight, because he assumed that in the absence of the resistance of air, pendular motion would continue indefinitely.
24 Hobbes (1656a, 1: 317-8, also 215, 320).
25 *Ibid*. 328, also 215.
26 Cannon and Dostrovsky (1981: 5).
27 *Ibid*. Later, it was recognised that, in the case of the simple pendulum, each element of the system would undergo simple harmonic motions having the same period. See, e.g., Hooke (1935a: 211, for 15 January 1675/6), who told friends that 'the vibrations of a string were not isocrone but that the vibration of the particals [i.e., partials] was'.
28 Galilei (1638: 95-108); see also Cohen (1984: 85-97).
29 Galilei (1638: 103).
30 *Ibid*. 107.
31 *Ibid*. 108.
32 *Ibid*. 104.
33 Mintz (1962: 19).
34 Aubrey (1978: 315).
35 Pacchi (1968). There are two catalogues at Chatsworth House: Hobbes MS E.1.A (compiled late 1620s) and Hobbes MS E.2 (compiled c.1631).
36 Hulse (1968) identifies the two music books.
37 Price (1981: 109-18); see also Hulse (1986).
38 Hulse (1986) identifies the music listed separately; but Hobbes MS

Notes

E.2. contains twenty-seven books and manuscripts lumped under one category, 'De musica', which cannot be identified.

39 Hobbes (1655, 1656a; 1650a, 1650b); MacDonald and Hargreaves (1952: 9-14, 41-2, 76). Goldsmith, in Hobbes (1640: vii-xx), compares the earlier texts with Hobbes (1650b).
40 Hobbes (1651: 626).
41 See Hobbes (1656b, 1682) for the debate; Macdonald and Hargreaves (1952: 29, 37-41) for bibliographical details; and Hobbes (1656b, 5: 22) for Bramhall's charge against Hobbes's 'rare piece of sublimated stoicism'.
42 Barker and Goldstein (1984); Salmon (1989: especially 202-5).
43 Hobbes (1656b, 5: 242-3).
44 *Ibid*. 243; Hobbes (1642-3: 421-34): 'The basis of the Stoics' fate; and that God is not the cause of any evil'.
45 Gould (1970: 152; 1974).
46 See Wilson (1965: 9) for the changes in England; Long (1971a) for the Stoic background; and Hood (1967) for Hobbes's definition.
47 See Epictetus (n.d.: 14-5) for freedom and determination; Manley (1980: 243-8) for the English assimilation of Stoic theories of natural law; and Grendler (1963) for similarities between the political philosophies of Hobbes and the neo-Stoic, Charron.
48 Hobbes (1656a, 1: 9).
49 Hobbes (1644, 5: 215-48); Macdonald and Hargreaves (1952: 23-4).
50 Shapiro (1973: 143-72 *et passim*).
51 Shapiro (1974: 243-54).
52 *Ibid*. 244, 247-8, 265.
53 Shapiro (1973: 147).
54 *Ibid*. 146.
55 According to Nussbaum (1978: 157), Aristotle did not clearly distinguish 'perceptual alterations from those that lead directly to limb motion'. The same was true of Descartes (*supra*). Hobbes, however, made this distinction by introducing a material 'reaction'.
56 Shapiro (1973: 169 and n.116).
57 Hobbes (1656a, 1: 426).
58 *Ibid*. 215, 217, 321-4, 326-32, 334-5, 337-9, 341-2, 344, 374-83, 425-6, 448, 474, 481, 504, 509, 519.
59 *Ibid*. 430: 'by supposing motive power *in* the sun, we suppose motion also; for power to move without motion is no power at all' [italics mine].
60 *Ibid*. 324-5, 449, 450, 474, 482; Hobbes (1655, 1: 264, 336, 366, 392).
61 Hobbes (1656a, 1: 448).

62 *Ibid.* 449.
63 *Ibid.* 451.
64 *Ibid.* 449.
65 *Ibid.* 403; Hobbes (1650a, 4: 54).
66 Hobbes (1650a, 4: 8).
67 Hobbes (1656a, 1: 406).
68 *Ibid.* 407.
69 *Ibid.* 406.
70 *Ibid.* 392–404, 448; Hobbes (1650a, 4: 3–8, 10–11, 31, 34).
71 Hobbes (1656a, 1: 392, 486).
72 *Ibid.* 392–3, 407, 449, 466; Hobbes (1650a, 4: 4, 6, 11, 55–6, 60–1, 63).
73 Hobbes (1656a, 1: 397, 403, 408).
74 Hobbes (1656a, 1: viii–ix, 407), who was remembered in Harvey's will.
75 Harvey (1628: 75–6).
76 *Ibid.* 76.
77 Harvey (c.1616–18: 273; 1649: 60).
78 Harvey (1651: 111 *et passim*). See Webster (1967) and Frank (1980: 36–7), the latter of whom tentatively dates the contents, which were written between 1630 and 1647–8.
79 Harvey (1651: 247–8).
80 Harvey (1651: 242; also 243, 257, 448, 463, 465).
81 E.g., Harvey (1628: 44–5, 47).
82 Harvey (1651: 241).
83 *Ibid.* 243.
84 *Ibid.* 247; the blood's pulsations vary in 'speed or slowness', 'vehemency or weakness etc.'.
85 *Ibid.* 293–300.
86 *Ibid.* 296–9.
87 Harvey (1628: 39, 50–1; 1651: 97, 100, 250, 297, 299): The blood has a pulse ('harmony'), as well as a period ('rhythm'), so that Harvey (1651: 217) could write that the blood 'moves and dances like an animal'.
88 Harvey (1649: 38, 65; 1651: 243, 253–8, 374, 381).
89 Twenty years after Harvey's death, Leeuwenhoek saw spermatozoa for the first time with the aid of a microscope.
90 Harvey (1651: 147–8, 183, 189–90, 227–8, 230, 232, 239–40, 353, 357, 443, 448, 463–5); cf. Hobbes (1678, 7: 129, 136).
91 Harvey (1651: 239, 349–51, 445–6, 452–3). For the brain as an embryo, see Onians (1951: 111 n.5); see also Pagel (1967: 270–6).
92 Harvey (1651: 237), perhaps after Cicero, who used nod (Lat.: *nutus*)

in its figurative sense on a number of occasions; e.g., *Catilinarians* (3.9.21): all things are governed by the will [*nutu*] and the power of the gods. Harvey (1628: 127) equated nod and contraction, e.g., 'it is certain that all local movement in animals comes first and takes its beginning from the contraction of some particle', for '*neuron* is derived from *neuo*, that is I nod, I contract'. Although his etymology and definition are false, Harvey (1627: 79) supposed that nerve is the generic term for everything that is contractible; and it comprises, as its species, ligament, tendon, origin of muscle, fibre and flesh.

93 Hobbes (1656a, 1: 527).
94 *Ibid.*
95 Hobbes (1656a, 1: 25) first distanced himself from the 'scales' of traditional writers on logic; then, *ibid.* 334, asserted his position: that words such as '*fluid, soft, tough,* and *hard,* in the same manner as *great* and *little,* are used only comparatively; and are not different kinds, but different degrees of quality'.
96 I.e., by analogy to the Galilean pendulum, where tension is maximum at the perpendicular and minimum at the extremes.
97 For cycles, Hobbes (1656a, 1: 395-408, 410-44, 449-50, 466-84, 445-65, 508-31).
98 *Ibid.* 406-7; Hobbes (1650a, 4: 31; 1651: 118, 122).
99 Hobbes (1656a, 1: 407; 1650a, 4: 25, 31, 32, 67, 69; 1651: 118-9).
100 See this chapter II.4.2. (*infra*).
101 I.e., ratiocination or computation by adding, subtracting, multiplying and dividing, Hobbes (1656a, 1: 3-5), who also, *ibid.* 408-9, defined deliberative processes as a succession of appetites and aversions, i.e., plus or minus degrees of heat.
102 See Hobbes (1650a, 4: 69; 1656a, 1: 409).
103 Hobbes (1656a, 1: 409; 1650a, 4: 68-9; 1656b, 5: 12): since 'the *will* be an internal act of the soul...the *will* and the *word* are diverse things; and differ as the *thing signified,* and the *sign*'.
104 Hobbes (1650a, 4: 23-4, 28-30; 1656a, 1: 55-64).
105 Hobbes (1650a, 4: 18, 29; 1650b, 4: 110).
106 Hobbes (1650a, 4: 29; 1651: 93, 96, 127; 1656a, 1: 399, 409).
107 Hobbes (1651: 82; 1650a, 4: 26).
108 Hobbes (1656a, 1: 9-10, 391)
109 *Ibid.* 399-402. Hobbes (1650a, 4: 54) focused on healthy creatures, whose organs are 'equally tempered'; hence, he used dreams rather than illness as the principal example of incoherence.
110 I.e., the Stoic version of *sophrosyne*; see Hobbes (1650b, 4: 110) and North (1966).
111 Hobbes (1656a, 1: 135-8, 323-4).

112 Tracy (1969: 358).
113 Cowley (1668, 2: 377), who was created M.D. at Oxford, which was to become the leading centre for the study of physiology in the second half of the seventeenth century.
114 *Ibid.* 2: 377–459.
115 Rostvig (1962).
116 Cowley (1668, 2: 384).
117 *Ibid.* 384–5; see also North (1966).
118 Cowley (1668, 2: 388).
119 *Ibid.* 383. *Pan huper sebastus: pan(h)upersebastos*, probably a nonceword and certainly Byzantine (W.D. Anderson, personal communication).
120 Cowley (1668, 2: 459).
121 *Ibid.* 384.
122 Hobbes (1651: 129–30).
123 Hobbes (1650a, 4: 50–1; 1651: 124, 167, 172; 1656a, 1: 168): our desire for knowledge is called 'curiosity' and from this arises 'not only the invention of names, but also supposition of such causes of all things as they thought might produce them. And from this beginning is derived all *philosophy*'.
124 Hobbes (1656a, 1: 56–7).
125 Kieffer (1964: 1–18).
126 Hobbes (1656a, 1: 55–6, 106). Misnomers: calling 'any thing a name, which is not the name thereof'; hasty inference: 'pronouncing rashly'; but man is not the measure, for Hobbes's criterion is universal nature ('Nature it selfe cannot erre').
127 *Ibid.* 56.
128 *Ibid.* 57.
129 Inwood (1985: 106–7, 160).
130 Gould (1970: 109–12).
131 Sambursky (1959: 46).
132 Todd (1976) details the Peripatetic criticism.
133 E.g., Hobbes (1642–3, 1644); see also Knudsen and Pederson (1968).
134 Scott (1970: 6), to whom I am indebted for the convenient shorthand way of summarising Descartes' conception of the universe; and Shapiro (1974: 243–4).
135 See Charleton (1654) and Digby (1645).
136 Westfall (1971: 99–109, 138–9, 535–7).
137 See Colie (1966) for other solutions to this classical problem, *ex nihilo nihil fit*.
138 Hobbes (1656a, 1: 71–2), italics mine.
139 *Ibid.* 112.

140 *Ibid.* 425. The atomists conceived fluidity as consisting 'of small grains of hard matter, in such manner as meal is fluid, made so by grinding of the corn', and the same view was held by Descartes. But Hobbes, *ibid.* 417, disagreed: fluidity is 'of its own nature as homogeneous as either an atom, or as vacuum itself'.
141 Hobbes (1656a, 1: 425).
142 *Ibid.* 445.
143 *Ibid.* 426.
144 In Descartes' theory, cohesion arises from simple repose or juxtaposition, whereas in Gassendi's theory, cohesion derives from the union of atoms by hooks and claws or by entwining antlers. See Millington (1942); Hesse (1962: 106) points out the difficulties of Descartes' theory in relation to solids.
145 Hobbes (1656a, 1: 419).
146 *Ibid.*: Lucretius 'ought...to have proved, that there are some bodies extremely hard, not relatively as compared with softer bodies, but absolutely, that is to say, infinitely hard; which is not true'.
147 *Ibid.* 212, 335: even hard bodies are deformable (i.e., yield), for 'when a point moved, how little soever the impetus thereof be, falls upon a point of any body at rest, how hard soever that body be, it will at the first touch make it yield a little'; and 'though from the compression of two stones we cannot with our eyes discern any swelling outwards towards the sides, as we perceive in two bodies of wax; yet we know well enough by reason, that some tumour must needs be there, though it be but little'.
148 *Ibid.* 343; for flexion (bowing, bending) 177, 184, 192, 195-7, 294-6, 303-7, 342-3, 407, 476, 478-9.
149 *Ibid.* 475-6. Flexible bodies, *ibid.* 343, easily 'suffer such transposition of their parts'; but bodies of 'innumerable degrees of hardness', *ibid.* 419, 475, require the application of greater force and are broken asunder...by solution of their continuity begun in the outermost superficies, and proceeding successively to the innermost parts'.
150 E.g., Galilei (1638: 51-2).
151 E.g., Hobbes (1656a, 1: 466-7): the 'pores' in the skin are filled with fluid passing in and out.
152 Galilei (1638: 7), who investigated what happens when a heavy weight is hung at the end of a horizontal beam but did not consider either the bending or the compression of fibres that takes place on the under side of the beam.
153 *Ibid.* 10.
154 Elasticity is implied in the term 'restitution', which Hobbes did use and which denotes the return of an elastic material to its original

form when released from strain. As early as 1641, according to Brandt (1928: 116-9), Hobbes attributed the cause of rebound to restitution.
155 Bernstein (1980).
156 For endeavour, Hobbes (1656a, 1: 206-7 definition).
157 For resistance, *ibid*. 211-2 definition.
158 For rest as endeavour motion, *ibid*. 342, 351, 526-7.
159 For initial moments, *ibid*. 342 'things…have the beginning of their restitution within themselves', 407 'animal motion…is the very first endeavour, and found even in the embryo', 516 'endeavours or moments', 529 'all endeavour being the beginning of motion'.
160 For impetus, *ibid*. 207-8 definition, 212 ('I define FORCE *to be the impetus or quickness of motion multiplied either into itself, or into the magnitude of the movent, by means whereof the said movent works more or less upon the body that resists it.*'), 218-45, 269-72.
161 For force, ibid. 214 ('motion is considered sometimes from the effect only which the movent works in the moved body, which is usually called *moment*. Now *moment is the excess of motion which the movent has above the motion or endeavour of the resisting body.*'), 351-61, 364, 372-3, 516.
162 *Ibid*. 205.
163 *Ibid*. 218.
164 For quantity of motion, ibid. 207, 218; for 'magnitude' of motion, 112, 115, 133, 203. See also Sacksteder (1981a: 582-4).
165 Hobbes (1656a, 1: 348): action and reaction 'proceed in the same line, but from opposite terms', for 'seeing reaction is nothing but endeavour in the patient to restore itself to that situation from which it was forced by the agent; the endeavour or motion both of the agent and patient or reagent will be propagated between the same terms; yet so, as that in action the term, *from which*, is in reaction the term *to which*. And seeing all action proceeds in this manner, not only between the opposite terms of the whole line in which it is propagated, but also in all the parts of that line, the terms *from which* and *to which*, both of the action and reaction will be in the same line.'
166 *Ibid*. 342. For mechanical change (mutation, transmutation, i.e., displacement or 'change of situation'), *ibid*. 70, 87, 118, 123, 126, 131, 149-54, 323, 342, 364, 389-90.
167 *Ibid*. 127-8.
168 For work, *ibid*. 103, 120-1, 123, 125, 150, 212, 214, 217, 245, 327, 342, 384, 394, 405, 436, 464, 480, 497, 523-4, 527, 530.
169 *Ibid*. 123, italics mine.

170 Sacksteder (1982a: 60).
171 Hobbes (1656a, 1: 122-3, 128, 392, 419, 491).
172 *Ibid.* 344, italics mine.
173 *Ibid.* 347-8.
174 Hobbes (1656a, 1: 97). The atomists maintained that matter (magnitude) was composed of indivisible minima, whereas Aristotle, *Physica* (6.1-231.b.3, 233.b.15, 6.10-241.a.16) asserted that a magnitude or continuum cannot be resolved into indivisibles, because a quantity is its own indivisible; that is, a plenum cannot allow of the existence of ultimate particles or atoms. Hobbes (*infra*) will reconcile these two beliefs, which are separately treated by Sorabji (1983) and Drabkin (1950: 162-98).
175 *Ibid.* 445-6.
176 E.g., as in Mersenne's Laws.
177 Hobbes (1656a, 1: 426).
178 *Ibid.* 445.
179 *Ibid.* 447-8.
180 I.e., the method of exhaustion devised by Eudoxus and reproduced by Euclid, *Elements* (Book V).
181 Hobbes (1656a, 1: 477).
182 *Ibid.* 211.
183 *Ibid.* 206.
184 Sacksteder (1981a: 577).
185 Hobbes (1656a, 1: 320).
186 See Helmholtz (1877: 21) for an example.
187 I.e., the spiral of Archimedes, which is the curve traced by a point moving with uniform speed along a straight line which revolves with uniform angular speed about a fixed point on the line.
188 Hobbes (1656a, 1: 307-9), whose approach reconciles the two beliefs. See also Drabkin (1950: 170 n.12).
189 Hobbes (1656a, 1: 268-73); see Jones (1974).
190 Hobbes (1656a, 1: 288).
191 For the way, *ibid.* 213.
192 *Ibid.* 111.
193 *Ibid.* 207-10.
194 Sambursky (1959).
195 Hobbes (1656a, 1: 135).
196 *Ibid.* 137-8; see also this chapter III.5.1. (*infra*) for Hobbes's argument that substance is defined by its attributes (i.e., predicates).
197 *Ibid.* 3, 66, 407; Hobbes (1650a, 4: 26, 50, 51, 71).
198 E.g., Hobbes (1651: 134-42).
199 Sacksteder, especially (1990).

200 Hobbes used the term 'conscious' only once in the final statement of his philosophy (1650a, 4: 42), preferring the older term, 'conscience', which had a twofold meaning: (1) internal recognition of (or the 'power' which decides upon) right and wrong as regards one's motives and actions; and (2) awareness of one's self and of one's actions. He employed the terms 'sense' and 'phantasm' but not 'sensation' and 'representation' (Sacksteder 1978), the latter of which is a reaction or motion outward equivalent to the Stoic apprehension – grasping, as in the contraction of the hand into a fist (Sandbach 1971).
201 Hobbes (1651: 95).
202 E.g., Hobbes (1650a, 4: 10-1; especially 1651: 90-3).
203 See Ch.4. (*infra*).
204 Hobbes (1651: 134).
205 *Ibid.* 138.
206 Hobbes (1656a, 1: 348-9; 1650a, 4: 23, 25-8, 47).
207 Hobbes (1656a, 1: 349-50).
208 Metals possess the dual properties of elasticity and plasticity (ductility), the one or the other property being brought into play according to the amount of force applied. Hobbes probably acquired this knowledge (also how metals may be tempered by heat) when, with Petty, he learned various chemical protocols from Davison, a Scottish chemist and physician resident in Paris. See Frank (1980: 102).
209 Hobbes (1656a, 1: 70).
210 Hobbes (1651: 140): 'In summe, all Passions that produce strange and unusuall behaviour, are called by the generall name of Madnesse. But of the severall kinds of Madnesse, he that would take the paines, might enrowle a legion. And if the Excesses be madnesse, there is no doubt but the Passions themselves, when they tend to Evill, are degrees of the same.'
211 *Ibid.*; Hobbes (1650a, 4: 54-9).
212 Hobbes (1651: 99).
213 Hobbes (1656a, 1: 64).
214 Davidson (1907: 36-51).
215 Hobbes (1656a, 1: 2).
216 *Ibid.* 1-91.
217 *Ibid.* 309-17.
218 Sacksteder (1982a: 55).
219 Hobbes (1656a, 1: 87-8).
220 *Ibid.* 92-202.
221 *Ibid.* 92, 411.

222 *Ibid.* 101-38 body and accident, 139-386 disposition and relative disposition.
223 *Ibid.* 76, 116-7; Hobbes (1651: 689): 'the Universe is All'.
224 *Ibid.* for common accidents (magnitude – including 'consistency' and 'figure' – and motion) e.g., 202, 404, 511; for particular accidents (e.g., of sound – strong/weak, grave/acute/, primary/derivative, uniform/not uniform, durable/less durable) 486.
225 Hobbes (1656a, 1: 28).
226 See Sacksteder (1981b: 472) on Hobbes's 'manner of reducing hypothetical and categorical propositions to each other'.
227 Kieffer (1964) and Mates (1961).
228 Hobbes (1656a, 1: 203-386, 387-532).
229 *Ibid.* 203-4.
230 *Ibid.* 386.
231 *Ibid.* 388.
232 Hobbes (1656a, 1: 87-8): 'such things as I have said are to be taught last, cannot be demonstrated, till such as are propounded to be first treated of, be fully understood. Of which method no other example can be given, but that treatise of the elements of philosophy, which I shall begin in the next chapter [Part 2], and continue to the end of the work'.
233 *Ibid.* xiii.
234 Galileo (1632: 399) used a pendulum to demonstrate that two contrary motions agree naturally in the same movable body.
235 E.g., like the motion of fluid in an air thermoscope, for which see Hobbes (1656a, 1: 521-2), whose instructions for making this 'organ' show a debt to Mersenne's 1644 modification of the standard type. See Barnett (1956: 278).
236 Hobbes (1640: 8, 11-2; 1650a, 4: 11-2; 1651: 88, 89; 1656a, 1: 396): imagination is '*sense decaying*', 'little by little'.
237 Hobbes (1656a, 1: 72, 74, 398, 401, 406-10).
238 Mersenne (1957: 270, 442).
239 Hobbes (1651: 105).
240 Sacksteder (1980, 1981a, 1982a, 1988).
241 According to Sambursky (1959: 86-7), the Stoics transposed geometrical figures into material shapes and regarded them as held together by *pneuma* tensions which pervade every body and define its physical state: 'After substitution of a cord of a given length for a geometrical line, the various shapes of the cord are compared and the straightened cord is seen as the extremal case as against the curved ones. A problem of the calculus of variations is thus stated in an intuitive way: among all curves of a given length the straight

line represents the curve between whose extremities lies the greatest distance.' A similar trend to physicalise geometry may be observed in Archimedes, Chrysippus' contemporary.

242 Butler (1636: 89), whose phonetic spelling I have modernised.
243 *Ibid.* 71.
244 *Ibid.* 90.
245 The strictest form of fugue is canon, which means rule. The relationship between melodies (traditional patterns or formulae) and laws (*nomoi*) was explored by Plato, *Laws* (4.722, 734, 7.799, 800) and is commented on by Anderson (1966: 82-3, 99-100). Plato did not care for innovation in the making of melodies. This is not Hobbes's position.
246 Butler (1636: 81).
247 Hobbes (1656a, 1: 92; 1650a, 4: 28-9).
248 Hobbes employed a number of instruments, including experiment, as part of his technique of comparing, accepting and rejecting. Although these instruments have yet to be fully analysed, one deserves special mention here – equipollence – the counterposing to a belief its equally well-supported negation or opposite. Equipollence was used by ancient sceptics to attack any belief and thereby induce suspension of belief without presupposing the truth of some other belief. The main sceptical threat, therefore, is the possibility of alternatives to our beliefs rather than the inadequacy of the reasons we have for them.
249 'Science corrects but enlarges prudence', as Sacksteder (1988: 6) points out.
250 Hobbes (1656a, 1: 7).
251 I.e., before 'wit' has been acquired 'by method and instruction', for which see Hobbes (1651: 134-9); hence, pre-rational includes children and fools (dullards).
252 I.e., the ant and bee are emblems of wisdom, Hobbes (1650b: 120-1; 1651: 225-7).
253 Hobbes (1651: 404, 534, 576).
254 See Anderson (1966) for the classical antecedents.
255 Hobbes (1656a, 1: 395); for his method of study, see Sacksteder, especially (1982a).
256 I.e., philosophy or knowledge of causes and effects, Hobbes (1650a, 4: 28-9; 1656a, 1: 3).
257 Hobbes (1651: 216-7, 545): the precepts of natural reason are 'written' in the heart.
258 *Ibid.* 454-5, where the two laws are reduced to 'reason' (universal nature, i.e., tension) and 'equity' (peace, i.e., concord).

CHAPTER 3: CALLING TO MIND

1. Glanvill (1665: lviii).
2. *Ibid.* 15: 'our *Souls*...are indeed our *selves*'.
3. *Ibid.* 73.
4. *Ibid.* 12-48.
5. *Ibid.* 19.
6. *Ibid.* 21.
7. *Ibid.* 23.
8. *Ibid.* 24.
9. *Ibid.* 26.
10. Balz (1918: 13) did not develop his insight that, for Hobbes, 'the human body retains the prior motion as a dampened but persistent organic reverberation; and in this resides the possibility of memory'.
11. Glanvill (1665: 37-8).
12. *Ibid.* 34-5.
13. Prudovsky (1989).
14. According to Schwoerer (1988: 136), the order for the burning was given by Charles II on the assumption that Hobbes's books justified resistance theory.
15. See Hermann and Chaffin (1988).
16. E.g., Montaigne (1603: 219-310).
17. Plato, *Theaetetus* (190e-195b, 196d-199c) and *Philebus* (39a).
18. Sorabji (1972) and Lloyd (1987: 375-6).
19. Aristotle, *Posterior Analytics* (99b36-100a8).
20. Tracy (1969: 262-3).
21. Riese (1959: 150),
22. Plato, *Meno* and *Phaedo*.
23. More (1652: 14-5).
24. See, e.g., Chalmers (1937); Freudenthal (1983); Hesse (1962); Jammer (1957).
25. Boyle (1662: 223-4).
26. Glanvill (1665: 174).
27. Hobbes (1656a, 1: 400-1).
28. The Alexandrian anatomist, Erasistratus, made the association, according to Clarke (1968a), who also indicates that between 1600-55 knowledge derived chiefly from the writings of the ancients, particularly Galen, together with a few modifications made in the sixteenth century, whereas between 1655-65 contributions of the greatest importance were made to brain anatomy and physiology.
29. Hobbes (1656a, 1: 392, 403, 486, 506, 507).
30. Before Harvey, most writers supposed that the brain had an

independent function, although a few (e.g., Coiter) recognised that the regular pulsating motion of the brain was synchronous with the arteries.

31 According to the older tradition of brain anatomy, continued by Descartes (1637, 1664), the pineal gland (penis), superior coliculi (the testes) and the inferior colliculi (the nates or testes inferior) were attached, in descending order, to the brain stem. See, e.g., Harvey (c.1616-18: 323) and Clarke (1968a). Harvey and Hobbes both resorted to the metaphor of the 'fecund' mind. Unlike Descartes, however, neither man gave primacy to one or the other gender for reasons suggested in Ch.2. (*supra*).
32 Glanvill (1665: 31).
33 *Ibid.* 30-1.
34 Digby (1645: 334-5). In England virginal was the generic term for plucked keyboard instruments.
35 *Ibid.* 336.
36 Descartes' treated the passions as feelings, i.e., as experiences of the soul derived from alien causes, whereas Hobbes treated the passions as tendencies not feelings, i.e., as the sole springs of action. See Gardner, Metcalf and Beebe-Center (1937).
37 Digby (1645: 344).
38 *Ibid.* 345.
39 *Ibid.* 341.
40 *Ibid.* 352.
41 *Ibid.* 310.
42 *Ibid.* 347.
43 Glanvill (1665: 32).
44 Digby (1645: 349).
45 *Ibid.* 350-1: when atoms, or 'similitudes of bodies', are not 'often repaired', they 'moulder away' and forgetting takes place.
46 Glanvill (1665: 29-30).
47 White (1665), with whom Hobbes carried on a number of friendly but systematic disputes; e.g., Hobbes (1642-3).
48 White (1665: 36-41).
49 *Ibid.* 38.
50 Digby (1645: 340).
51 See Münxelhaus (1976) for medieval depictions. According to McKinnon (1978), the fallacy of the weights was suspected by Vincenzo Galilei and definitely exposed by his son, Galileo.
52 Ancient *musica speculativa* classed canonics, the use of the monochord, as a branch of arithmetic; see Kassler (1982). But Mersenne (1957: 30) pointed out that the monochord was called 'the *harmonic*

or *canonic* rule, because it measures the pitch of sounds as the ordinary ruler of the geometers measures straight lines and the compass describes circles'.

53 See Ch.4.I.1.1. (*infra*); see also Gunther (1923-67, 10: 80). Dostrovsky (1974-75: 199) points out that Hooke's wheel demonstrated experimentally 'for the first time, that which Galileo had demonstrated conceptually, namely, the correctness of identifying pitch with frequency or, more precisely, interval with relative frequency'.
54 Kassler and Oldroyd (1983: 592-3).
55 *Ibid.*; see also Kassler (1979, 1: 539-42) and Gouk (1980).
56 For a summary of Hooke's work, see 'Espinasse (1956); for a bibliography of secondary sources relating to that work, see Hunter and Schaffer (1989: 294-304).
57 T. Hobbes, *Dialogus physicus de natura aeris* (London, 1661), translated in Shapin and Schaffer (1985: 345ff.)
58 F. Linus, *Tractatus de corporum inseparabilitate* (London, 1661).
59 North, *The Autobiography*, 100. Other contemporaries attributed the tract to one Francis Line, *alias* Hall, perhaps because Boyle thought the funicular hypothesis was congruent with Jesuit beliefs, and Line, a Jesuit, was in England when the tract was printed. See Webster (1962-66: 481). The funicular hypothesis was adopted by North's legal mentor, Hale, whose work was attacked publicly by Hooke, More and Wallis and privately by North and his brother, Francis.
60 Both Hobbes and Linus utilised equipollence, for which see Ch.2.n.248.
61 E.g., Boyle (1965-66, 3: 117; 4: 12, 416, 418, 422, 455, 457; 5: 141, 150, 517-8, 520, 6: 741, 750, 753); for penetration of dimensions, divisibility and indivisibility, vaccum and plenum, see Boyle (1662), Drabkin (1950: 191-3), Jones (1974) and Webster (1962- 66).
62 Webster (1962-66).
63 *Ibid.* contains a well-argued case for Boyle. Nevertheless, he did not consider Boyle's aristocratic status, his self-admitted weakness in mathematics, or his treatment of Hooke as a servant rather than an equal. In short, I believe the case for Hooke has yet to be adequately argued. For a possible approach, see Centore (1970: 58-60).
64 See Boyle (1965-66, 6: 486-7).
65 Aubrey (1978: 318).
66 Hooke (1935a: 108, also for discussions about Hobbes 302, 439).
67 Hooke (1935a: 379); 'Espinasse (1956: 122).
68 Shapiro (1973: 188-207) on Hooke (1665: 54-67).
69 Hooke (1705: 81, 130, 136, 183).

70 Hooke (1935a: 11, 14-5, 22, 68, 69, 176, 332, 379, 390, 419). The contents of Hooke's library were sold in 1693/4 and 1703; see Feisenberger (1975: 69, 70, 76, 81, 89, 91-2, 95, 99, 103, 105, 108, 111-3).

71 E.g., Hooke (1935a: 289, 10 May 1677): 'I explaind to the Society the reason of the strength of lightning from motion according to Divers swiftnesses moving Divers Lengths of bodys &c.'; see also Centore (1970: 98, 104-5); Jammer (1957: 188-90); Shapiro (1973: 188- 207).

72 Singer (1976) and Oldroyd (1980) completely ignore the vibratory nature of Hooke's theory of brain function, the latter concluding that Hooke conceived the brain 'as a kind of butter factory, in which the process workers make up and store pats of butter of different shapes and sizes'.

73 Hobbes (1656a, 1: 508).

74 Oldroyd (1980: 17-20) transcribes the fragment.

75 Hooke (1665: [viii]).

76 Hooke (1683-85: 553).

77 Hesse (1966: 82): 'That he chose to interpret "analysis" and "synthesis" differently from his contemporaries was not a mistake, for the extension of these ideas from mathematics, with its convertible propositions, to natural science, with its nondemonstrative induction of causes, is not decidable logically, but only by a particular understanding of what the structure of scientific reasoning is.'

78 Keynes (1960) provides a checklist of the manuscripts.

79 Hooke (c.1668: 7), whose 'True Method', or 'Philosophical Algebra', consisted of two 'Branches': one on 'the manner of Preparing the Mind, and Furnishing it with fit Materials to work on'; the other (?never written) on 'the Rules and Methods of proceeding or operating with this so collected and qualify'd Supellex'.

80 Hesse (1964, 1966), Oldroyd (1972, 1987) and Westfall (1983) neither consider Hooke's conception of method within the tradition of self-knowledge and self-restraint nor pay attention to his continuation of the tradition deriving from Archimedes.

81 Hobbes (1641: 139, 1656a, 1: 13-5) asserted that an idea got by sensation may be deceptive and that weakness of memory requires us to use 'marks'.

82 Hooke (c.1668: 35-8 *et passim*), for whom, *ibid.* 19, 34, 44, 65, standard denoted a reduction to number, weight and measure. The sciences that assist this reduction are geometry, arithmetic and algebra, since those who are 'very well skill'd in Geometry and Arithmetick, the more demonstrative Parts, and Algebra the

more inventive Part of it' will have their minds furnished 'as it were with Numbers, Weights, and Measures to inquire into, examine and prove all things'. See also Gunther (1923-67, 7: 462).
83 Hooke (c.1668: 9).
84 Hooke (1676a: 597-605).
85 See Kassler and Oldroyd (1983). Bacon (1626, 9: 143) had suggested making 'an instrument like a funnel, the length of six inches or more; the narrow part whereof may fit the hole of the ear, and the broader end swell much larger, like a bell'.
86 Hooke (c.1668: 40), whose analogue would have been a drum membrane (see this chapter III.5.2. *infra*).
87 *Ibid.* 12.
88 Hooke (1676a: 602).
89 *Ibid.* 601.
90 Hooke (c.1668: 13): 'the Apperture [of the Eye] is not opened in an Instant but by degrees'; for his method of constructing an artificial eye, see Hooke (1680-2: 71-148).
91 E.g., Hooke (c.1668: 36).
92 Hooke (1676a: 603).
93 Hooke (1680-2: 134-6, section 6).
94 *Ibid.* 135.
95 *Ibid.* 138-48 (section 7).
96 Partially printed at the end of Hooke (c.1668: 65-70, p.65); see also Hooke (1683-85: 520): 'By Point...I do not here understand an imaginary nothing, which, in speculative Geometry, is defin'd to be a Negation of Quantity, or an Entity that hath no Part or Quantity; but I understand such a Point as hath Quantity and Extention, but yet so small and minute, as that the sense cannot distinguish that it hath any Parts'.
97 Hooke (c.1668: 66).
98 Hooke (1680-2: 134).
99 *Ibid.* According to Shapiro (1973: 188-206), Hooke 'made a notable contribution to the continuum theory of light with his principle of "interference"', which, nevertheless, fell short of the true principle, because Hooke 'could not take the necessary step and consider white light as a mixture of different frequencies'.
100 Hooke (1680-2: 134).
101 Hooke (1683-5: 550).
102 *Ibid.* 551.
103 Hooke (1665: 93).
104 Kirk, Raven and Schofield (1983: 205); Sambursky (1959: 24-5, 123-4).

105 Hooke (1661: 7).
106 *Ibid.* The similarity of Hooke's hypothesis to that of Hobbes is remarked on by Millington (1942: 261), who does not develop this insight. On 8 July 1680 Hooke restated his hypothesis in a meeting of the Royal Society, 'but it was desired, that some further experiments should clear it'. See Gunther (1923-67, 7: 560).
107 Hooke (1665: 11-31).
108 *Ibid.* 15.
109 *Ibid.*
110 *Ibid.* 16.
111 *Ibid.* 27-8.
112 See, e.g., Gunther (1923-67, 6: 388, 15 February 1672/3) and Hooke (1678b: 262).
113 Hooke (1665: 56-7).
114 *Ibid.* 56.
115 For this study, which began before 1666, see Centore (1970: 92-117).
116 Jammer (1957: 189).
117 Hooke (1682: 183-5), whose hypothesis of the cause of gravity – a 'way of working at a distance' – follows from his discussion of how the 'Sound in the Ear, which is a real Motion in some part thereof, is produced by the internal Motion of the Parts of the Bell some Miles perhaps distant', because the internal motion of the bell is transmitted through a fluid medium.
118 Mersenne (1957: 500ff.), who, *ibid.* 535-7, resorts to atoms and pores ('little vacua') to explain the vibration of bells as a boiling motion of atoms: the air pushes them out of place, but the hooks draw them back into place.
119 Boyle (1662: 62, 63, 239), who (1685) reported the bell experiments without naming Hooke.
120 Gunther (1923-67, 6: 376).
121 *Ibid.* 377.
122 *Ibid.* 377-8: as the vibrations of the glass increase in frequency, the flour ebbs and flows more rapidly.
123 *Ibid.* 378; see also Hooke (c.1668: 39, 40, 41).
124 Galilei (1638: 101-2) had observed that streaks appeared when a hissing sound was produced by scraping a brass plate with a sharp iron chisel.
125 Wallis (1677); see also Dostrovsky (1974-5: 204-9). There are no points of absolute rest in a vibrating bell, for the nodes of the higher tones are not those of the fundamental one. I have been unable to discover when this was first understood.

Notes

126 Hooke (1935a: 403, 411, 431, 433, 443, 446, 449); Gunther (1923-67, 7: 561).
127 Hooke (1935a: 209-10); see also Gunther (1923-67, 6: 265-8) and Oldroyd (1987: 154).
128 Hooke (1705: xxiii); see also Hooke (1935a: 448, 8 July 1680): 'Formed the experiment of the glasse vibrating. 6.4.8. places', and Gunther (1923-67, 7: 560).
129 Hooke (1680-82: 136-7).
130 Gunther (1923-67, 7: 608).
131 Hooke (1705: 191).
132 Hooke (1935a: 4, 191, 322; 1935b: 84, 94, 95, 97, 112, 162, 165).
133 North, *The Musicall Grammarian*, 105.
134 Raven (1906: 237-43) reprints Jenkins' composition, commonly referred to as 'The Five Bells Consort', and compares it to the changes called 'Grandsire Doubles'.
135 Hooke (1935a: 4, 6, 7, 220): 6 August 1672, 10 and 16 September 1672, 16 March 1675/6.
136 Brown (1979): The term 'brother' was reserved for blacksmith-clockmakers originally members of the Blacksmiths' Company.
137 See Edwardes (1977: 106) for one of Tompion's bells, made in 1671.
138 Hooke (1935a: 6).
139 For bell (striking) clocks, see Hooke (1935a: 255-6, 297, 383, 418): 10 November 1676, 24 June 1677, 3 November 1678, 19 July 1679; perhaps also Hooke (1935b: 114): 16 April 1689.
140 Hall (1950-51: 169). On 5 September 1667 Hooke wrote to Boyle (1965-66, 6: 508-9): 'I have lately contrived a new way of wheel work for clocks...which I think does much excel all the ways yet known: and indeed I think it the very perfection of wheel work, and capable of the highest perfection, that can be expected in that kind. There has been nothing like it yet practised. Many other things I long to be at, but I do extremely want time.'
141 Hooke (1705: iv).
142 Hooke (1678a: 331-56); see also Centore (1970: 63-91).
143 Hooke (1678a: 333).
144 *Ibid.* 349-50.
145 *Ibid.* 338-41.
146 Hooke (1683-85: 550); see Hooke (1674: 18-22) for an earlier 'measuring Clew' or 'Mensurator'.
147 Gunther (1923-67, 7: 598-9): 28 June 1682, italics mine.
148 See this chapter II.3.1. (*supra*); see also Hooke (1665: [viii], [xv]) and Hooke (1678b: 368).

149 Harvey (c.1616-18: 99, 297): 'Why and how air is requisite for all animals that breathe, as also how air is necessary for a candle and for fire, I WH have seen'.
150 Wilson (1960: 163-4).
151 *Ibid.* 163; see also Lysaght (1937), McKie (1953, 1983), Mendelsohn (1964: 58-9), Turner (1955-6).
152 Hooke (1677: 163) regarded heat and light as the two 'most spirituous and most potent Agents in nature'.
153 Hooke (1665: 12).
154 Hooke (1705: 191).
155 For penetration, Hooke (1935a: 36; 1935b: 121, 123, 128, 131-2 and n.2; 1665: 22, 76, 84, 151, 234; 1678a: 340-2, 345; 1705: 29, 31, 49, 78, 115, 191-2); for 'penetration of dimensions', Derham (1726: 7) and Gunther (1923-67, 6: 265, 325, 7: 533-4, 712-4).
156 Hooke (c.1668: 61, also 44; 1935a: 30, 84-5, 103, 124, 251, 433; 1935b: 228); Gunther (1923-67, 6: 326, 7: 533-4).
157 On 2 May 1678, at one of the Royal Society meetings discussing the structure of the lungs and the use of the 'air or respiration', Hooke observed that 'air was the pabulum of the animal spirits, and...the principle cause both of the heat and animal motion'. See Gunther (1923-67, 7: 486).
158 Hooke (1691-92, edited according to modern practice). For his hypothesis of sparks, which differed from that of Descartes, see Hooke (1665: 44-7); see also Boyle (1685) and Gunther (1923-67, 6: 159, 7: 504, 746).

CHAPTER 4: THE *DAIMON* WITHIN
1 Wilkins (1648, 2: 167ff.).
2 I.e., as in Hero's 'theorems' (experiments or tricks) for musical automata – mechanical singing birds, self-sounding trumpets and self-acting organs worked by water or by a windmill.
3 Wilkins (1648, 2: 171). Drebbel, a Netherlander, went to England about 1605 and died there. His inventions included a *perpetuum mobile*, in which water, driven along a spiral tube by the contraction and expansion of an enclosed body of air, caused the tube to rotate and, thus, to wind up a clock. See *Ibid.*, 2: 211-4 and Taylor (1945: 156).
4 Harris (1961).
5 Bacon (1626, 8: 95); for the nitre concept after c.1657, see Frank (1980).
6 Gregory (1938).
7 Bacon (1605: 106, 1626, 8: 95): 'The vital spirits of animals are a

substance compounded of an airy and flamy matter; and though air and flame will not well mix, when free; yet they may when bound in by a fixing body.'

8   Rees (1980: 553).
9   Rees (1986: 422).
10 Rees (1977) ignores the contact. According to Aubrey (1978: 308-9), Hobbes 'assisted his Lordship in translating severall of his *Essayes* into Latin'. Bacon's *Essayes*, first published in 1597, went through a number of editions, some with additions; in 1625 an enlarged edition was published and afterwards reprinted many times. It was probably this edition to which Hobbes contributed, since the two men worked together before 1628-29, when Hobbes's translation of Thucydides was published.
11 Fearing (1964: 2).
12 Hooke (Ch.3.III.5.1. *supra*) likewise used a solid to model the ether, although he did not restrict himself to this type of model, e.g., Hooke (1682: 183-4):

> I have already...produced several Experiments, whereby I have shewn how mechanically to produce...an Attraction towards the acting Body. The first was that of a Body placed upon a wooden Rod, the one End of which was kept in its place by a Spring, and the other was struck by a Hammer, whereby it plainly appeared, that at every Stroke the Body was moved on the Rod towards the Hammer that struck. Here the Æther was resembled to a Solid. By the second Experiment, where a Ball poised in Water descended towards the striking Part, I shewed how the same Effect might be done by a fluid Medium, as in the other was done by a Solid. In the third was shewn how a Fluid also might be affected by a like Pulse; for that the Water it self, by means of a vibrative Motion in the Parts of the Glass, acquired a Motion towards the vibrating Parts.

The last is Hooke's glass bell experiment.

13 Hobbes (1656a, 1: 324).
14 See Ch.3.III.5.2. (*supra*).
15 Hooke (1678a: 345, also 343): the particles of solids 'do immediately touch each other; that is, the Vibrative motions of the bodies do every one touch each other at every Vibration'.
16 *Ibid*. 342: fluid 'bulks differ from solids only in this, that all fluids consist of two sorts of particles, the one this common Menstruum near the Earth, which is interspersed between the Vibrating particles appropriated to that bulk, and so participating of the motions and

Vibrations thereof: And the other, by excluding wholly, or not participating of that motion'.
17 *Ibid.* 345.
18 E.g., Hesse (1966b) and Moyer (1977).
19 Williams (1956: 76).
20 Truesdell (1960: 53-8).
21 Bacon (1626, 8: 281, 9: 72, 75, 78-9, 89-91, 94, 97-9, 113-4, 120-1 *et passim*), Hobbes (1656a, 1: 487-8, 492-3) and Mersenne (1957: especially 294ff.); see also Dostrovsky (1974-5: 190-3, 196). Hooke (1935a: 211) seems to have made an advance on the theories of earlier writers, because on 15 January 1675/6 he wrote about the 'breaking' of the air in pipes.
22 North, *Theory of Sounds*, f.134.
23 *Ibid.* f.134.
24 North, *General Preface*.
25 'Introduction' to North, *Cursory Notes*, pp. [65]-[69].
26 North, *The World*, ff.1-18v, f. 18v. Korsten (1981) treats North as a life-long Cartesian, in part because he ignores the writings on music.
27 Porter (1985: 386).
28 Hobbes (1651: 83).
29 North, *The Autobiography*, 86.
30 *Ibid.* 144-5.
31 *Of Humane Capacity*, f.34v.
32 *Ibid.* f.44v.
33 *Theory of Sounds*, f.87.
34 *Ibid.*
35 See Hine, Chan and Kassler (1987); Chan, Kassler and Hine (1988) for the early and late periods.
36 North (1677: 5-7); see also Chenette (1967: 94-5).
37 Shapiro (1973: 207-58); Ziggelaar (1980: 185-6).
38 Shapiro (1973: 219).
39 In the case of the voice and wind instruments, it is not the instrument but an enclosed quantity of air which vibrates.
40 *Untitled Essay*, f.262v.
41 *The Life*, 2: 277; see also Hooke (1935a: 211, 223, 256, 259, 274, 275): 15 January 1675/6, 28 March 1676, 10, 21, 26 November 1676, 15, 19, 23 February 1676/7.
42 *Theory of Sounds*, f.95: 'The fabrick of the ear is very considerable, with regard, not onely to the perceiving, but judging of sounds. The place of the sensible touch, is reputed to be the drum membrane, for by the modes of attaque upon that, wee judg the

modes of the percussion, as quik, dull, continued, or otherwise as the case is.'
43 *Some Essays*, ff.13-15.
44 *Ibid.* f.15. North's writings on music contain the first suggestion that a conductor ('president') should regulate a consort of instruments.
45 *Power*, f.89. The implication is that apparent extension is due to the amplitude of vibrations, which, in turn, constitutes the scanning function of mind.
46 *Cursory Notes*, 152.
47 *Theory of Sounds*, ff.99-99v and *Untitled Essay*, f.254v. Cohen (1984) assays earlier writers who attempted to explain why the ratios of simple consonances stop after 6:5, but none offer North's explanation, which is based on the 'dullness of our materiall engin'.
48 I.e., human perception of sound is creative, since the mind makes an 'in phase' interpretation. Cf. Helmholtz (1877): when we listen to a series of four or more consecutive harmonic vibrations we do not hear a series of partial tones. Our hearing faculty blends the partial tones into a compound whole (whence their name, *s.v.* 'Tone', *OED* I.2.) and perceives a single musical tone of definite pitch. Phenomena such as musical tones, therefore, are the products of sensory perception. In his private critique of North (1677), Newton took a different point of view, for which see Chenette (1967: 207) and Chan, Kassler and Hine (1988: 58-9).
49 *The Musicall Grammarian*, 104.
50 *Theory of Sounds*, f.105v.
51 *Ibid.* ff.99v-100,
52 *Change*, ff.94-102v: all 'sensible formes' are due to the 'workings' of the imagination and not to the nature of objects.
53 *The Musicall Grammarian*, 105.
54 *The Autobiography*, 3: 'certeinly nature calls for that which is good for itself. And setting aside wantonness, which is easy to be perceived and may be as easily checked in children, their appetites are the best Indications of what is good for them'.
55 *Cursory Notes*, 148.
56 *Ibid.* 144.
57 *Ibid.* 145.
58 *Ibid.*
59 *Of Humane Capacity*, f.42; see also f.37: 'It is a comon fancy, that wee bring into the world with us, as innate, the knowledge of our hands, fingers, etc. and that a child new borne can tell which finger is pricked, and the like. But I thinck otherwise, and that naturally and originally we have no knowledge of our selves and our parts, and that

wee learne it all by experience; all that wee bring is to know wee are well, or ill'.
60 *Ibid.* f.40v. By instinct, North, *The Autobiography*, 5, denoted our original nature, that which derives, '*ex traduce*', from our parents.
61 *Of Humane Capacity*, f.37v.
62 *Ibid.* f.38.
63 *Ibid.* f.42v.
64 See, e.g., *The Life*, 2: 202-3, for 'non-sanity of mind'.
65 *Untitled Essay*, f.250v.
66 *The World*, f.9.
67 *Untitled Essay*, f.255: the 'analitick' method moves 'from the proposition to the axiom...as under the name algebra, is accounted the culmen of human understanding'; hence, *ibid.* f.261, the acts of reason are 'litle els, but the deposing of fantasmes and prejudices and reducing things to simple ideas, such as the practise of algebra shews'.
68 *Theory of Sounds*, f.74v.
69 *Change*, f.95.
70 *Cursory Notes*, 1-25. After c.1703 North tended to focus on secondary causes; e.g., in *Theory of Sounds*, he made only passing reference to the ether as 'interstitiall' or 'finer' matter.
71 *Some Essays*, f.14.
72 *Of Humane Capacity*, ff.34v-37.
73 *Change*, f.97
74 *Essay*, f.80v.
75 *Of Humane Capacity*, f.44v.
76 *Theory of Sounds*, f.92v.
77 *Essay*, f.80.
78 *Change*, f.97v
79 *Cursory Notes*, 8.
80 *Essay*, f.81.
81 E.g., *The Musicall Grammarian*, 101-2 and n.12, 197.
82 *Musicall Recollections III*, f.52v.
83 Not counting the various drafts and fragments, the sequence is: (1) *Cursory Notes* (c.1698-c.1703), (2) *Musicall Recollections I-III* (c.1708-c.1722), (3) *Theory of Sounds* and *The Musicall Grammarian* (1728-c.1733).
84 *Musicall Recollections III*, f.48v: 'musick is a true pantomime, or resemblance of humanity in all its states, motions, passions and affections. And in every musicall attempt reasonably designed, humane nature is the subject, and so penetrant that thoughts, such as mankind occasionally have, and even speech it self, share

in the resemblance so that an hearer shall put himself into the like condition, as if the state represented were his owne. It hath been observed that the termes upon which musicall time depends, are referred to men's active capacities. So the melody should be referred to their thoughts and affections'.

85 *The Musicall Grammarian*, 100-1, 174. Wit, for North, is not a sudden flash of 'conceipt' or 'humour'; rather, it is a settled, constant, habitual sufficiency of the understanding, whereby the aspiring composer is enabled to achieve sharpness in invention, subtlety in expression and dispatch in execution.

86 *The Musicall Grammarian*, 219ff., is the first naturalist account of the origin and development of music.

87 Hobbes (1650a, 4: 30, 38-9, 54, 56-8; 1650b, 4: 85-7).

88 Hobbes (1656a, 1: 78).

89 Hobbes (1651: 139).

90 *Ibid.* 135; see also Hobbes (1650a, 4: 55-6).

91 Hobbes (1651: 142): Madmen are called 'sometimes [by the name] *Daemoniacks*, (that is, possessed with spirits;) sometimes *Energumeni* (that is, agitated, or moved with spirits)'.

92 Hobbes would have known about false strings from at least two sources: the lutenists employed by the Cavendish family; and Mersenne (1636-7: 79).

93 Holder (1694: 19-20). For his indebtedness to Hooke, see Kassler and Oldroyd (1983) and to Francis North, see Chenette (1967).

94 Holder (1694: 154), who hints at a continuum theory of pleasure and pain. In an emission theory, e.g., Charleton (1654), minute 'sonorific' particles ('species') enter the ear and move the auditory nerve. The particles that in their configuration accommodate to the pores of the nerve make a gentle, smooth or equal impression on the nerve's filaments, whereas those that do not accommodate to the pores make a rough, harsh or unequal impression.

95 Bastholm (1950); Clarke (1968b).

96 Bastholm (1950); Davis (1973).

97 See Hierons and Meyer (1964).

98 Willis (1681) identified the various 'seats' as follows: perception in the corpora striata; imagination and phantasie in the corpus callosum; instincts in the corpora quadrigemina; passions in the pons; vital centres (for the regulation of heart beat, respiration, digestion) in the cerebellum and its attendant structures; and memory in the cephalic cortex.

99 Willis (1683: 24).

100 Willis (1670, 1681) and Frank (1980).

101 Willis (1683: 48). The implication is that the incorporeal, rational soul is masculine.
102 For tubulated, *ibid*. windpipe 8, 12, 14-7, 25; nerves 25, 27, 59, 88; membranes 89; muscle fibres 27; body compared to hydraulic organ 33-4. Willis used the term 'pores' (Gk: *poroi*) to denote channels. The tubes in the body serve as channels, and even the air has pores, *ibid*. 70.
103 *Ibid*. measured, tempered 3, 4, 45, 62, 63, 73, 88, 94-5; beyond measure, distempered 31, 45, 47, 48, 49, 51, 52, 71, 90. Part II, on pathology, deals specifically with gestures that are too loose or too tight; for specific mention of 'beyond' or 'above measure', *ibid*. 203, 208, 210, 211.
104 *Ibid*. 56.
105 *Ibid*. 71-2.
106 For the military metaphor, *ibid*. army 24, 43, 56, 145; battle, conflict, *see* strife; command 43, 56; company 7, 25; defend, defense 47, 90, 96; enemy 50-1, 53, 54, 211; guards, *see* watchmen; invade 182, 193, 214; legion 25, 43; rank(s) 89, 163; regiment(s) 88, 166, 180, 185, 198, 211, 212, 228; soldiers 25, 53, 96, 211; strife 41, 42, 43, 54, 130, 215; troops 95, 145, 180; truce, 232; watchmen 7, 57, 78, 89, 95, 96.
107 *Ibid*. 56.
108 *Ibid*. unpaginated front matter; see also Meier (1982).
109 Willis (1681: unpaginated 'Table' of 'hard words').
110 Willis (1683: 105-234).
111 For mines, incentives (i.e., the charge of powder in subterranean passages), *ibid*. 203, 215-8, 220-1, 225-33.
112 *Ibid*. 157: '*copula*' (Lat.: line, string, cord) results from *copulo* (Lat.: to couple, join, as in a mixture or combination).
113 E.g., Frank (1980).
114 Willis (1681: 105).
115 Willis (1683: 24); see also *ibid*. (1) spirits become elastic, i.e., combustible bodies (like sulphur or hot things) 23, 24, 91, 157, 170, 171, 205; (2) the copula (mixture) 227, compared to gunpowder 15, 167; (3) the letting off (elastic virtue or explosive endeavours) in the muscles 157, 163, 167, 205, 227, 228; (4) the animal spirits exploded (separated) one from another 227; (5) the muscle exploded (filled up, inflated) 9, 17.
116 For instantaneous ('like Lightning'), *ibid*. 10, 54, 56, 58, 183.
117 Mendelsohn (1964: 39).
118 Willis (1683: 56), who defined 'Pneumatic' (1681: unpaginated 'Table') as 'Windy, or belonging to wind or breath'.

119 North, *The Autobiography*, 146-7.
120 *Ibid.* 146, italics mine.
121 *Ibid.* 147, italics mine.
122 *Ibid.* 188. Masters, who attended Francis North during his last illness, was 'a plain man nurse', according to Roger North, who added, 'that is all I care for in a physician'.
123 According to North, *The Life*, f.188v, his sister-in-law, Lady Frances North, 'had a great happyness in Dr. Willis, who regarded her not as a patient, but as if she had bin a neer relation. For when he lived at Oxford he was phisitian to her family and to her in particular. ... And [in London]...he watched her diligently, and...did almost weekly visit her to know how matters stood with her'. North provided a graphic description of the lady's illness, for the probable treatment of which, see Miller (1922).
124 E.g., *The Musicall Grammarian*, 100-1, the muscles of the mouth and throat are acoustic vibrators, because they are expanded and contracted, so that, *Theory of Sounds*, f.141, the voice generates sound in the same way as the 'reedall' or reed pipe in organs.
125 *Ibid.* f.134.
126 *Ibid.* f.134v. North, *Cursory Notes*, 119, 264, probably learned about the tube trumpet from Shore, the supposed inventor of the tuning fork and trumpeter-in-ordinary to James II.
127 *Theory of Sounds*, ff.134v-135.
128 *Of Humane Capacity*, f.43.
129 *Ibid.* f.41v.
130 *Ibid.* ff.43v, 45v.
131 *Ibid.* f.43v.
132 Willis (1683: 205).
133 *Ibid.* 208.
134 See Crane (1962) for an illuminating treatment of this textbook tradition.
135 I.e., the belief satirised by Swift (1726).
136 Hobbes (1650a, 4: 38).
137 On dullness as a medical concept, see Cranefield (1961) and Spiegel (1973). On children that are 'almost uncapable of learning the infant skill of it self', because they 'allways ly dull' and so become 'dull, and approaching to that, they call changeling', see North, *Of Humane Capacity*, f.37v.
138 E.g., *Cursory Notes*, 3-4, 5 (gunpowder fired), 14, 23-25 (glass drops), 65-6, 74-5 (fulminating gold, gunpowder fired) and *Solutiones phænomenon*, ff.39-68v, 47v-48, 60v, 61; see also Chan, Kassler and Hine (1988: 99, 104, 105).

139 Brodsley, Frank and Steeds (1986: 1).
140 Hobbes (1662, 7: 32-5, repeated, though not verbatim, 1678, 7: 130-1).
141 Hobbes seems to have grasped Hooke's Law that any increase of string tension strains the lath proportionately: the greater the draw, the greater the bend. If we substitute a soundboard for the lath, the same law applies. When the string is forcibly bent, the tension increases and the soundboard is overstrained. When the string is released, the soundboard recovers; but recovery is checked as soon as the string is drawn straight at its tuned tension.
142 Hooke (1665: 33-44); see also Brodsley, Frank and Steeds (1986), who mention Hobbes's friend, Sorbières, as a source of information about glass drops but fail to make the connection with Hobbes.
143 Hobbes (1656a, 1: 457-8). For exterior ballistics, see Galilei (1638: 289-94), who compared the curve (parabola) of the path of a bullet with the curve of a stretched string.
144 E.g., Hall (1983: 126).
145 Williams (1956).
146 North, *General Preface & Life*, 102.
147 *General Preface & Life*, 103.
148 *Ibid*. 109. The failure was the more notable because most members of the North family were 'addicted' to music.
149 *Ibid*. 142.
150 *Ibid*. 131.
151 *Ibid*. 138.
152 *Ibid*. 133-4.
153 *Ibid*. 34.
154 *Ibid*. 151.
155 *Ibid*. 153. According to Willis (1683: 153), apoplexy 'denotes percussion, and...is called a...Blasting'.
156 *General Preface & Life*, 154.
157 *Ibid*. 155.
158 *Ibid*. 156; see also Hobbes (1650a, 4: 56-8), on levity and other defects of the mind.
159 *General Preface & Life*, 161.
160 *The Lives*, 2: 249.
161 *The Autobiography*, 148-52. North set out his own regimen of health in order to avoid doctors, and so retain his Stoic self-sufficiency. He rejected blood letting, as well as 'preventive physic' (i.e., drugs). Then, *ibid*. 150,

> ...when I have been very ill, and with the symptoms of want of

good temper, which makes folk run to doctors, as in or fearing a fever, I have let all pass, and eat and drank with my friends as usual, though uneasy and improper, being disposed to endure anything rather than submit and own myself sick that brought upon me the ordinary importunity of catechization, how I did, and this and the other medicine. When I have been forced to own an indisposition I have retreated all diet into water gruel, and not a little, but a very great quantity, which I thought would clear me, and I have ever found my distempers wear off of themselves.

There were two reasons for North's medical scepticism. First, he had numerous occasions to witness the physicians' methods of treatment, which he sometimes referred to as 'tortures'. Second, he did not respect 'doctoral reason', which he supposed was from authority rather than from demonstration.

162 *The Lives*, 2: 249-50.
163 *Ibid.* 236-7, 238-9, 242-4, 245.
164 In a letter dated 31 December 1691, North, *The Autobiography*, 228, wrote: 'His [Sir Dudley's] disease was asthma, that brought a fever and inflammation of the lungs, in spite of blooding and all extreme remedies. He had the incomparable Dr. Paman perpetually with him, and Dr. Ratcliff, who in formality was (sure) a sufficient warrant to die.' For Paman, a colleague of Hooke and a lifelong friend of the North family, see Chan and Kassler (1989: 41).
165 *The Lives*, 2: 252.
166 *The Life*, 2: 321.
167 *Ibid.*, 2: 322.
168 *Ibid.*, 2: 328.
169 *Ibid.*, 2: 231.
170 *Ibid.*, 2: 202.
171 *Ibid.*, 2: 203-4. Cortex is a drug made from the bark of a tree.
172 *Ibid.*, 2: 205-6.
173 Willis (1683: 93) defined cachexy as an '*Atrophie*' in the solid parts, caused by digestion ('chyme') made 'dull by Fumes and Vapours'.
174 *The Life*, 2: 213.
175 *Ibid.*, 2: 208.
176 *Ibid.*, 2: 205.
177 *Ibid.*, 2: 216.

CHAPTER 5: SOUNDING THE DEPTHS

1. Aubrey (1978: 315-6). See Gunther (1923-67, 4: 139) for Hooke's statement (3 July 1663) that Hobbes's 'hand...shook as fast one way as his head did the other'.
2. Hooke (1935a: 9, 12, 15, 17, 19, 26, 27, 29, 54, 99, 166), who chiefly recorded the state of his health and only occasionally, his morality, e.g., *ibid.* 76 (23 December 1673): 'extreamly troubled with vapours and the chimeras of my youth'.
3. *Ibid.* 26.
4. *Ibid.* 15.
5. *Ibid.* 77, 172, 184, 226, 232, 369, 384, 447.
6. North, *The Autobiography*, 22.
7. North used the word 'crisis' in its several medical senses, including, *ibid.* 18, 35, 194, as a psychological event associated with a specific stage of life.
8. Korsten (1981: 15-7), Chan and Kassler (1989).
9. North, *The Autobiography*, 153-6, p. 156, contains reflections on whether or not suicide is justifiable.
10. Hobbes (1651: 718).
11. Bacon (1605: 106).
12. Long (1971b: 83-4).
13. Hobbes (1641: 138), whose objections to Descartes' *Meditations* relate chiefly to making statements and drawing inferences and start from the premiss, *ibid.* 142, that 'no idea is innate; for what is innate is always present'. Hence, we can have no idea of the soul or of God, both of which are 'inconceivable'; but, *ibid.* 141, we can understand the name of God as 'a *substance*'. Hobbes understood 'that God exists; but I do this not through an idea but as a result of reasoning'.
14. Hooke (c.1668: 39-40).
15. E.g., Mayow (1674: 198) and Willis (1692: 367-8). According to Hunt (1978: 138), even though Harvey (1628) alluded to heart sounds, the diagnostic value of these sounds 'was almost entirely ignored by the physicians who studied the heart during the century and a half following Harvey's great work'.
16. Auenbrugger (1761: 3): 'I here present the Reader with a new sign which I have discovered for detecting diseases of the chest. This consists in the Percussion of the human thorax, whereby, according to the character of the particular sounds thence elicited, an opinion is formed of the internal state of that cavity.' The story is apochryphal that Auenbrugger treated his patients like beer barrels; see Jarcho (1961).
17. Auenbrugger (1761: 5); for the practice of percussion in England and

Scotland, see Keel (1988).
18 Laennec (1826, 1: 383; 1846: 524, 548).
19 E.g., Bowditch (1846: 248) and Guttmann (1879); for 'auscultatory percussion', the two methods used in combination, e.g., Bowditch (1846) and Flint (1866).
20 Guttmann (1879: 117-8).
21 Gee (1893: 101, 105).
22 Flint (1866: 254).
23 *Ibid.* 96.
24 Alison (1861: 297-306): If the body is a resonating system, some sort of sympathetic resonance must be established between patient and physician.
25 King (1959).
26 *Ibid.* treats educational developments that impeded or facilitated the introduction of auscultation; Gottlieb (1964) proceeds by eras (e.g., the era of clinical physiology) and provides the achievements of 'great men'; Foucault (1973) focuses on visual perception at the expense of other kinds of perception; Gandevia (1960) and Rieser (1978) survey instrumentation.
27 Laennec (1846: 771), who derived a number of names from Greek sources (e.g., aegophony, bronchophony), argued that 'the art of reasoning chiefly lies in a well-formed language', and 'nothing is more injurious to the progress of science than to wrest words from their received acceptation on insufficient grounds, or to invent bad ones'. But Williams (1840: 27-8n.) cautioned that 'if we attempt to construct words from the only legitimate classical source, the Greek, we find ourselves hampered by a want of scientific precision in the meaning of certain words: instance the want of distinction between *sound* and *noise*'.
28 E.g., Williams (1840: 29) complained that 'nothing injures the purity of a language more than the introduction of foreign words', whereas Flint (1866) objected to the lack of euphony of the English terms 'ronchi' and 'rattles', which were used in place of Laennec's French term, *râles* (in the absence of a satisfactory substitute, he anglicised the term as rales).
29 Stokes (1882: 575). Because disagreements were widespread, Gee (1893: 307) concluded his treatise with the following observation:

> IN the foregoing pages I have taken great pains with the terminology; and I have used technical words with strict adherence to their original meaning. I have not taken upon myself to pervert the meaning of words already well defined, nor have I invented new words to denote signs already well denominated. Much of

the difficulty of teaching auscultation and percussion to students is due to neglect of these plain rules, which everyone who uses technical terms may be expected to follow, or to give good reasons for not following.

30 Laennec (1826, 1: 424-5, musical notation corrected in 1846: 544), who initially compared the sound produced in the neck to that of a jew's harp, even though the body instrument executed the tones of its *chant* in a legato and staccato manner, rather than legato only, and from time to time a drum-like sound appeared. Later, he made a more '*bizarre*' comparison: the body instruments producing the *chant* were like instruments of war and the *chant* itself, like a military march.

31 See Horine (1941) and Siraisi (1975). According to Galen (1821-33, 7: 69ff., 734-50), Herophilus modelled his pulse theory on Aristoxenus, *Elementa rhythmica*.

32 For the system of Marquet, see Underwood (1947: 662), who states that the crotchet indicates a natural pulse. But it is tempo that sets the norm, because notation is to be read off as a system of relations, like music.

33 These and other efforts led to the technology of sphygmography, stethography and spirometry, whereby body sounds and movements were measured and recorded by instruments such as sphygmometers, tonometers, oscillometers, spirometers, etc.

34 Laennec (1826, 2: 381-5).

35 Williams (1840: 203).

36 E.g., Guttmann (1879: 372). In antiquity Caelius Aurelianus (1950: 867, also 421, 721, 827, 875) described *borborygmi* and observed that when the stomach is filled with gas, parts of the abdomen 'resound like a drum' when struck with the flat palm.

37 E.g., Hughes (1854: 219, 239, 283) and Williams (1840: 203, 211). According to Skoda (1853: 175):

> The normal sounds of the heart are generally indicated by the expression "tic-tac"; its abnormal sounds being comprised under the terms of bellows, sawing, rasping, filing murmurs, etc. The tic-tac may be stronger or weaker than natural, or altered in its timbre; we are therefore obliged to speak of over-strong, or over-weak, or too ringing – and consequently abnormal – normal heart sounds. This tic-tac I call the sounds (*Töne*) of the heart, and speak of normal and abnormal sounds. By murmurs (*Geräusche*) I understand the abnormal sounds of the heart indicated above, blowing, sawing, rasping, etc.

38 This belief is called 'Cratylism', after the approach taken by Cratylus in Plato's dialogue of the same name.
39 Laennec (1846: 48).
40 Gee (1893: 117 n.1).
41 Skoda (1853: x, xiii–xiv).
42 Guttmann (1879: 116-7) stated that such terms had 'long been abandoned, as they are quite unsupported by physical science'.
43 E.g., Williams (1840: 27-8), who followed the German penchant for compound terms – 'stroke-sounds', 'breath-sounds', 'voice-sounds' and 'heart-sounds', which, though lacking in euphony, were 'more expressive and concise than those in common use; and being simple, they readily admit the addition to them of epithets descriptive of their character'.
44 Skoda (1853: 8-10).
45 Guttmann (1879: 102) pointed out that 'a small violin may yield a fuller sound than a large one. Similarly in the human voice difference in sonorousness does not arise from difference in the size of the vocal cords'.
46 Walshe (1860: 74), who proposed the following types: for loudness, diminished/increased; for pitch, lowered/raised; for quality, hardened or otherwise modified/softened; and for duration, lessened/not sensibly changed. See also Stokes (1882: 39-40).
47 Flint (1866: 177) observed that pitch is 'a feature to which attention had not been called prior to the publication by the author to which reference has already been made', that is, by Flint (1852).
48 Williams (1840: 26).
49 Herschel (1817-45, 4: 777). Timbre was not explained until the work of Helmholtz (1877; 1st edn. 1863); see also Rich (1919).
50 Kassler (1984c).
51 According to the translator of Skoda (1853: ix), the French and German schools produced taxonomies with endless subdivisions, although he singled out Fournet for his 'flatulent nosological vocabularies'.
52 Jackson (1958, 1: 278); see also Riese (1959: 43-4, 167-9).
53 Hoeline (1980: 1100); see also Temkin (1959).
54 Duffin (1986); but see Laennec (1846: 559): 'All the sounds which take place inside the body and which can be heard with the naked ear, arise from the movements of whatever substance happens to be in contact with a gas'. As examples, he enumerated *borborygmi*, Hippocratic fluctuation, crepitation in inspiration, pulsations of the heart in some cases of emphysema, cracking of the fingers in pneumarthroses, and crackling of the knees in rheumatism.

55 Williams (1840: 216-7).
56 *Ibid.* 313-7, contains an account of 'Experiments on the production of Sound by the motion of Water through a Tube'. For similar experiments, see Skoda (1853: i–iv) and Kamm and Pedley (1989).
57 Cassirer (1957, 1: 190).
58 Hobbes (1656a, 1: 14).
59 Guttmann (1879: 73).
60 Bell (1951: 357).
61 Hobbes (1641: 144).

References

1. WORKS OF ROGER NORTH

NB: One of four periods is assigned to North's undated writings as follows: very early (pre-c.1698), early (c.1698-c.1707), middle (c.1708-c.1720) and late (c.1721-c.1730). Both published and unpublished writings are listed in alphabetical order by title. BL stands for British Library, London.

Change of Philosophicall Methods [middle], BL Add MS 32549: ff.94-102v.
Cursory Notes of Musicke (c.1698-c.1703) ed. M. Chan and J.C. Kassler, Kensington, N.S.W., 1986.
Essay on the Reciprocall Forces of Body and Spirit influencing Each Other [middle], BL Add MS 32549: ff.77-81.
General Preface [c.1718-22] *& Life of Dr. John North* [1728] ed. P. Millard, Toronto, Buffalo, London, 1981.
Musicall Recollections I-III [short title, middle], BL Add MS 32531: ff.8-23v, 32534: ff.1-82v, 32536: ff.1-90.
Notes of Me [c.1688-98], BL Add MS 32506: ff.1-194.
Of Humane Capacity [after c.1698], BL Add MS 32526: ff.34v-47.
Power of Humane Understanding [after c.1698], BL Add MS 32526: ff.88-89v.
Solutiones phænomenon [middle], BL Add MS 32549: ff.39-68v.
Some Essays, concerning the Manner of our Sence, or Perception of Things [after c.1698], BL Add MS 32526: ff.8v-33v.
The Autobiography ed. A. Jessopp, London and Norwich, 1887.
The Life of the Right Honourable Francis North [1st draft, after c.1698], BL Add MS 32511: ff.180-250v.
The Life of the Right Honourable Francis North [1728, 1st edn. 1740 ed. M. North], 3d edn., 2 vols., London, 1819.
The Lives of the Norths ed. A. Jessopp, 3 vols., London, 1890.
The Musicall Grammarian 1728 ed. M. Chan and J.C. Kassler, Cambridge, 1990.
The World Part I [my title; before c.1698], BL Add MS 32546: ff.1-18v.
Theory of Sounds shewing, the Genesis, Propagation, Augmentation and Applications of Them reduced to a Specifick Inquiry into the Cripticks of Harmony and Discord, with Eikons annexed esposing them to Occular Inspection 1728, BL Add MS 32535: ff.74-149.

Untitled Essay [late?], BL Add MS 32546: ff.247-261v.

2. OTHER WORKS

Alison, S.S. 1861, *The Physical Examination of the Chest in Pulmonary Consumption and its Intercurrent Diseases*, London.

Ammann, P.J. 1967, 'The Musical Theory and Philosophy of Robert Fludd', *Journal of the Warburg and Courtauld Institutes*, 30: 198-227.

Anderson, W.D. 1965, *Matthew Arnold and The Classical Tradition*, Ann Arbor.

――― 1966, *Ethos and Education in Greek Music: The Evidence of Poetry and Philosophy*, Cambridge, Mass.

Ariotti, P. 1971-72, 'Aspects of the Conception and Development of the Pendulum in the 17th Century', *Archives for the History of Exact Sciences*, 8: 329-410.

Aubrey, J. 1978, *Aubrey's Brief Lives* ed. O.L. Dick, Harmondsworth, Middlesex.

Auenbrugger, L. 1761, *Inventum novum. A Facsimile*, London, 1966.

Bacon, F. 1605, *The Advancement of Learning and New Atlantis* ed. A. Johnston, Oxford, 1986.

――― 1626, *Sylva sylvarum*, vols. 8 and 9 of *The Works*, a new edn., London, 1818.

Balz, A.G.A. 1918, *Idea and Essence in the Philosophies of Hobbes and Spinoza*, New York.

Barker, P. and Goldstein, B.R. 1984, 'Is Seventeenth Century Physics Indebted to the Stoics?', *Centaurus*, 27: 148-64.

Barnett, M.K. 1956, 'The Development of Thermometry and the Temperature Concept', *Osiris*, 12: 269-341.

Bastholm, E. 1950, *The History of Muscle Physiology from the Natural Philosophers to Albrecht von Haller: A Study of the History of Medicine*, Copenhaven.

Bell, E.T. 1951, *Mathematics: Queen and Servant of Science*, New York, Toronto, London.

Bernstein, H.R. 1980, 'Conatus, Hobbes, and the Young Leibniz', *Studies in the History and Philosophy of Science*, 11: 25-37.

Bogard, P.A. 1979, 'Heaps and Wholes: Aristotle's Explanation of Compound Bodies', *Isis*, 70: 11-29.

Bolzan, J.E. 1976, 'Chemical Combination according to Aristotle', *Ambix*, 22: 134-44.

Boring, E.G. 1942, *Sensation and Perception in the History of Experimental Psychology*, New York.

Bowditch, H.I. 1846, *The Young Stethoscopist*, New York and London, 1964.

Boyle, R. 1662, 'New Experiments Physico-mechanical, touching the Spring of the Air, and its Effects; made, for the Most Part, in a New Pneumatical Engine' [1st edn. 1660], reprinted in Boyle 1965-66, 1: 1-242.
―――― 1685, 'An Essay of the Great Effects of Even Languid and Unheeded Motion', reprinted in Boyle 1965-66, 5: 1-37.
―――― 1965-66, *The Works* ed. T. Birch, 6 vols., London.
Brandt, F. 1928, *Thomas Hobbes' Mechanical Conception of Nature*, Copenhagen and London.
Brodsley, L., Frank, C. and Steeds, J.W. 1986, 'Prince Rupert's Drops', *Notes and Records of the Royal Society*, 41: 1-26.
Brown, J. 1979, 'Guild Organisation and the Instrument-making Trade, 1550-1830: The Grocers' and Clockmakers' Companies', *Annals of Science*, 36: 1-34.
Butler, C. 1636, *The Principles of Musik, in Singing and Setting: With the Two-fold Use therof, [Ecclesiasticall and Civil,]*, London.
Caelius Aurelianus 1950, *On Acute and On Chronic Diseases* ed. and tr. I.E. Drabkin, Chicago.
Cannon, J.T. and Dostrovsky, S. 1981, *The Evolution of Dynamics: Vibration Theory from 1687 to 1742*, Springer-Verlag.
Cassirer, E. 1957, *The Philosophy of Symbolic Forms, Volume One: Language*, tr. R. Manheim, New Haven.
Centore, F.F. 1970, *Robert Hooke's Contributions to Mechanics: A Study in Seventeenth Century Natural Philosophy*, The Hague.
Chalmers, G.K. 1937, 'The Lodestone and the Understanding of Matter in Seventeenth Century England', *Philosophy of Science*, 4: 75-95.
Chamberlain, D.S. 1971, 'Wolbero of Cologne (d.1167): A Zenith of Musical Imagery', *Mediaeval Studies*, 33: 114-26.
Chan, M. and Kassler, J.C. 1989, *Roger North: Materials for a Chronology of his Writings*, Kensington, N.S.W.
Chan, M., Kassler, J.C. and Hine, J.D. 1988, *Roger North's The Musicall Grammarian and Theory of Sounds: Digests of the Manuscripts with an Analytical Index of 1726 and 1728 Theory of Sounds*, Kensington, N.S.W.
Charleton, W. 1654, *Physiologia Epicuro-Gassendo-Charltoniana: Or a Fabrick of Science Natural, upon the Hypothesis of Atoms*, London.
Chenette, L.F. 1967, 'Music Theory in the British Isles during the Enlightenment', Ohio State University doctoral dissertation.
Clarke, E.S. 1968a, 'Brain Anatomy before Steno', *Steno and Brain Research in the Seventeenth Century* ed. G. Scherz, Oxford, 27-34.
―――― 1968b, 'The Doctrine of the Hollow Nerve in the Seventeenth and Eighteenth Centuries', *Medicine, Science and Culture* ed. L.G. Stevenson and R.P. Multhauf, Baltimore, 123-41.

Cohen, H.F. 1984, *Quantifying Music: The Science of Music at the First Stage of the Scientific Revolution, 1580-1650*, Dordrecht.
Colie, R.L. 1966, *Paradoxia Epidemica: The Renaissance Tradition of Paradox*, Princeton.
Cowley, A. 1668, *The English Writings* ed. A.R. Waller, 2 vols., Cambridge, 1905-06.
Crane, R.S. 1962, 'The Houyhnhnms, the Yahoos, and the History of Ideas', *Reason and the Imagination: Studies in the History of Ideas 1600-1800* ed. J.A. Mazzeo, New York and London, 243-53.
Cranefield, P.F. 1961, 'A Seventeenth Century View of Mental Deficiency and Schizophrenia: Thomas Willis on "Stupidity or Foolishness"', *Bulletin of the History of Medicine*, 35: 291-316.
Davidson, W.L. 1907, *The Stoic Creed*, Edinburgh.
Davis, A.B. 1973, *Circulation Physiology and Medical Chemistry in England 1650-1680*, Lawrence, Kansas.
Dear, P. 1988, *Mersenne and the Learning of the Schools*, Ithaca and London.
Derham, W. 1726, *Philosophical Experiments and Observations of the Late Eminent Dr. Robert Hooke*, London.
Descartes, R. 1632, *Treatise on Man* [1st Lat. edn. 1662], French Text [1664] tr. T.S. Hall, Cambridge, Mass., 1972.
―――― 1637, *Discourse on Method, Optics, Geometry, and Meteorology* tr. P.J. Olscamp, Indianapolis, New York, Kansas City, 1965.
Diderot, D. 1966, *Rameau's Nephew and D'Alembert's Dream* tr. L. Tancock, Harmondsworth, Middlesex.
Digby, K. 1645, *Two Treatises: In the One of which the Nature of Bodies; in the Other, the Nature of Mans Soule, is looked into: In Way of Discovery of the Immortality of Reasonable Soules* [1st edn. 1644], London.
Dijksterhuis, E.J. 1969, *The Mechanization of the World Picture* tr. C. Dikshoorn, London, Oxford, New York.
Dostrovsky, S. 1974-75, 'Early Vibration Theory: Physics and Music in the Seventeenth Century', *Archive for History of Exact Sciences*, 14: 169-218.
Drabkin, I.E. 1950, 'Aristotle's Wheel: Notes on the History of a Paradox', *Osiris*, 9: 162-98.
Drake, S. 1970, 'Renaissance Music and Experimental Science', *Journal of the History of Ideas*, 31: 483-500.
Duffin, J.M. 1986, 'The Medical Philosophy of R.T.H. Laennec (1781-1826)', *History and Philosophy of the Life Sciences*, 8: 195-219.
Edmonds, J.M. (ed. and tr.) 1957, *The Fragments of Attic Comedy after Meineke, Bergk, and Kock augmented*, 3 vols. in 4, Leiden.
Edwardes, E.L. 1977, *The Story of the Pendulum Clock*, Altrincham.

Epictetus n.d., *The Teaching of Epictetus: Being the 'Encheiridion of Epictetus,'* with Selections from the *'Dissertations'* and *'Fragments'* tr. T.W. Rolleston, London.

'Espinasse, M. 1956, *Robert Hooke*, Melbourne, London, Toronto.

Fearing, F. 1964, *Reflex Action: A Study in the History of Physiological Psychology*, New York and London.

Feisenberger, H.A. (ed.) 1975, *Sale Catalogues of Eminent Persons, Vol. II: Scientists*, London.

Flint, A. 1852, 'On Variations of Pitch in Percussion and Respiratory Sounds, and their Application to Physical Diagnosis', *Transactions of the American Medical Association*, 5: 73-123.

────── 1866, *A Practical Treatise on the Physical Exploration of the Chest, and the Diagnosis of Diseases affecting the Respiratory Organs* [1st edn. 1866], 2d edn., revised, Philadelphia.

────── 1874, *Compendium of Percussion and Auscultation, and the Physical Diagnosis of Diseases Affecting the Lungs and Heart* [1st edn. ?1864], 5th edn. revised, New York.

Fodor, J. 1975, *The Language of Thought*, New York.

Foucault, M. 1973, *The Birth of the Clinic: An Archeology of Medical Perception* tr. A.M. Sheridan, London.

Frank, R.G. 1980, *Harvey and the Oxford Physiologists: Scientific Ideas and Social Interaction*, Berkeley, Los Angeles, London.

Freeman, K. 1952, *Ancilla to the Pre-Socratic Philosophers: A Complete Translation of the Fragments in Diels, Fragmente der Vorsokratiker*, Oxford.

Freudenthal, G. 1983, 'Theory of Matter and Cosmology in William Gilbert's *De magnete*', *Isis*, 74: 22-37.

Galen 1821-33, *Claudii Galeni Opera omnia*, ed. C.G. Kuhn, 22 vols., Leipzig.

────── 1951, *A Translation of Galen's Hygiene (De sanitate tuenda)* by R.M. Green, Springfield, Illinois.

Galilei, G. 1632, *Dialogue concerning the Two Chief World Systems – Ptolemaic and Copernican* tr. S. Drake, Berkeley and Los Angeles, 1953.

────── 1638, *Dialogues concerning Two New Sciences* tr. H. Crew and A. de Salvio, New York, 1954.

Gandevia, B. 1960, 'The Evolution of the Stethoscope and the Techniques of Auscultation and Percussion', *The Medical Journal of Australia*, 782-7.

Gardner, H.M., Metcalf, R.C. and Beebe-Center, J.G. 1937, *Feeling and Emotion: A History of Theories*, New York.

Gee, S.J. 1893, *Auscultation and Percussion: Together with the Other*

Methods of Physical Examination of the Chest [1st edn. 1870], 4th edn., London.

Glanvill, J. 1665, *Scepsis scientifica: Or, Confest Ignorance, the Way to Science; in an Essay of the Vanity of Dogmatizing, and Confident Opinion* [1st edn. 1661] ed. J. Owen, London, 1885.

Godwin, J. 1979, *Robert Fludd: Hermetic Philosopher and Surveyor of Two Worlds*, London.

Gottlieb, L.S. 1964, *A History of Respiration*, Springfield, Illinois.

Gottschalk, H.B. 1971, 'Soul as Harmonia', *Phronesis*, 16: 179-98.

Gouk, P. 1980, 'The Role of Acoustics and Music Theory in the Scientific Work of Robert Hooke', *Annals of Science*, 37: 573-605.

Gould, J.B. 1970, *The Philosophy of Chrysippus*, Leiden.

────── 1974, 'The Stoic Conception of Fate', *Journal of the History of Ideas*, 35: 17-32.

Gregory, J.C. 1938, 'Chemistry and Alchemy in the Natural Philosophy of Sir Francis Bacon, 1561-1626', *Ambix*, 2: 93-111.

Grendler, P.F. 1963, 'Pierre Charron: Precursor to Hobbes', *The Review of Politics*, 25: 212-24.

Gunther, R.T. 1923-67, *Early Science in Oxford*, 15 vols., Oxford.

Guttmann, P. 1879, *A Handbook of Physical Diagnosis. Comprising the Throat, Thorax, and Abdomen* [1st edn. 1872] tr. from the 3d German edn., London.

Hahm, D.E. 1977, *The Origins of Stoic Cosmology*, Ohio State University Press.

Hale, D.G. 1971, *The Body Politic: A Political Metaphor in Renaissance English Literature*, The Hague and Paris.

Hall, A.R. 1950-51, 'Robert Hooke and Horology', *Notes and Records of the Royal Society of London*, 8: 167-77.

────── 1983, 'Gunnery, Science, and the Royal Society', *The Uses of Science in the Age of Newton* ed. J.G. Burke, Berkeley, Los Angeles, London, 111-41.

Hall, T.S. 1969, *Ideas of Life and Matter: Studies in the History of General Physiology 600 B.C. – 1900 A.D.*, 2 vols., Chicago and London.

Harris, L.E. 1961, *The Two Netherlanders: Humphrey Bradley and Cornelis Drebbel*, Cambridge.

Harvey, W. c.1616-18, *The Anatomical Lectures* ed. G. Whitteridge, Edinburgh and London, 1964.

────── 1627, *De motu locali animalivm 1627* ed. and tr. G. Whitteridge, Cambridge, 1959.

────── 1628, *An Anatomical Disputation concerning the Movement of the Heart and Blood in Living Creatures [De motu cordis]* tr. G. Whitteridge, Oxford, 1976.

―――― 1649, *The Circulation of the Blood: Two Anatomical Essays* tr. K.J. Franklin, Oxford, 1958.
―――― 1651, *Disputations touching the Generation of Animals [De generatione animalium]* tr. G. Whitteridge, Oxford, 1981.
Helmholtz, H. von 1877, *On the Sensations of Tone as a Physiological Basis for the Theory of Music*, 2d English edn., tr. A.J. Ellis, New York, 1954.
Hermann, D.J. and Chaffin, R. (eds.) 1988, *Memory in Historical Perspective: The Literature before Ebbinghaus*, Springer-Verlag.
Herschel, J.F. 1817-45, 'Sound' [1830], *Encyclopedia Metropolitana; or, Universal Dictionary of Knowledge*, 27 vols., London, 4: 747-825.
Hesse, M. 1962, *Forces and Fields: The Concept of Action at a Distance in the History of Physics*, New York.
―――― 1963, *Models and Analogies in Science*, London and New York.
―――― 1964, 'Hooke's Development of Bacon's Method', *Proceedings of the Tenth International Congress of the History of Science*, 2 vols., Paris, 1: 265-8.
―――― 1966a, 'Hooke's Philosophical Algebra', *Isis*, 57: 67-83.
―――― 1966b, 'Hooke's Vibration Theory and the Isochrony of Springs', *Isis*, 57: 433-41.
Hewes, G.W. 1977, 'Language Origin Theories', *Language Learning by a Chimpanzee: The Lana Project* ed. D.M. Rumbaugh, New York, San Francisco, London, 3-53.
Hierons, R. and Meyer, A. 1962, 'Some Priority Questions arising from Thomas Willis's Work on the Brain', *Proceedings of the Royal Society of Medicine*, 55: 287-92.
―――― 1964, 'Willis's Place in the History of Muscle Physiology', *Proceedings of the Royal Society of Medicine*, 57: 687-92.
Hine, J.D., Chan, M. and Kassler, J.C. 1987, *Roger North's Writings on Music to c.1703: A Set of Analytical Indexes with Digests of the Manuscripts*, Kensington, N.S.W.
Hobbes, T.
NB: The abbreviations HEW and HLW refer respectively to *The English Works of Thomas Hobbes of Malmsbury* ed. W. Molesworth, 11 vols., London, 1839-45 (reprinted, Scientia Aalen, 1962); and *Thomae Hobbes Malmesburiensis Opera philosophica quae latine scripsit* ed. W. Molesworth, 5 vols., London, 1839-45.
―――― 1640, *The Elements of Law Natural and Politic* ed. F. Tönnies, 2d edn. with a new Introduction by M.M. Goldsmith, London, 1969.
―――― 1641, 'The Third Set of Objections & Replies containing the Controversy between Hobbes and Descartes', *Descartes: Philosophical*

Writings, A Selection ed. and tr. E. Anscombe and P.T. Geach, The Open University, 1970.

——— 1642-43, *Thomas White's De mundo examined* tr. H.W. Jones, London, 1976.

——— 1644, *Tractatus opticus*, HLW 5: 215-48.

——— 1650a, *Human Nature, or The Fundamental Elements of Policy. Being a Discovery of the Faculties, Acts, and Passions, of the Soul of Man, from their Original Causes: According to Such Philosophical Principles, as are not commonly known or asserted*, HEW 4: 1-76.

——— 1650b, *De corpore politico: or The Elements of Law, Moral and Politic, with Discourses upon several Heads: as of The Law of Nature; of Oaths and Covenants; of Several Kinds of Government; with The Changes and Revolutions of them*, HEW 4: 77-228.

——— 1651, *Leviathan* ed. C.B. Macpherson, Harmondsworth, Middlesex, 1968.

——— 1655, *De corpore*, HLW 1: xii + 431pp.

——— 1656a, *Elements of Philosophy. The First Section, concerning Body*, HEW 1: xiv + 508pp.

——— 1656b, *The Questions concerning Liberty, Necessity, and Chance, clearly stated and debated between Dr. Bramhall, Bishop of Derry, and Thomas Hobbes of Malmesbury*, HEW 5: vi + 455pp.

——— 1662, *Seven Philosophical Problems and Two Propositions of Geometry. With an Apology for Himself and His Writings. Dedicated to the King in the Year 1662* [English tr. 1682], HEW 7: 1-68.

——— 1678, *Decameron Physiologicum*, HEW 7: 69-180.

——— 1682, *An Answer to a Book published by Dr. Bramhall, late Bishop of Derry; called "Catching of the Leviathan." Together with an Historical Narration concerning Heresy, and the Punishment thereof*, HEW 4: 279-384, 385-408.

Hoeline, K.A. 1980, 'Classification versus Typology: A Difference of Practical Importance', *JAMA: The Journal of the American Medical Association*, 244: 1099-1100.

Holder, W. 1694, *A Treatise on the Natural Grounds, and Principles of Harmony*, London.

Hood, F.C. 1967, 'The Change in Hobbes's Definition of Liberty', *The Philosophical Quarterly*, 17: 150-63.

Hooke, R.

NB: The abbreviation, *PW*, refers to Hooke (1705) below.

——— 1661, *An Attempt for the Explication of the Phenomena observable in an Experiment published by the Hon. Robert Boyle, Esq., in the 35th Experiment of his Epistolical Discourse touching the Aire*, London, reprinted in Gunther 1923-67, 10: [vi] + 50pp.

——— 1665, *Micrographia: Or Some Physiological Descriptions of Minute Bodies made by Magnifying Glasses with Observations and Inquiries thereupon*, London, reprinted in Gunther 1923-67, 6: 54-67.

——— c.1668, 'A General Scheme, or Idea of the Present State of Natural Philosophy, and how its Defects may be remedied by a Methodical Proceeding in the making Experiments and collecting Observations. Whereby to compile a Natural History, as the Solid Basis for the Superstructure of True Philosophy', *PW*, 1-70.

——— 1674, *An Attempt to prove the Motion of the Earth from Observations*, London, reprinted in Gunther 1923-67, 8: 18-22.

——— 1676a, 'A Curious Dissertation concerning the Causes of the Power & Effects of Musick' [title added posthumously], ed. Gouk 1980, 597-605.

——— 1676b, *A Description of Helioscopes, and Some Other Instruments*, London, reprinted in Gunther 1923-67, 8: 119-52 + plate.

——— 1677, *Lampas: Or, Descriptions of Some Mechanical Improvements of Lamps & Waterpoises. Together with Some Other Physical and Mechanical Discoveries*, London, reprinted in Gunther 1923-67, 8: 154-208, plates.

——— 1678a, *Lectures de potentia restitutiva, or of Spring explaining the Power of Springing Bodies*, London, reprinted in Gunther 1923-67, 8: 331-56.

——— 1678b, *Lectures and Collections*, London, reprinted in Gunther 1923-67, 8: 217-71.

——— 1682, 'A Discourse of the Nature of Comets', *PW*, 149-85.

——— 1680-82, 'Lectures of Light, explicating its Nature, Properties, and Effects, &c. [in 7 sections]', *PW*, 71-148.

——— 1683-85, 'Lectures concerning Navigation and Astronomy' [also other dates than those cited], *PW*, 451-572.

——— 1686-87, 'Lectures and Discourses of Earthquakes, and Subterraneous Eruptions' [also other dates than those cited], *PW*, 277-450.

——— 1691-92, Untitled Lecture, 4 February, Cambridge, Trinity College MS 0.11a.14f-14h.

——— 1705, *The Posthumous Works* [ed. R. Waller], New York and London, 1969.

——— 1935a, *The Diary* [1672-1680] ed. H.W. Robinson and W. Adams, London.

——— 1935b, 'The Diary [1688-1690]' ed. Gunther 1923-67, 10: 69-265.

Horine, E.F. 1941, 'An Epitome of Ancient Pulse Lore', *Bulletin of the History of Medicine*, 10: 209-49.

Hughes, H.M. 1854, *A Clinical Introduction to the Practice of Auscultation*, and *Other Modes of Physical Diagnosis, in Diseases of the Lungs and Heart* [1st edn. 1845], 2d edn., London.

Hulse, L. 1986, 'Hardwick MS 29: A New Source for Jacobean Lutenists', *The Lute*, 26: 62-72.

Hunt, F.V. 1978, *Origins in Acoustics: The Science of Sound from Antiquity to the Age of Newton*, New Haven and London.

Hunter, M. and Schaffer, S. (eds.) 1989, *Robert Hooke: New Studies*, Woodbridge, Suffolk.

Hutchison, K. 1983, 'Supernaturalism and the Mechanical Philosophy', *History of Science*, 21: 297-333.

——— 1984, 'Reformation Politics and the New Philosophy', *Metascience*, 1: 4-14.

Inwood, B. 1985, *Ethics and Human Action in Early Stoicism*, Oxford.

Jackson, J.H. 1958, *Selected Writings*, 2 vols., London.

Jammer, M. 1957, *Concepts of Force: A Study in the Foundations of Dynamics*, New York.

Jarcho, S. 1961, 'Auenbrugger, Laennec, and John Keats: Some Notes on the Early History of Percussion and Auscultation', *Medical History*, 5: 167-72.

Joachim, H.H. 1903, 'Aristotle's Conception of Chemical Combination', *Journal of Philology*, 29: 72-86.

Jones, H.W. 1974, 'A Seventeenth-Century Geometrical Debate', *Annals of Science*, 31: 307-33.

Kamm, R.D. and Pedley, T.J. 1989, 'Flow in Collapsible Tubes: A Brief Review', *Journal of Biomechanical Engineering*, 8: 177-9.

Kassler, J.C. 1979, *The Science of Music in Britain, 1714-1830: A Catalogue of Writings, Lectures and Inventions*, 2 vols., New York and London.

——— 1982, 'Music as a Model in Early Science', *History of Science*, 20: 103-39.

——— 1984a, 'Man – A Musical Instrument: Models of the Brain and Mental Functioning before the Computer', *History of Science*, 22: 59-92.

——— 1984b, 'Apollo and Dionysos: Music Theory and the Western Tradition of Epistemology', *Music and Civilization* ed. R. Maniates, E. Strainchamps and C. Hatch, New York, 457-71.

——— 1984c, '*Organon*: Musical and Logical Instrument', *Problems & Solutions* ed. J.C. Kassler and J. Stubington, Sydney, 123-48.

——— 1986, 'The Emergence of Probability reconsidered', *Archives Internationales d'Histoire des Science*, 36: 17-44.

Kassler, J.C. and Oldroyd, D.R. 1983, 'Robert Hooke's Trinity College "Musick Scripts", his Music Theory and the Role of Music in his Cosmology', *Annals of Science*, 40: 559-95.

Keel, O. 1988, 'Percussion et diagnostic physique en Grande Bretagne au 18e siècle: l'exemple d'Alexander Monro secundus', *XXXI Congrès International d'Histoire de la Mèdecine, Actes* ed. R.A. Bernabeo, Bologna, 869-75.
Keynes, G.L. 1960, *A Bibliography of Dr. Robert Hooke*, New York.
Kieffer, J.S. 1964, *Galen's Institutio logica*, Baltimore.
King, L.S. 1959, 'Auscultation in England, 1821-1837', *Bulletin of the History of Medicine*, 33: 446-53.
Kirk, G.S., Raven, J.E. and Schofield, M. 1983, *The Presocratic Philosophers*, 2d edn., Cambridge.
Knudsen, O. and Pedersen, K.M. 1968, 'The Link between "Determination" and Conservation of Motion in Descartes' Dynamics', *Centaurus*, 13: 183-6.
Korsten, F.J.M. 1981, *Roger North (1651-1734): Virtuoso and Essayist*, Amsterdam.
Kostelijk, P.J. 1950, *Theories of Hearing: A Critical Study of Theories and Experiments on Sound Conduction and Sound Analyses in the Ear*, Leiden.
Laennec, R.T.H. 1826, *De l'auscultation médiate ou traité du diagnostic des maladies des poumons et du coeur* [1st edn. 1819], 2d edn. entièrement refondue, 2 tom., Paris.
────── 1846, *A Treatise on Mediate Auscultation, and on Diseases of the Lungs and Heart* tr. from the Latest Edition, London.
Leibniz, G.W. von 1714, *Leibniz Selections* ed. P.P. Wiener, New York, 1951.
Littler, T.S. 1965, *The Physics of the Ear*, Oxford.
Lloyd, G.E.R. 1970, *Early Greek Science: Thales to Aristotle*, New York.
────── 1987, *Polarity and Analogy: Two Types of Argumentation in Early Greek Thought*, Bristol.
Long, A.A. 1971a, 'Freedom and Determinism in the Stoic Theory of Human Action', *Problems in Stoicism* ed. A.A. Long, London, 173-99.
────── 1971b, 'Language and Thought in Stoicism', *Problems in Stoicism* ed. A.A. Long, London, 75-133.
────── 1982, 'Soul and Body in Stoicism', *Phronesis*, 27: 34-57.
Lysaght, D.J. 1937, 'Hooke's Theory of Combustion', *Ambix*, 1: 93-108.
Macdonald, H. and Hargreaves, M. 1952, *Thomas Hobbes: A Bibliography*, London.
Manley, L. 1980, *Convention 1500-1700*, Cambridge, Mass. and London.
Mates, B. 1961, *Stoic Logic*, Berkeley and Los Angeles.
Mathieson, T.J. 1975, 'An Annotated Translation of Euclid's Division of a Monochord', *Journal of Music Theory*, 19: 236-58.

Mayow, J. 1674, *Medico-physical Works being a Translation of Tractatus quinque medico-physici*, Edinburgh and London, 1957.

McKie, D. 1953, 'Fire and the Flamma Vitalis: Boyle, Hooke and Mayow', *Science and History* ed. E.A. Underwood, 2 vols., London, 1: 469-88.

—— 1983, 'Some Early Work on Combustion, Respiration and Calcination', *Ambix*, 1: 143-65.

McKinnon, J.W. 1978, 'Jubal vel Pythagoras, Quis sit Inventor Musicae?', *The Musical Quarterly*, 64: 1-28.

Meier, R.Y. 1982, '"Sympathy" in the Neurophysiology of Thomas Willis', *Clio Medica*, 17: 95-111.

Mendelsohn, E. 1964, *Heat and Life: The Development of the Theory of Animal Heat*, Cambridge, Mass.

Mersenne, M. 1636-37, *Harmonie universelle, contenant la theorie et la pratique de la musique, où il est traité de la nature des sons & des mouvemens, des consonances, des dissonances, des genres, des modes, de la composition, de la voix, des chants, & de toutes sortes d'instrumens harmoniques*, Paris.

—— 1957, *Harmonie universelle: The Books on the Instruments* tr. R.E. Chapman, The Hague.

Meyer, A. and Hierons, R. 1965, 'On Thomas Willis's Concepts of Neurophysiology', *Medical History*, 9: 1-15, 142-55.

Michael, E. and Michael, F.S. 1989, 'Two Early Modern Concepts of Mind: Reflecting Substance vs. Thinking Substance', *Journal of the History of Philosophy*, 27: 29-48.

Miller, W.S. 1922, 'Thomas Willis and his De phthisi pulmonari', *American Review of Tuberculosis*, 5: 934-49.

Millington, E.C. 1942, 'Theories of Cohesion in the Seventeenth Century', *Annals of Science*, 5: 253-69.

Mintz, S.I. 1962, *The Hunting of Leviathan: Seventeenth-Century Reactions to the Materialism and Moral Philosophy of Thomas Hobbes*, Cambridge.

Montaigne, M.E., Seigneur de 1603, *The Essayes* tr. J. Florio, London and New York, 1898.

More, H. 1652, 'An Antidote against Atheism', *Philosophical Writings* ed. F.I. Mackinnon, New York, 1969.

Moyer, A.E. 1977, 'Robert Hooke's Ambiguous Presentation of "Hooke's Law"', *Isis*, 68: 266-75.

Münxelhaus, B. 1976, *Pythgagoras musicus: Zur Rezeption der pythagoreischen Musiktheorie als quadrivialer Wissenschaft in lateinischen Mittelalter*, Bonn-Bad Godesberg.

North, H. 1966, *Sophrosyne: Self-knowledge and Self-restraint in Greek Literature*, Ithaca.

North, F. 1677, *A Philosophical Essay of Musick directed to a Friend*, London.
Nussbaum, M.C. 1978, *Aristotle's De Motu Animalium*, Princeton.
Oatley, K. 1978, *Perceptions and Representations: The Theoretical Bases of Brain Research and Psychology*, London.
Oldroyd, D.R. 1972, 'Robert Hooke's Methodology of Science as Exemplified in his "Discourse of Earthquakes"', *The British Journal for the History of Science*, 6: 109-30.
——— 1980, 'Some "Philosophicall Scribbles" attributed to Robert Hooke', *Notes and Records of the Royal Society of London*, 35: 17-32.
——— 1987, 'Some Writings of Robert Hooke on Procedures for the Prosecution of Scientific Inquiry, including his "Lectures of Things Requisite to a Ntral [*sic*] History"', *Notes and Records of the Royal Society of London*, 41: 145-67.
Onians, R.B. 1951, *The Origins of European Thought about the Body, the Mind, the Soul, the World, Time, and Fate*, 2d edn., Cambridge.
Pacchi, A. 1968, 'Una "biblioteca ideale" di Thomas Hobbes: Il MS E2 dell'archivo di Chatsworth', *Acme: Annali della facolta di lettere e filosofia del'Universita degli Studi di Milano*, 21: 5-42.
Pagel, W. 1958, 'Medieval and Renaissance Contributions to Knowledge of the Brain and its Functions', *The History and Philosophy of Knowledge of the Brain and its Functions* ed. F.N.L. Poynter, Oxford, 95-114.
——— 1967, *William Harvey's Biological Ideas: Selected Aspects and Historical Background*, Basel and New York.
Palisca, C.V. 1992, 'Was Galileo's Father an Experimental Scientist?', *Music and Science in the Age of Galileo* ed. V. Coelho, Dordrecht, 143-51.
Porter, R. 1985, 'Making Faces: Physiognomy and Fashion in Eighteenth-Century England', *Études Anglaises*, 38: 385-96.
Price, D.C. 1981, *Patrons and Musicians of the English Renaissance*, Cambridge.
Prudovsky, G. 1989, 'The Confirmation of the Superposition Principle: On the Role of a Constructive Thought Experiment in Galileo's *Discorsi*', *Studies in the History and Philosophy of Science*, 20: 453-68.
Rabelais, F. 1530-4, *The Histories of Gargantua and Pantagruel*, tr. J.M. Cohen, Harmondsworth, Middlesex, 1982.
Randall, D.B.J. 1983, *Gentle Flame: The Life and Verse of Dudley, Fourth Lord North (1602-1677)*, Durham, N.C..
Raven, J.J. 1906, *The Bells of England*, London.
Rees, G. 1977, 'The Fate of Bacon's Cosmology in the Seventeenth Century', *Ambix*, 24: 27-38.
——— 1980, 'Atomism and "Subtlety" in Francis Bacon's Philosophy',

Annals of Science, 37: 549-71.
—— 1986, 'Mathematics and Francis Bacon's Natural Philosophy', *Revue Internationale de Philosophie*, 159: 399-426.
Riese, W. 1959, *A History of Neurology* (New York, 1959).
Rieser, S.J. 1978, *Medicine and the Reign of Technology*, Cambridge.
Rich, G.J. 1919, 'A Study of Tonal Attributes', *American Journal of Psychology*, 30: 121-64.
Rist, J. 1985, 'On Greek Biology, Greek Cosmology and Some Sources of Theological Pneuma', *Prudentia*, supplementary number: 27-47.
Robinson, F.G. 1972, *The Shape of Things Known: Sidney's Apology in its Philosophical Tradition*, Cambridge, Mass.
Rose, S. 1973, *The Conscious Brain*, London.
Rostvig, M.-S. 1962, *The Happy Man: Studies in the Metamorphoses of a Classical Ideal*, 2d edn., 2 vols., Oslo and New York.
Sacksteder, W. 1978, 'Hobbes: Teaching Philosophy to Speak English', *Journal of the History of Philosophy*, 16: 33-45.
—— 1980, 'Hobbes: The Art of the Geometricians', *Journal of the History of Philosophy*, 18: 131-46.
—— 1981a, 'Hobbes: Geometrical Objects', *Philosophy of Science*, 48: 573-90.
—— 1981b, 'Some Ways of doing Language Philosophy: Nominalism, Hobbes, and the Linguistic Turn', *Review of Metaphysics*, 34: 459-85.
—— 1982a, 'Hobbes' Logistica: Definition and Commentary', *Philosophy Research Archives*, 8: 55-94.
—— 1982b, 'Hobbes: Man the Maker', *Thomas Hobbes: His View of Man* ed. J.G. van der Bend, Amsterdam, 77-88.
—— 1982c, *Hobbes Studies (1879-1979): A Bibliography*, Bowling Green, Ohio.
—— 1984, 'Man the Artificer: Notes on Animals, Humans and Machines in Hobbes', *Southern Journal of Philosophy*, 22: 105-21.
—— 1988, 'Three Diverse Sciences in Hobbes: First Philosophy, Geometry and Physics', Boulder, Colorado.
—— 1990, 'Hobbes's Science of Human Nature', *Hobbes Studies*, 3: 35-53.
Salmon, J.H.M. 1989, 'Stoicism and Roman Example: Seneca and Tacitus in Jacobean England', *Journal of the History of Ideas*, 50: 199-225.
Sambursky, S. 1959, *Physics of the Stoics*, London.
Sandbach, F.H. 1971, 'Phantasia Kataleptike', *Problems in Stoicism* ed. A.A. Long, London, 9-21.
Scaltsas, T. 1990, 'Soul as Attunement: An Analogy or a Model?', *Greek Studies in the Philosophy and History of Science* ed. P. Nicolacopoulos,

Dordrecht, 109-19.
Schrödinger, E. 1956, *Mind and Matter: The Tarner Lectures delivered at Trinity College, Cambridge, in October 1956*, Cambridge, 1967.
Schwoerer, L.G. 1988, *Lady Rachel Russell*, Baltimore.
Scott, W.L. 1970, *The Conflict between Atomism and Conservation Theory 1644 to 1860*, London and New York.
Shapin, S. and Schaffer, S. 1985, *Leviathan and the Air-Pump: Hobbes, Boyle, and the Experimental Life*, Princeton.
Shapiro, A. 1973, 'Kinematic Optics: A Study of the Wave Theory of Light in the Seventeenth Century', *Archives for History of Exact Sciences*, 11: 143-72.
―― 1974, 'Light, Pressure, and Rectilinear Propagation: Descartes' Celestial Optics and Newton's Hydrostatics', *Studies in the History and Philosophy of Science*, 5: 239-96.
Singer, B.R. 1976, 'Robert Hooke on Memory, Association and Time Perception', *Notes and Records of the Royal Society of London*, 31: 115-31.
Siraisi, N.G. 1975, 'The Music of Pulse in the Writings of Italian Academic Physicians (Fourteenth and Fifteenth Centuries)', *Speculum – A Journal of Mediaeval Studies*, 50: 689-710.
Skoda, J. 1853, *A Treatise on Auscultation and Percussion* [1st edn. 1837], tr. W.O. Markham from the fourth edn. [1850], London.
Smart, C. c.1756-63, *Jubilate agno* re-ed. W.H. Bond, London, 1954.
Solmsen, F. 1950, 'Tissues and the Soul', *Philosophical Review*, 59: 435-68.
―― 1961, 'Greek Philosophy and the Discovery of the Nerves', *Museum Helveticum*, 18: 150-67, 169-97.
Sorabji, R. 1972, *Aristotle on Memory*, London.
―― 1983, *Time, Creation and the Continuum: Theories in Antiquity and the Early Middle Ages*, London.
Spiegel, R.E. 1970, *Galen on Sense Perception: His Doctrines, Observations and Experiments on Vision, Hearing, Smell, Taste, Touch and Pain, and their Historical Sources*, Basel.
―― 1973, *Galen on Psychology, Psychopathology, and Function and Diseases of the Nervous System*, Basel.
Stokes, W. 1882, *A Treatise on the Diagnosis and Treatment of Diseases of the Chest. Part I. Diseases of the Lung and Windpipe* [1st edn. 1837] ed. A. Hudson, London.
Swift, J. 1726, *Gulliver's Travels: A Facsimile*, Delmar, New York, 1976.
Taylor, F.S. 1945, 'The Origin of the Thermometer', *Annals of Science*, 5: 253-69.
Temkin, O. 1959, 'The Dependence of Medicine upon Basic Scientific

Thought', *The Historical Development of Physiological Thought* ed. C.McC. Brooks and P.F. Cranefield, New York, 6-21.

Tobias, J.V. (ed.) 1970-72, *Foundations of Modern Auditory Theory*, 2 vols., New York and London.

Todd, R.B. 1976, *Alexander of Aphrodisias on Stoic Physics: A Study of the De mixtione*, Leiden.

Tracy, T.J. 1969, *Physiological Theory and the Doctrine of the Mean in Plato and Aristotle*, The Hague and Paris.

Truesdell, C. 1960, *The Rational Mechanics of Flexible or Elastic Bodies 1638-1788*, Zurich.

Turner, H.D. 1955-56, 'Robert Hooke and Theories of Combustion', *Centaurus*, 4: 297-310.

Underwood, E.A. 1947, 'Apollo and Terpsichore: Music and the Healing Art', *Bulletin of the History of Medicine*, 17: 639-73.

Virchow, R. 1958, *Disease, Life, and Man: Selected Essays* tr. L.J. Rather, Stanford.

Wallis, J. 1677, 'Dr. Wallis's Letter to the Publisher concerning a New Musical Discovery', *Philosophical Transactions of the Royal Society*, 12: 839-42.

Walshe, W.H. 1860, *A Practical Treatise on the Diseases of the Lungs: Including the Principles of Physical Diagnosis* [1st edn. 1851], 3d edn., revised and much enlarged, London.

Webster, C. 1962-66, 'The Discovery of Boyle's Law, and the Concept of the Elasticity of Air in the Seventeenth Century', *Archives for the History of Exact Sciences*, 2: 441-502.

——— 1967, 'Harvey's *De generatione*: Its Origins and Relevance to the Theory of Circulation', *British Journal for the History of Science*, 3: 262-74.

Westfall, R.S. 1971, *Force in Newton's Physics: The Science of Dynamics in the Seventeenth Century*, London and New York.

——— 1983, 'Robert Hooke, Mechanical Technology, and Scientific Investigation', *The Uses of Science in the Age of Newton* ed. J.G. Burke, Berkeley, Los Angeles, London, 86-110.

White, T. 1665, *An Exclusion of Scepticks from all Title to Dispute: Being an Answer to The Vanity of Dogmatizing*, London.

Wilkins, J. 1648, 'Mathematical Magic: Or, the Wonders that may be performed by Mechanical Geometry not before treated of in this Language', *The Mathematical and Philosophical Works of John Wilkins* [1802], 2 vols. in 1, London, 1970, 2: 89-246.

Williams, C.J.B. 1840, *The Pathology and Diagnosis of Diseases of the Chest, comprising a Rational Exposition of their Physical Signs, with an Appendix; containing Various Opinions and Experiments on the Motions and Sounds of*

References

the *Heart, and on the Bronchi* [1st edn. 1828], 4th edn., much enlarged, London.

Williams, E. 1956, 'Hooke's Law and the Concept of the Elastic Limit', *Annals of Science*, 12: 74-83.

Willis, T. 1670, 'De motu musculari', *Affectionum quae dicuntur hystericae & hypochondriacae pathologia spasmodica vindicata*, London.

────── 1681, *Cerebri anatome: Cui accessit nervorum descriptio et usus* [1664], tr. S. Pordage in *The Remaining Medical Works of Thomas Willis*, partially reprinted in *The Anatomy of the Brain and Nerves* ed. William Feindel, Montreal, 1965.

────── 1683, *De anima brutorum* [1672], tr. S. Pordage as *Two Discourses concerning the Soul of Brutes, which is that of the Vital and Sensitive of Man*, Gainesville, Florida, 1971.

────── 1692, *The London Practice of Physick, being the Practical Part of Physick contain'd in the Works of the famous Dr. Willis*, London.

Wilson, C. 1965, *England's Apprenticeship 1603-1763*, London.

Wilson, L.G. 1959, 'Erasistratus, Galen, and the *Pneuma*', *Bulletin of the History of Medicine*, 33: 293-314.

────── 1960, 'The Transformation of Ancient Concepts of Respiration in the Seventeenth Century', *Isis*, 51: 161-72.

Ziggelaar, A. 1980, 'How did the Wave Theory of Light take shape in the Mind of Christiaan Huygens?', *Annals of Science*, 37: 179-87.

Index

Agricola, Martin (1486-1536),
   Musica instrumentalis Deudsch, x,
   125
Alembert, Jean le Rond d' (1717-83),
   20-4, 234
Alison, Somerville Scott (1813-77),
   222, 267
   The Physical Examination of the
      Chest, xi, 214-15, 217-18,
      223, 272
Almighty, *see* God
Ancients, *see* Greeks, Romans
Anderson, Warren D., viii, 29,
   242, 272
Apollo, 211
Archimedes (c.287-212 B.C.), 87,
   238, 245, 248, 252
Aristophanes (c.444-c.380 B.C.), 28-9
Aristotle (384-322 B.C.), 29, 37,
   50, 68, 77, 272, 274, 280-1,
   283, 285-6
   categories (predicaments), 97
   change, 33-4
   cosmology, 50-1, 66-7
   De anima, 36, 235
   De generatione et corruptione, 160
   equilibrium, balance, 34
   experience, 114
   heart, 72, 114
   mechanics, 4, 55, 63, 66-7
   memory, remembering,
      recollection, 113-14, 285
   Physica, 236, 245
   Posterior analytics, 249
   self as a lever, 72
   sense perceptions, 114, 239
   prime mover, 50, 72
   soul, 35, 113-14
   virtues, 94
   see also Peripatetics
Aristoxenus (fl. c.318 B.C.), 29

Elementa harmonica, 235
Elementa rhythmica, 268
Aubrey, John (1626-97), 128, 162,
   238, 251, 266, 272
   report on Hobbes, 59, 128,
      208-9, 257
Auenbrugger, Leopold (1722-1809),
   266, 272, 280
   and music, 213-14
   identification of body sounds,
      213-14, 226-7, 266
Aurelius, *see* Marcus Aurelius
   Antoninus
Australian Academy of the
   Humanities, viii
Australian Research Committee, viii

Bacon, Francis (1561-1626), 162, 256,
   266, 272, 276-7, 283-4
   analogies, metaphors, 161, 211,
      231, 253
   and music, 165
   Essayes, 257
   instrumental aids, 253
   spiral, 161-2
   spirit, spirits, 161-2, 256-7
   Sylva sylvarum, 188, 196, 272
   sympathy, affinity, 161-2
Begué, Sigfrido Martín, viii, ix
Behemoth (beast), 51
Bernstein, H.R., 82-3, 272
Bible, 61, 74, 236
   Genesis, 124
   Job, 51
   Joshua, 16, 233
Blacksmiths' Company, 255
Boethius (c.480-524 or 5),
   The Consolation of Philosophy, 117
Bosch, Hieronymus (c.1450-1516),
   viii
   Garden of Earthly Delights, ix, 42

Index

Bowditch, Henry Ingersoll (1808-92), 222, 267
The Young Stethoscopist, xi, 217, 223, 272
Boyle, Robert (1627-91), 127, 233, 249, 251, 254-6, 273, 278, 282, 285
  Boyle's Law, 127-8, 163, 286
  magnetism, 116
  New Experiments Physico-mechanical, touching the Spring of the Air, and its Effects, 127-8
  replies to criticism, 127
Bramhall, John (1594-1663), 61-2, 239, 278
British Library, London, viii
Butler, Charles (d. 1647), 168, 181, 248, 273

Caelius Aurelianus (fl. 5th century), 268, 273
Cartesian, *see* Descartes, René
Cassirer, Ernst, 231, 273
Cavendish, William, 1st Earl of Devonshire (d. 1626), 59
Cavendish, William, 2nd Earl of Devonshire (1591?-1628), 59
Cavendish, William, 3rd Earl of Devonshire (1617-84), 59
Cavendish family, 59, 261
Cecilia, *Saint*, 27-8
Charles II (1630-85), 206, 249
Charleton, Walter (1619-1707), 242, 261, 273
Charron, Pierre (1541-1603), 239, 276
Chladni, Ernst Florenz Friedrich (1756-1827), 144-5
Christ, *see* Jesus Christ
Christians and Christianity, 61
Chrysippus of Soli (280-207 B.C.), 50-1, 62, 77, 248
Cicero, Marcus Tullius (106-43 B.C.), 97-8, 240-1
  Catilinarians, 241
  Nature of the Gods, 5, 16, 209, 212, 216, 219, 226, 229, 231
  Paradoxa Stoicorum, 185
Cleanthes (c.331-c.230 B.C.), 35, 50

Clement, William (fl. 1672-76), 149
Clockmakers' Company, 149, 273
Coiter, Volcher (1534-76), 250
Cowley, Abraham (1618-67), 73, 242, 274
  'Of My self', 74
  Several Discourses by Way of Essays, in Verse and Prose, 73
Cratinus (c.525-422 B.C.), 28-9
Creator, *see* God
Cutler, *Sir* John (1608?-1693), 127

D'Alembert, *see* Alembert, Jean le Rond d'
Davison, William (fl. 1635-60), 246
Deity, *see* God
Dennett, Daniel C.,
  Liber, 1
Derham, William (1657-1735), 256, 274
Descartes, René (1596-1650), x, 49, 115-16, 119, 128, 166, 236-8, 250, 256, 258, 274, 277-8, 281, 285
  analogies, metaphors, 43-6, 63, 78, 118-19, 150
  and music, 44-5
  brain, 43-7, 118-20, 150, 188, 194, 250
  cohesion, 243
  cosmology, Cartesian universe, 77-9, 85, 119, 242-3
  De homine figuris, ix, 43, 45
  Discours de la méthode, ix, 47
  ghost in machine, 166
  heart, 43-4
  mechanical theory, 43-4, 63, 77-9, 85, 88-9, 100, 109, 119, 156, 166
  Meditations, 266
  memory, remembering, 117-21, 150
  mental representation, 44-5, 110, 120
  nerve and muscle, 43-4, 46-7, 119, 150, 188, 194-5, 237
  particles, 78-9, 89
  sensory perception, 44,

46-7, 109, 118-19, 150, 239
soul, mind, 43-8, 108, 115, 119-20, 250
spirits, 43-4, 118, 188, 194
Devil, 40
Devonshire, Earls of, *see* Cavendish, William
Dicaearchus (fl. 3rd century B.C.), 29
Diderot, Denis (1713-84), 20-6, 234-5
  D'Alembert's Dream, 20-6, 274
  Rameau's Nephew, 20, 24, 26, 274
Digby, Kenelm (1603-65), x, 119-24, 242, 250, 274
Diogenes Laertius (fl. 2nd century), *Lives of the Philosophers*, 233
Divinity, *see* God
Drebbel, Cornelis (1572-1633), 160-1, 256, 276
Duckworth, Richard (fl. 1668), *Tintinnalogia*, 151

Empedocles of Acragas (fl. c.460 B.C.), *On Nature*, 32-3
Epictetus (fl. 1st century), 239, 275
Epicureans (followers of Epicurus), 50, 69, 80, 88-9, 131, 245
Epicurus (342-270 B.C.), 50, 78
Erasistratus of Ceos (fl. 300-260 B.C.), 249, 287
Erinyes (Ministers of Justice), 31
Euclid (fl. c.280 B.C.), 238, 281
  Elements, 245
Eudoxus of Cnidus (fl. c.366 B.C.), 245

Fletcher, Phineas (1582-1650), *The Purple Island*, 9, 233
Flint, Austin (1812-86), 227, 267, 269, 275
Fludd, Robert (1574-1637), 38-43, 236, 272, 276
  Utrius cosmi...historia, ix, 40-1
Fourier, Jean-Joseph (1768-1830), 233
Fournet, Jules (fl. 1830-40), 269
Franklin, James, viii

Gafori, Franchino (1451-1522), *Theoria musice*, x, 126
Galen, Claudius (129-c.200), 33-6, 236, 249, 268, 275, 281, 285, 287
Galilei, Galileo (1564-1642), 54, 57, 59, 87, 237-8, 243, 251, 264, 275, 283
  and music, 54, 57-8, 186, 238, 250-2, 254
  cohesion, 81-2
  Discorsi e dimostrazioni matematiche, intorno a due nuove scienze, 54, 275
  elasticity, 54
  law of length, 55, 58
  pleasure and pain, 57-8
  spiral, 82, 87
  superposition, 111
  vibrations, oscillations, pulsations, 55-8, 63, 103, 165, 241, 247
Galilei, Vincenzo (c.1520-91), 238, 250, 283
Gassendi, Pierre (1592-1655), 78
  brain, 188, 194
  cosmology, 78-9, 243
  magnetism, 116
  mechanical theory, 78-9, 89
  memory, 117, 121
  nerve and muscle, 188, 194-5
  particles, atoms, 78-9, 89
  spirits, 188, 194-5
Gaukroger, Stephen, viii
Gee, Samuel Jones (1839-1911), 225, 267-9, 275-6
Glanvill, Joseph (1636-80), 108-9, 115, 122, 135, 249-50, 276
  and music, 109, 111, 117
  attacks Hobbes, 108-12, 115, 117
  brain, 110, 117-19
  criticism of Peripatetic theory, 122
  memory, remembering, 109-11, 118
  particles, 117
  soul, 108-11, 117, 249
  spirit, spirits, 109-10, 119
  sympathy, 110, 116-17
God, 38, 40, 50-1, 61, 68, 71, 73-4, 79, 94, 99, 103, 105-7, 129, 210, 236-7, 239, 266

Index

Almighty, 182
 always acts geometrically, 159
 conserves motion, 77-9, 85, 119
 Creator, creation, 49, 77-8, 99, 159, 237
 identical with universe, 51
 immutable, transcendental, 79
 intervenes, 85
 laws, 73, 77, 106-7
 Trinity, 36
Godolphin, Sidney (1610-43), 211
Greeks, 1, 11, 28, 33, 225, 267, 281, 284-5
 Hellenic, 73
 pre-Socratic, 30-3, 275, 281
Gresham College, 127, 133
Guttmann, Paul (1834-93), 267-8, 270, 276

Hale, Matthew (1609-76), 251
Hall, A.R., 152, 276
Hall, Francis, see Line, Francis
Haller, Albrecht von (1708-77), 234
Hardwicke, Baron, see Cavendish, William, 2nd Earl of Devonshire
Harvey, William (1578-1657), 36, 38, 68, 70, 162, 236, 240-1, 249-50, 266, 275-7, 283, 286
 analogies, 36-8, 67-8, 240, 250
 and music, 36-7, 68, 240
 beginnings, 241
 brain, 37-8, 67-8
 circulation, cycle, 66-8, 157, 240
 cosmology, 68-9, 241
 De generatione animalium, 67-8, 277, 286
 De motu cordis, 66, 276
 heat, 67-8, 157
 health and disease, 68
 heart, 37-8, 67-8
 life, 67-8, 157
 nerve and muscle, 37-8, 67, 241
 pleasure and pain, 67
 respiration and combustion, 157, 256
 spirit, 67
 vibration, pulsation, 67-8, 240
Hellenic times, see Greeks

Helmholtz, Hermann von (1821-94), 234, 245, 269, 277
 pitch theory, 17-19, 259
Heraclitus of Ephesus (fl. c.510 B.C.), 28
 compares soul to spider, 140
 cosmic harmony theory, 30-3, 35
Hermes, 108
Hero of Alexandria (fl. 3rd century B.C.), 160, 256
 Automata, 160
 Pneumatica, 160
Herophilus (fl. c.300 B.C.), 268
Herschel, *Sir* John Frederick William (1792-1871), 269, 277
 and music, 228
Hippocrates (c.460-c.357 B.C.), 210, 269
His Master's Voice, Nipper logo, 28
HMV, see His Master's Voice
Hobbes, Thomas (1588-1679), 2-4, 49-50, 52-4, 61, 66, 77, 108, 112, 115-17, 127-30, 162, 171, 174, 176, 208, 236-52, 254, 257-8, 261, 263-4, 266, 270, 272-3, 276-8, 281-3, 284
 analogies, metaphors, 2-4, 49, 64, 69-72, 79, 84, 91, 99-105, 109-10, 162, 167, 186, 198-9, 208, 241, 247, 250
 analysis, synthesis, 96
 and music, as musician, 49, 52-4, 58-9, 69, 70-2, 84, 91-2, 99-100, 103-4, 111-12, 185, 208, 238-9, 261
 and sound, 50, 165, 199-200, 247
 as neo-Stoic, 51-2, 61, 208
 beginnings, initial moments, 70, 72, 76, 82, 84, 89-93, 99, 104, 199, 242, 244
 Body, 59-60, 64, 68-9, 79, 82-3, 85, 92, 95-9, 118, 128, 167, 199, 278
 body as habit, 88, 90, 110, 185-6, 198-9, 209, 236, 264
 body moving through body, 76-7, 79-81, 87

brain, 64, 66, 102, 117-18, 186
cause and effect, 51, 61, 69, 71, 76, 83-5, 93, 97, 186, 239, 242, 244, 248
change, mutation, transformation, 70, 81, 83-4, 86, 88-90, 100, 200, 244
circulation, cycles, 66, 70, 90, 118, 162, 241
cohesion, 79-82, 106-7
consciousness, 90-1, 102, 246
continuum theory, continuity, 3-4, 49-50, 53-4, 63, 69-70, 79, 82-5, 88-9, 103, 108, 111-12, 117, 135, 198-9, 243, 245
cosmology, universe, 51, 55, 62, 68-70, 76, 79, 82-5, 105-7, 110, 247
criticism of biblical interpreters, 61
criticism of Epicureans, 50, 80, 89, 243, 245
criticism of mechanical philosophers, 63, 79, 243
criticism of Peripatetics, 50, 63, 89, 97
criticism of vacuum experiments, 11, 233
De corpore politico; or the Elements of Law, 95, 278
Dialogus physicus de natura aeris, 127, 251
elasticity, spring, 3-4, 71, 81-2, 84-5, 93, 103, 162, 198-9, 243-4, 246
'end of knowledge is power', 105
endeavour, tendency, effort, 63, 70, 79-85, 88, 90, 92, 96, 102-3, 105, 110, 198-9, 244, 250
energy fills space, 79
energy source, 199-200
equilibrium, balance, 57, 88, 100-2, 209
erring, sources of error, 71, 75-6, 93, 102, 232
ether, fluid plenum, 64-6, 69-70, 80, 82, 85, 118, 141, 162, 182, 200
ethics, morality, virtuous life, 49, 51-2, 62, 71-3, 76, 88, 93-5, 98-9, 102, 105-7, 210-11, 246
experience and study, 49, 51, 70-1, 88, 91-4, 100, 102, 104-6, 196, 248
explosives, 199-200
fire and burning, 65, 86, 199-200
force, power, 3-4, 62, 69, 71, 73, 80, 82-5, 88, 90, 94, 100-1, 103, 105-7, 110, 198-9, 209, 232, 239, 243-4, 246
fracture, breaking, 72, 81-2, 101, 199, 243
freedom and determinism, 52, 61-2, 69-73, 83, 93, 105-7
gravity, weight, 70, 209
glass drops, 198-9, 264
God's will, law, 51, 71, 79, 105-7
health, indisposition, 59, 72, 91, 93-4, 186, 208-9, 241, 266
heart, 49, 64-6, 102, 106, 118, 186, 248
heat, 65-6, 69-70, 86, 100-1, 141, 192, 199-200, 209, 241, 246
hostile reception of work, 3-4, 112, 249
human nature, *Human Nature*, 95, 167, 185-6, 211, 278
ideas, 212, 252, 266
identity of indiscernibles, 88-9
individuality, identity, 72, 89-90, 94, 186
instrumental aids, 55, 86-7, 105, 211, 238, 247-8
Leviathan, viii, x, 49, 52, 99, 106, 166, 278, 282, 285
life, 66, 73-4, 90, 93, 100, 102
light, 62-5, 68-70, 86, 99, 186, 199-200
madness from untempered passions, 73, 93, 185-6, 246, 261
magnetism, 68-9, 116
mathematical points, 86-7
memory, remembering, recollection, 102, 110-12, 117-18, 129, 247, 249, 252
mental computations, 18, 71, 75,

Index

85-6, 96, 98, 101-2, 109-10, 212, 241
mental representation, phantasms, 64, 98, 117-18, 174
movement, animal motion, 70-1, 74, 87, 90, 92, 94, 186, 212, 239, 244, 261
names, speech, utterance, 75, 89-91, 94, 97, 104-5, 212, 231, 241-2, 266
natural and acquired wit, art and science, 91-5, 99, 103-5, 248
natural and right reason, 95, 105-6, 186, 248
natural law, law of universal nature, 51, 76, 79, 88, 90, 94, 100, 105-7, 209, 242, 248
nerve and muscle, 49, 64, 66, 70, 186, 209
noises accompanying internal motions of body, 93
particles, 65, 69, 86, 101, 103, 200
parts and wholes, 76, 85-6, 96
philosophy as medium, method, 76, 93-6, 99, 106, 247, 284
plasticity, 93, 246
pleasure and pain, feeling, 65-6, 70, 101, 212
reality, 75, 105, 212
reason an accidental attribute of man, 196
relief from ignorance, 64, 75
rule of action, 62, 76, 88, 93
self as bundle of taut strings, 51, 72-3, 101-3, 109-10, 186, 208-9
self-knowledge, 2, 71-2, 210-11, 246
self-restraint as exercise of tension, 2, 49, 72-3, 92-4, 102, 106, 210
senses, 66, 75, 83, 243, 252
sensory perception, 'sense', 18, 64-6, 70, 74-5, 85, 90-1, 104, 129, 209, 243, 246-7, 252
signs, 75-6, 98, 231, 241
sleep and dreams, 72, 90-1, 110, 118, 241
social (sympathetic) passions,

social concord, 49, 101, 106
soul, mind, 49, 74-5, 85, 91, 93-4, 98, 105, 110, 209, 212, 231, 241, 252-3, 264
spiral, 82, 87, 245
spirit, spirits, 65-6, 70, 261
superposition and interference, 3, 111-12
sympathy, affinity, 69, 72, 101, 116-17, 162
time, instant, 56-7, 79, 80-4, 86, 89, 93, 96, 100, 102-3, 110, 129, 238, 253
total mixture, penetration, 3, 80-1, 111
Tractatus opticus, 63, 174, 278
truth, true philosophy, 49, 61, 75-6, 93-4, 96, 105-6, 252
understanding, intellect, 75-6
vibrations, oscillations, pulsations, reciprocal or contrary motions, 3-4, 50, 55-7, 63-6, 69-70, 79-85, 87, 90, 99-106, 110, 117-18, 141, 162, 199-200, 209, 238-9, 244, 247, 249

Hobbians, 112
Hoeline, Kurt A., 228-9, 278
Hogarth, William (1697-1764)
Credulity, Superstition and Fanaticism, xi, 197
Holder, William (1616-98), 186-8, 261, 278
Homer (before 700 B.C.)
'Hymn to Hermes', 108
Odyssey, 235
Hooke, Robert (1635-1702), x, 126-30, 147-9, 160, 165, 171, 176, 208-10, 216, 236, 251-8, 261, 264-6, 273, 275-83, 285-7
analogies, metaphors, 2, 129, 132, 136, 139-43, 145, 149-50, 156, 158-9, 162-4, 208, 253, 257
analysis, synthesis, 130, 252
and music, 131-4, 136-8, 141-7, 149-51, 154, 156, 158-9, 163-5, 171, 186, 208, 210, 276, 279-80

and sound, sound producers, 126, 131-3, 137-8, 142, 144, 146, 150, 157, 159, 165, 199, 210, 213, 254, 258
body, human body, 131, 134, 139, 141-4, 147, 153-4, 157, 159, 163-5, 213, 252, 257
brain, 130, 135, 137, 139-40, 149-50, 156-7, 252
cause and effect, 130, 132, 141, 143, 146, 164, 256
change, 'transmutation', 158-9, 199
circulation, 129-30, 150, 157, 162
clocks, clockwork, 126, 151-2, 161, 171, 255
cohesion, 141-2, 254
continuum theory, 4, 150, 253
developing Hobbes's theory, 4, 129-30, 135, 141, 158, 254
diary, 128, 144, 149, 210, 238, 279
elasticity, spring, resilience, 4, 143, 153-4, 158, 163-5, 199, 277, 279
energy source, 150, 157, 159, 199
equilibrium, balance, 141-2, 152, 154, 164
erring, sources of error, 131
ether, fluid plenum, 141, 143, 146, 163, 182, 257-8
ethics, morality, 266
experiments, 126, 131, 143-7, 149-50, 153-4, 158, 171, 254, 257
explosives, 200
fire and burning, combustion, 157-9, 200, 256
force, power, 4, 128-9, 131, 135, 150, 152, 154, 156, 161, 163-5
fracture, breaking, 132, 150, 199
glass drops, 199
gravity, 'Of Gravity', weight, 128, 143-4, 146-7, 152-3, 254, 257
health, indisposition, 134-5, 150, 208-10, 213, 266
heart, 130, 213
heat, 128, 131, 141-2, 157-8, 162, 192, 256

Hooke's Law, 127-8, 154-6, 163-5, 183, 234, 264, 282, 287
human nature, 130
ideas, 130, 135-7, 156
identification of body sounds, 213
instrumental aids, 126-7, 131, 139, 150, 153-6, 171, 211, 213, 252-3, 255, 277
Lampas, x, 153, 279
Lectures de potentia restitutiva, x, 155, 163, 279
life, 130, 136, 150
light, lightning, 128, 132-4, 142, 157, 252-3, 256, 279
magnetism, 128, 147
mathematical point, 137, 253
memory, remembering, recollection, 129-31, 134-7, 139-40, 150, 285
mental computations, 129-30, 134-9, 150
Micrographia, 141, 279
motions of earth, 143, 257-8
motions of moon, 145
movement, animal motion, 256
nerve and muscle, 133, 150
nodal points and lines, 145-6, 149, 158, 254
particles, 138, 141-2, 146, 154, 158-9, 162-3, 238, 257-8
'Philosophical Scribbles', 129, 283
pleasure and pain, feeling, 131-2, 134, 159
reason accidental attribute of man, 196
respiration, 157, 159, 161, 200, 256
self as a ringing bell, 149-50, 159
self-knowledge, 2, 130, 210-11, 252
self-movers, automata, 161
self-restraint, 2, 129-31, 210, 252
senses, 129-34, 137-9, 143, 210, 253
sensible motions proportional to bulk, 133-4
sensory perception, sense, 129, 131, 134-9, 150, 159, 254

Index

signs, 213
soul, soul/point, mind, 129-30, 134-7, 139-40, 150, 156-7, 159, 252
spiral, 135, 139, 150, 153-6
spirits, spirituous, 256
superposition and interference, 136, 138, 150, 253
sympathy, 132-3, 136
time, moments, 129, 133, 135, 137-9, 150, 154-6, 165, 171, 238
total mixture, penetration, 141, 158, 256
truth, true philosophy, 130
understanding, intellect, 129-31, 139
vibrations, oscillations, pulsations, 126, 128, 132-4, 137-8, 141-2, 151-2, 154, 159, 164-5, 238, 251-5, 257-8
vibratory modes, patterns, 139-47, 149-50, 153, 158, 257
wave fronts, 135, 150
waves of compressed energy, 199
waves of sound, 199
Hornbostel, Erich M. von, 233
Hughes, Henry Marshall (1805-58), 268, 279-80
Hunt, Frederick Vinton, 11, 280
Huygens, Christiaan (1629-95), 170, 287
Traité de la lumière, 170

Jackson, John Hughlings (1835-1911), 228, 269, 280
James II (1633-1701), 263
Jammer, Max, 143, 280
Jenkins, John (1592-1678), 149
  'The Bells' or 'The Five Bells Consort', 149, 255
Jesuits, 251
Jesus Christ, 36, 237
  see also Christians and Christianity
Job, *see* Bible
Joshua, *see* Bible
Jubal, 124, 282

Kassler, Michael, viii
Keeper of the Great Seal, 201, 206

Laennec, René Théophile Hyacinthe (1781-1826), 227, 229, 267-9, 274, 280
  and music, 216, 219, 222, 268
  identification of body sounds, 214-16, 222-4, 226, 269
  instrumental aids, 214-15, 222, 229
  names employed in diagnosis, 219, 225-7, 267
  A Treatise on Mediate Auscultation, xi, 219, 281
Laszlo, Pierre, viii
Leeuwenhoek, Anton van (1632-1723), 240
Leibniz, Gottfried Wilhelm (1646-1716), 18, 234, 272, 281
Leviathan (beast), 51, 74, 237
Line, Francis (1595-1675),
  identified with Franciscus Linus or Francis Hall, 127, 251
  Tractatus de corporum inseparabilitate, 127, 251
Linus, Franciscus, *see* Line, Francis
Lipsius, Justus (1547-1606), 61
Long, A.A., 212, 281
Lucretius, Carus T. (94-55 B.C.), 80, 243

Marcus Aurelius Antoninus (121-180), *Meditations* ['On Himself'], 49, 61-2, 69, 76, 79, 88, 93, 105
Marquet, François (1687-1759), 268
  Nouvelle méthode facile et curieuse, pour connoitre le pouls, xi, 220-1
Masters, John (fl. 1654-80), 192-3, 263
Mayow, John (1641-79), 266, 282
Memory (mother of the Muses), 108
Mersenne, Marin (1588-1648), 59, 102, 237, 247, 274
  and music, 54, 102, 112, 143, 165, 186, 250-1, 254, 258, 261
  experiments with stretched strings, 54, 187
  Harmonie universelle, ix-x,

22, 39, 47, 54, 60, 148, 187, 282
Mersenne's Laws, 54, 141-2, 245
Universae geometriae, mixtaque, synopsis et bini refractionum demonstratum tractatus, 63
Millard, Peter, 202, 271
Molesworth, Sir William, 63, 277
Montaigne, Michel Eyquem, Seigneur de (1553-92), 249
Essayes, 124, 129, 139, 282
More, Henry (1614-87), 115-16, 249, 251, 282
attacks Hobbes, 115
Museo del Prado, Madrid, viii

Neo-Stoics, *see* Stoics and Stoicism
Newton, Sir Isaac (1642-1727), 4, 53, 79, 130, 174, 259, 276, 280, 285-6
Nipper (dog), *see* His Master's Voice
Non-Hobbian theories, *see* Hobbes, Thomas
North, Sir Dudley (1641-91), 201, 204-5, 265
his lady, Anne North *née* Cann (fl. 1670-1714), 204
North, Francis, 1st Baron Guilford (1637-85), 201, 205-7, 251, 263
and music, 169, 171-4, 186, 261
his lady, Frances North *née* Pope (1647-78), 193, 263
A Philosophical Essay of Musick, x, 172-3, 283
North, John (1645-83), 201-5
and music, 201, 203
his mother, *Lady* Anne North *née* Montague (c.1613-81), 203
North, Roger (1651-1734), viii, 2, 193, 200-8, 210, 251, 258-61, 263-6, 271-3, 277, 281
analogies, metaphors, 2, 165-8, 174, 178, 180-5, 193, 195, 198, 201, 204, 206, 209, 260-1, 263
analysis, 181, 260
and music, 148-9, 165-8, 170-4, 178, 180, 183-5, 193-5, 198, 201, 258-61, 263
and sound, sound producers, 165-6, 169-70, 174, 176, 182, 193-5, 198, 209, 258-9, 263
as writer of lives, 166-8, 201-7
beginnings, 179
body, human body, 167-9, 174, 180-4, 195-6, 203, 205, 210, 259
brain, cerebellum, central processing unit, 167, 171, 174, 183-4, 195, 203, 207
cause and effect, law of causality, 180-4, 202, 204, 206
change, alteration, transformation, 168, 170, 177-8, 182-3, 193, 200-1, 203-4, 207
circulation, 195, 202
clocks, clockwork, 169, 171, 181
consciousness, 171, 177-9, 184
cosmology, universe, 181-4
criticism of mechanical philosophers, 166, 193-6
developing Hobbes's theory, 4, 166-7, 171, 174, 182
elasticity, spring, resilience, 165-6, 168-9, 182-4, 194-8, 200-1, 204
endeavour, tendency, effort, 179, 183, 206
energy source, 167, 182, 192-5
equilibrium, balance, 169, 183, 205
erring, sources of error, 180, 192
ether, 181-2, 260
ethics, morality, virtuous life, 166, 180-1, 196, 210
experience and study, 179-80, 196, 203, 259-60, 263
experiments, 180
explosives, 182-3, 198, 202-3, 263
fire and burning, combustion, 167, 183, 195, 198, 202-3, 205-7
force, power, 169, 171, 174, 176-8, 180-3, 193-6, 198, 201, 203-4
fracture, rupture, 198, 201, 204
glass drops, 199, 204, 263
gravity, weight, 169, 195, 202, 205-6

Index

health, indisposition, 168, 179-80, 192-3, 196, 198, 201-7, 209-10, 260, 263-6
heat, 192, 202
heart, 183
human nature, 166, 168, 180, 185, 201, 204-5, 260-1
ideas, 177-8, 180-1, 259-60
individuality, identity, 196, 201
instrumental aids, 181, 260
life, 167-8, 171, 179-80, 182-3, 196, 201
madness, sanity, 193, 196, 201, 260
mathematical point, 183
memory, remembering, 171, 176-8, 180, 203
mental computations, 176-80, 184, 259, 260
mental representations, images, 171, 174, 176, 178, 184, 193, 196
movement, animal motion, 168, 179-80, 184-5, 194-6, 198, 203
names conventional, 177
nerve and muscle, 167, 171, 180, 184, 194-6, 203, 263
noises accompanying movements of body, 198
Notes of Me, 166, 192, 271
particles, 169-70, 183
pleasure and pain, feeling, 179, 192-3, 205-7, 210
reality, 177, 179, 193
reason accidental attribute of man, 196
relief from ignorance, 179
respiration, breathing, 167, 205
self as musical activity, 167-85
self-knowledge, 2, 179, 205, 210, 259-60, 263
self-restraint as exercise of tension, 2, 180, 195, 201-2, 206
self-sufficiency, 205, 264
senses, 168, 170-1, 176, 178-80, 183-4, 258
sensory perception, sense, 176-7, 179-81, 183, 193, 259
signs, 178, 184, 203

sleep and dreams, 171, 193, 203, 206-7
soul, mind, 166-7, 171, 174-81, 184-5, 196, 201-3, 205, 207, 210, 259
spirit, pneumatic substance, 167-8, 181-5, 201-2, 204-7, 260
spirits, 180, 181-2, 193-5, 201-2
superposition, 174
sympathy, 184, 194
Theory of Sounds, x, 166, 175, 271, 273
time, moments, 169-71, 174, 177, 185, 194, 216
total mixture, penetration, 182
truth, 180
understanding, intellect, 168, 180-1, 196, 260-1
vibrations, oscillations, pulsations, 165-6, 168-77, 183, 193-4, 198, 201-2, 259
waves of compressed energy, 182, 194-5
waves of sound, 170, 182
North family, 264-5

Odysseus, 235

Paman, Henry (1626-95), 265
Peripatetics (followers of Aristotle), 50, 77, 89, 97, 117, 122, 131, 242
Petty, William (1623-87), 246
Philolaus (fl. 5th century B.C.), 29
Pigot, Thomas (d. 1686), 145
Piorry, Pierre (1794-1879), 226
Plato (c.429-347 B.C.), 115-16, 235, 237, 248, 286
  cosmology, 116-17
  Cratylus, 269
  Laws, 248
  memory, remembering, recollection, 113, 116, 129
  Meno, 249
  Phaedo, 113, 235, 249
  Philebus, 237, 249
  soul, 29, 113, 115-17, 159
  Theaetetus, 249
  Timaeus, 30, 33

truth, true beliefs, 113, 115, 117
  virtues, 94
Pope family, 263
  see also North, Francis (his lady)
Porphyry (fl. 3rd century), 97
Porter, Roy, 166, 283
Pre-Socratic Philosophers, see Greeks
Purcell, Henry (1659-95), 149
  'Bell Anthem' (Rejoice in the Lord alway), 149
Puritans, 73
Pythagoras of Samos (fl. 6th century B.C.), x, 36, 124-6, 235, 237, 282
  and music, 124
  theories of soul, 29, 53, 113, 159
Pythagoreans, x
  cosmic harmony theories, 30-2

Rabelais, François (1494-1553), 233, 236, 283
Rameau, Jean-François (fl. 18th century), 20, 23-4
Rameau, Jean-Philippe (1683-1764), 20, 24, 234
Ratcliffe, John (1650-1714), 205, 265
Rees, Graham, 161, 283-4
Riese, Walther, 115, 284
Romans, 94
Romieu, Jean-Baptiste (1723-66), 234
Royal Society, 108, 127-8, 143-5, 171, 198, 252, 254, 256, 276

Sachs, Curt, 233
Sacksteder, William, viii, 103, 284
Saint Cecilia, see Cecilia, *Saint*
Schaffer, Simon, 127, 285
Schrödinger, Erwin (1887-1961), 19-20, 234, 285
Scripture, see Bible
Seneca, Lucius Annaeus (d. 65), 94, 284
Shapin, Stephen, 127, 285
Shapiro, Alan E., viii, 63-4, 128, 258
Shore, John (c.1662-1752), 263
Simmias, 29, 235
Skoda, Josef (1805-81), 226-7, 268-70, 285

Smart, Christopher (1722-71), 237, 285
Socrates (469-399 B.C.), 113
Sorbières, Samuel de (1615-70), 264
Sorge, Georg Andreas (1703-88), 234
Stedman, Fabian (fl. 1668), *Tintinnalogia*, 151
Stoics and Stoicism, 8, 52, 62, 76, 89, 95-6, 111, 161, 185, 239, 241, 246-8, 264, 272, 274, 281, 284, 286
  apathy, preserving balance, 73, 206
  categories (predicaments), 96-7
  change, 77
  cohesion, 50
  continuum theory, 8, 50, 88-9, 103
  cosmology, 35, 50-1, 61, 70, 97, 276
  ethics, morality, virtuous life, 64, 94-5, 167-8, 210, 280-1
  fate, destiny, 61-2, 239, 276
  fiat, tenets, 52, 64, 76, 94, 167-8
  heat, 35, 51, 70
  incorporeals, sense of words, 212
  life is striving, 74
  neo-Stoic, 51, 208, 239
  paradox of great man and happy man, 73
  paradox that body moves through body, 80
  power of freedom, 62
  reason as essential function of mind, 94-5
  relief from ignorance, 64
  signs, 97-8
  soul, 35, 140, 161
  speech as symbol, 73
  spirit, 70, 73
  sympathy, 50, 162
  total mixture, penetration, 76-7
  see also Cleanthes, Chrysippus, Zeno
Stokes, William (1804-78), 267, 269, 285
Sutton, John, viii
Swift, Jonathan (1667-1745), 263, 274, 285

Index   299

Tartini, Giuseppe (1692-1770), 234
Tertullian (fl. 2nd century), 236
Thucydides (c.457-c.401 B.C.), 257
Tompion, Thomas (1639-1713), 149, 255
Trinity, *see* God
Tubalcain, 124

University of New South Wales: School of Science and Technology Studies, viii
University of Sydney Library: Rare Books and Special Collections, viii

Vulcan, x, 124-5

Wallis, John (1616-1703), 251, 254, 286
Walshe, Walter Hayle (1812-92), 227, 269, 286
Westfall, Richard, 78, 286
White, Thomas (1593-1676), 122-3, 250, 278, 286
Wilkins, John (1614-72), 160-1, 256, 286
Williams, Charles James Blasius (1805-89), 268-70
   and music, 229-30
   identification of body sounds, 224, 227, 229-30
   instrumental aids, 224, 230-1, 270
   names employed in diagnosis, 267, 269
   The Pathology and Diagnosis of Diseases of the Chest, xi, 224, 286-7
Williams, E., 164, 200, 287
Willis, Thomas (1621-75), 181, 188, 193, 261-6, 274, 277, 282, 287
   analogies, metaphors, 190-2, 262
   brain, 188, 190-1, 261
   energy source, 192
   explosives, 190, 262
   health and disease, 190-1, 264-5
   individuality, identity, 191, 196
   inflation theory, wind, 189-92, 262
   madness, 196
   mechanical theory, 189-90, 192
   nerve and muscle, 189-92, 262
   pleasure and pain, 189
   soul, 188-91, 262
   spirits, 181, 188-93, 262
   sympathy, 190-1
Wren, Christopher (1632-1723), 127, 145

Zeno of Citium (335-263 B.C.), 8, 35, 76